FROM WHERE WE CAME

A PHYSICIST'S PERSPECTIVE ON HUMAN ORIGIN, ADAPTATION, PROLIFERATION, AND DEVELOPMENT

CHRIS YOUNG KELLY

1

SOLVING HUMANS' OLDEST MYSTERY

"Where did we come from?" This simple question has confounded human beings for ages. It is reasonable to assume that someone might have raised this question as soon as we started to have communicable language and cognitive ability eons ago. The recent discovery of a fossil piece showing similar voicing capability as ours may date verbal communication to 500,000 years ago. Likely, it was not language as we know it today. Modern chimpanzees show a hint of the thinking process (i.e., cognition, implying that humans could think very early on). Without any hard evidence as to the origins of our language and intelligence, we might never know when or how this question was first asked.

It is commonly believed that we ask this question out of natural curiosity, which has been around since early in our existence. Humans have always been curious by nature indeed since the early days. Early humans were curious about practical matters, mostly things about which they had immediate concerns. For example, they might have been curious why some nuts (bitter almonds, for example) might cause breathing difficulties upon ingestion, why some plants had the ability to stop the bleeding from open wounds (e.g., yarrow), or why fire could not arise from damp wood. Such a non-tangible question of our origins could only be entertained when they did not have to worry about their livelihood and had tons of time on their hands.

Why might that question even be contemplated and in need of answers? Some believe there was a need to know all along.

WHO NEEDS TO KNOW?

Early humans' basic social units might have consisted of immediate families, close relatives, and friends during hunter-and-gatherer times. We do not have written records as to how these human clans were organized, but it would be reasonable to assume that our social structures were similar to those of our closest relatives: advanced primates. Evolution psychologists suggest that typical social group sizes were a few dozen—around 30 individuals—in those days, similar to modern-day chimps in their natural habitat. It could be as many as 150 in some rarer cases, but larger groups tend to disintegrate into smaller cliques unless rules and regulations are established and observed throughout.

Just try to imagine that we are members of such a social group during our early tribal days for the time being. To keep the units cohesive and survive, we encourage and foster innate empathy, compassion, and altruism. Similar to what we observe in modern-day primates, these emotions are reflected in how we take care of each other. Not all is well all the time, though. There are always occasional scuffles, vying for resources. The conflicts are usually reconciled between engaging parties by some material offering, a friendly jab on the chin, some backslapping, or guffawing at each other. Lives are, in general, peaceful, because we know each other intimately in these small groups, and the subsistence is quite serene and satisfying on most days.

But our lives are more complicated since there are unavoidable yet necessary interactions with other groups that stir commotions in the middle of the doldrums. According to a recent study, this type of social networking among early human groups is the main driving force of our complex civilization. What was the interaction between groups? In our xenophobic nature, the first instinct is to put up a defense to try to find out from where the other group had come through some forms of communication. During this probing dance, one of the first questions asked would most likely have been "Where are you from?" much like any partygoers striking up a conversation in modern days. Only when the interacting groups are deemed nonthreatening to each other would we start sharing food and stories, trading surpluses for shortages, and establishing alliances for common causes like hunting or fighting disasters.

Reaching out to other groups is, at times, intentional. In some cases, this is a means to look for mating opportunities outside of one's own unit. Whatever the motivation might be, the urge to know about us is part survival and part reproductive. A desire from this instinctual perspective should be enough motivation to care about from where we—or others—have come.

ANSWERS THROUGH THE AGES

These practical inquiries would have been reciprocated by the groups involved to keep the interaction going. Having done so numerous times, the groups must have had a few canned answers. These group-specific answers would have been left up to the smartest—the shamans or the sorcerers—to formulate. Shamans can cure simple problems like wounds or sicknesses and are the most-trusted person in the group. They can also imagine and abstract mundane daily activities into stories well-received by the members. Shamans are practically in every aspect of our lives—why not create a narrative to answer the question of from where we have come?

One of the most critical tasks for the shaman is to keep the social group or tribe together through myths. These stories are woven together to be mysterious and fantastic.

MYTHICAL ANSWERS

Most myths try to convince us that we are the creation of some mighty divine deity. We believe that we are unique, strong, powerful, fertile, smart, and excellent at getting resources for living. In other words, our origin makes us worthy as a group, belonging to each other as friends or formidable enemies to foreign groups. There are real benefits bestowed upon those who believe in the myths. Communicated properly, these beliefs would have undoubtedly improved the chances of being granted a bride/groom's hand, bartering for resources, or establishing alliances.

The shamans, as smart as they were, no doubt knew that the question of from where we have come had no real credible answers because they did not know themselves. It was best if members of the group just believed the myths to be the truth. Until the modern era, that is.

From the beginning of time as recent as mid-nineteenth century, mythical answers have dominated humans' imaginations. The myths do not have to be real or right—they just have to be convincing, so people are not bothered with lives' uncertainty hanging over their heads. A belief in something larger than life seems to be a human necessity.

Myths of from where we have come abound and vary, attesting to the imagination of sorcerers and the wise ones. There is a legend from the Boshongo people of Central Africa that claims they all came from Bumba, the great creator, who vomited out the universe and everything in it, including humans, as its last act of creation. Pachamama is a goddess revered by the Indigenous people of the Andes, according to *Wikipedia*. A Quechuan native in Peru told me the native's version during my trip there two years ago. Pachamama is the great-grandmother of everyone, as she was created from Mother Earth (i.e., the mud). In a 4,600-year-old myth of Fuxi and Nüwa, they are humans' first ancestors—the Adam and Eve of China. An alternative version about Nüwa says that she was all alone and created humans as her companions by molding them from the mud. Discovering that humans die eventually, she made humans with sexes—women and men—and dictated that they mate with each other so cular anthropology age, when the molecular genetics combined with traditional anthropology. We have since drastically enriched our evolutionary stories and continue to resolve more subtle and complex human histories.

These two periods focus on two different aspects of evolution. The fossil-study age gave us a macroscopic broad-stroke of our ancestral lineage, starting from 7,000,000 years ago, while the molecular anthropology age expands beyond the physical evolution and provide microscopic genetics on the DNA level. The latter also has been successful in unraveling the stories of our extended family story as far back as a few million years.

THE FOSSIL STUDY: CONFIRMING HUMAN EVOLUTION

Human curiosity in this period has been primarily stoked by the discovery and interpretation of human fossils. Since we first discovered Neanderthal fossils in the mid-1800s, we have accumulated thousands of fossil pieces, representing the remains of 6,000 early human individuals. Through the fossils, we now understand things like how and when early humans adapted to walk upright, live in hot and cold habitats, and the speed at which the children of early humans grew. Most importantly, we found out we are a branch of a large and diverse family tree. Fossil discoveries show that the human family tree has many branches and deeper roots than we knew about even a couple of decades ago. The number of branches on our evolutionary tree has nearly doubled since the discovery of the famed "Lucy" fossil skeleton in 1974.

While the existence of a more massive human evolutionary family tree is not in doubt, researchers continued to debate its size and shape because fossil records only offer a fragmented look at our ancient past and the number of branches. The debates concern the precise evolutionary relationships, essentially who is related to whom, when, and how. What we know about our ancestral line is dependent on what fossils reveal to us. There has even been some debate concerning evolutionary theories based on different interpretations of the same fossils. We keep repeating the claims that we have settled the arguments to the most plausible theory by its proponents until the next significant fossil discovery subverting the status quo.

TRANSITIONING TO MOLECULAR ANTHROPOLOGY STUDY

The discovery of DNA and its implications for biological traits in the 1960s led to significant advances in molecular biology and genetics and changed our reliance on fossils. Around the 1970s, a few visionaries saw that molecular genetics and anthropology were closely related. The groundswell of DNA knowledge and genetic studies culminated in a pioneering work, concluding in our origins with that single line summary: "All the living human beings today are descendants of a few ancestors who lived 200,000 years ago in sub-Saharan Africa."

The group of scientists responsible for this revelation was working at UC Berkeley, consisting of Rebecca L. Cann, Mark Stoneking, and Allan Wilson, in the mid-1980s (referred to as Cann et al. from this point on). Their breakthrough was not just in their conclusions, their adoption of rigorous scientific methodology to anthropology practically ushered in the molecular anthropology age. Their publication, entitled *Mitochondrial DNA and Human Evolution,* helped coin the moniker "Mitochondria Eve," commonly referred to as the ancestral mother by the general public these days.

The full transition from the time of fossil-study to molecular anthropology was not by any means smooth. Triggered by Cann et al.'s claim, the immediate reactions were reflective of the state of affairs around the mid-1980s. Quite a few debates continued for a while, highlighting how hard it was to alter deeply entrenched misconceptions, such as the earth being flat.

There were four significant debates in the aftermath of the publication that have expended our intellectual effort. The first is a clash between old and new academic groups. The other three argued about the age of modern humans, the lineage of modern humans, and finally, the location where modern humans' MRCA lived.

The Old Guards Versus The New

The first debate—or more appropriately, feud—was a clash between the new camps and the old: the traditional paleontologists and anthropologists and a new breed of molecular biologists and geneticists. The debate started in the mid-60s and was both academic and personal through at least the mid-90s.

As for the personal feud, the older camp held an incredulous attitude toward the new one. The traditional paleontologist and anthropologist camp worked tirelessly to establish the ages and locations of our ancestors and gave us a great start on our family tree. Then came the new breed of scientists who never had to spend a single day in hot, arid, ancient lands to sift through tons of rock, searching for human fossils. They have touted their new data coming from DNA as being so precise and scientific that the older group—the paleoanthropologists—were a bunch of bumbling old fools (their words, not mine). The new camp considered the older generation's research speculative at best.

Traditional anthropologists were particularly incensed at this new group of scientists, who were a minority at the time, as they had not even spent a single day in the field and did their anthropological work in air-conditioned laboratories. They reportedly settled the age-old debate in a single swoop, and from the United States, to boot.

Modern Humans' Single Ancestral Lineage

In the mid-1970s, it was common to believe that various modern humans evolved independently, likely from their current locations. For example, Peking Men are the ancestors of all Chinese, and Neanderthals give birth to all Europeans. As the venerable Richard Leakey claimed in 1977, "There is no single center where a modern man was born." This concept was dubbed multiregionalism.

There is, however, a logical difficulty in multiregionalism. If it were true, then it is unlikely all modern human groups flourished almost simultaneously in contradiction to fossil evidence (we will get to that later). This logical fallacy stemmed from not recognizing how mobile human beings have been—we now know that human beings were well-traveled as early as about 2,000,000 years ago. Once this point is conceded, either multiregionalism or single location sources are equally viable. The DNA study and discovery regarding modern humans not only does not contradict fossil evidence, but it also helps bridge gaps in the fossil records.

<u>Modern Humans' Age</u>

Another debate had to do with the relatively young age of modern humans—a mere 200,000 years—in contrast to the ranges of millions of years as commonly believed then. The modern humans' age should be at least as old as our fossils, in range of millions of years. What is hard for the traditional camps to accept this young age is partly due to the lack of a clear understanding of the term "modern humans" around that time.

Around late 1980's, there was a consensus that human beings like Neanderthals appeared somewhere in the Middle East around 100,000 years ago. They had to be the descendants of people as old as a few million years, based on fossil discoveries from Africa. It sounded reasonable to assume their ancestors were also modern humans' ancestors, thus modern humans should have a lineage in the range of a few million years old. These intelligent modern humans somehow showed up across Europe with the intelligence to create paintings and artifacts in caves around 40,000 years ago.

There is a discontinuity in this evolutionary theory. There have not been transitional fossils between the Neanderthals and modern humans found in the Middle East, between 100,000 and 40,000 years ago. The discovery by Cann et al. bridged this gap with a younger and newer breed of human beings from Africa without challenging the older ages of our more ancient relatives.

<u>Location Of "Garden Of Eden"</u>

There was also a disagreement as to the location of the "Garden of Eden" between two genetic research groups, even though both independently arrives at a similar age for modern humans and are from a single but different site. By contrast, one group concluded this was Africa and the other, South East Asia. The parties recognized that this is the process for eventually reaching an agreement with independent verifications, but I side with Cann et al.'s conclusions as to the location after going through both arguments. Besides, all follow-up studies corroborate the Africa location being our homeland.

THE ARRIVAL OF THE MOLECULAR ANTHROPOLOGY AGE

The years since the 1980s had been particularly consequential in scientific and technological advances to help us better answer that age-old human origin question.

We made significant progress in molecular biology, medicine, and genetics, helped along by advances in science and technologic infrastructure. We saw polymerase chain reactions (PCRs) widely used in DNA studies from the late 1980s, making the decoding of trace amounts of DNA possible. We saw the invention of fast DNA sequencing around 1992, leading to the possibility of quickly obtaining human genomes. The Human Genome Project's first draft was made public in 2001. CRISPR was invented in 2005, leading to the possibility that chromosomes could be edited gene by gene, opening up the opportunity for gene therapies that could potentially cure most genetic disorders and diseases.

The last 30 years also saw the continuously shrinking nanometer-scale integrated circuit, supercharging modern computers' calculating capabilities. The artificial intelligence running on top of the raw hardware power is now able to unravel how microscopic genomes dictate macroscopic aspects of our bodies, our daily lives, and our evolution.

The seemingly ongoing feud between the traditionalists and newcomers some 30 years ago has evaporated. These days, every evolutionary study has to embrace the newly emerged discipline of molecular anthropology, which merges traditional paleoanthropology and molecular genetics. Molecular anthropology has incorporated scientific and technological advances to form a multidisciplinary academic branch. I believe that modern molecular anthropology will continue to refine and enrich our evolutionary story. We know a fair amount about ourselves and we are about to learn a lot more moving forward.

THE CONTINUING QUEST TO COMPLETE THE ANSWERS

We believe that we now know more definitely about modern human's origin in the last 200,000. We also have a rough idea of our expanded family tree, including archaic relatives like the Neanderthals, but our origins are a little murky when we try to go further back beyond the Neanderthals.

We understand us—modern humans—better because we are getting better at molecular anthropology. Even so, a part of the reason we have not been successful in the big-picture understanding of our species is the lack of DNA—or molecular remnants—of our extinct relatives. While we have tons of DNA from modern humans at our disposal, it is a different story when it comes to early humans. DNA has a short shelf life once an organism dies and tends to break up into small segments if exposed to heat and moisture. Irrespectively, with tremendous effort, we constructed the full genome of Neanderthals who lived 40,000 years ago.

For even earlier ancestors and relatives, we will need to recover DNA as old as millions of years. Thanks to the imagination and innovation of visionary scientists, the molecular evolutionary history may be preserved a lot longer on rare occasions, albeit not necessarily in DNA form. As such, there may be the possibility that we can trace out family relationships among early humans on the microscopic level. Given the fast progress of molecular anthropology, we have seen modern and early humans connected on the family tree on the molecular level. We can even find previously unknown early human species, just like how we discovered our long-lost relatives, the Denisovans, a mysterious, extinct relative of ours.

MISSING FROM THE EXISTING ANSWERS: A PRINCIPLE BEHIND EVOLUTION

The overall approach to the subject of human evolution has always been phenomenological. We seek to explain what has happened through whatever the fossil and molecular evidence can give us. As a physicist, however, I have another layer of curiosity and a bigger picture in mind. As for modern human origin, the vast amount of information is concisely organized into that one-line summary is a manifestation of a hidden order, a ground-rule, a fundamental principle governed by physics. I believe, beyond knowing all the facts of what happened to us, a fundamental principle should be equally applicable to the understanding of the human evolution.

Physics is logical. It is believed nothing can arise without a cause, because causality rules in our world. If you ignore the nitty gritty details of our evolution in time, the answer to "Where did we come from?" entails two parts: cause and effect. All the action about evolution, our family tree, and the mechanism of evolution are the effects. There has to be an overriding driving force, or the cause, of evolution behind the actions. This search for an all-encompassing evolutionary principle, along with finding out what happened, has been my strongest motivation to get so deeply involved in the subject over the past few years.

LEARNING HUMAN EVOLUTION: A TWO-PRONGED APPROACH

To learn as much as possible about our evolution, I charted out a two-pronged approach for what I needed to do sometime in 2014. First, I needed to get up to speed on the existing knowledge about us. Realizing that I was a complete novice, I had to build the general background of biological anthropology and related subjects. Going back to school sounded like a good idea. Second, I would like to find and sort out the underlying principle behind human evolution. As it turned out, school and coursework did not satisfy my second wish, so I resorted to applying my physics and mathematics backgrounds and skills to research on whether the cause behind evolution is as fundamental as gravity to all motions in the universe.

Back To School

The primary course work included biological anthropology and anthropology. I also got involved in a few, less tangible courses I thought would let me compare my world view to that of contemporary academic versions of the 21st century.

Biological Anthropology: Getting The Hands Dirty

During my three months of biological anthropology course work, I found that I enjoyed the subject so much, I wondered why anthropology did not seem so significant to me years ago. I could have been a biologist or an anthropologist instead of a physicist. Well, it was too late to change that.

As I anticipated, the course work and textbooks did not address the core principle of evolution. I expressed the desire to sort out the fundamentals with my physical anthropology professor, a brilliant, open-minded senior graduate student from Berkeley, pursuing her anthropology degree, specializing in the brain activity of autistic people. We agreed that I would present a special topic on molecular anthropology to the class using Cann's study as the central theme. This topic served at least two purposes: first, it was an excellent supplement to the outdated textbook for the students' benefit; and second, it motivated me to bootstrap the general molecular genetics research. I was to make a presentation of the study from today's anthropological vantage point, including original premises, outcomes altering our concept of the emergence of modern humans, and the methodology drastically changing the course of anthropological studies.

Sorting Out The Evolutionary Principle

Preparing the special topic presentation was a great exercise since I had to compress my learning with a deadline. As well, it allowed me to contemplate the principle of evolution as an outsider looking in. I had a out-of-the-box idea of what the principles behind the development would be like by that time. The presentation would be the first time I test the waters for the nascent concept I thought was relevant to the evolution principle. After a few discussions with the professor, we felt that I was on the right track and should include this in the presentation. The professor even encouraged me to submit the idea to professional journals, which was certainly a vote of confidence for me as a novice. That was when the big picture of evolutionary principles started to emerge.

Supporting Background: Archaeology

The feud was pretty antagonistic between traditional paleoanthropologists and molecular geneticists in the late 1980s. The root cause was mainly due to a lack of mutual understanding of their respective points of view or disciplines. As a physicist, I tend to side with molecular geneticists, but to make sure I did not have myopic prejudice like the feuding parties, I planned to get to know paleoanthropology better to balance the perspectives. Since there was no specific paleoanthropology course for which fossil study was a significant part, I took archaeology instead.

I found out that archaeology requires a lot of skills that are deeply rooted in physics. One of the essential skills is to reliably determine the ages of fossils. These days, all you have to do is send a sample to a radiocarbon dating lab, and voila—you have your answers a few days later. Dating the vintage of fossils is based on a completely random process dictated by one of the four fundamental forces in nature. The operative word here is "random," which signifies a directionality of the progression of time. Similarly, the "randomness" is also responsible for the technique of luminescence dating. Although the forces involved are different, random process is still the underlying mechanism of being able to date samples' ages.

Another critical skill needed was comparative anatomy, a science requiring extensive training in taxonomy and anatomy for biological organisms. If it were not for this branch of science and scientists, we might never have been able to reconstruct how our ancient ancestors looked like and to construct a family tree of ours.

Attending classes in archaeology was a lot of fun, especially when the professor shared his personal fieldwork experience, which bore a resemblance to Indiana Jones's exciting life, sans the bullwhip. His class sometimes felt as if Professor Indiana Jones was coming alive at the podium. The only difference might have been that no student ever wrote "LOVE YOU" on her eyelids, and if she did, it was well-hidden to everyone except for the professor. Through his lively narration, photos, videos, and exotic location backdrops, he brought our evolutionary journey over the past 6,000,000 to 7,000,000 years to life. The archaeology sites are of particular interest to me for another reason: I found places I would like to visit and did. On a couple of occasions, I even participated in archaeological discoveries myself.

I gave a similar presentation on Cann et al.'s pioneering work to the archaeology classes. Since I was an old pro by then and was given more latitude on the subject matter and time, I dove into the substance of data acquisition and analysis, leading logically to their conclusions about modern humans. I also included a recent genetic study that pinpointed when we began putting on hides or pelts.

Prehistory, History, and Philosophy

These courses are not directly tangible to the evolutionary story, but they are about the stuff generated by fully-evolved modern humans. I was hoping that a refreshed perspective of history and philosophy would help forging a more objective perspective for human evolution.

It seems our physical evolution had reached its final stage, standing still from the onset hunting and gathering as well as agriculture ages after we left Africa about 70,000 years ago. That is not entirely true and there is abundant evidence pointing to our continued evolution. But from our species' biological point of view, there has been one major evolution event since then: the population explosion. As a result, demographers estimate that, about 40,000 years ago, the world's population was less than 1,000,000, compared to almost 10,000,000 by about 10,000 years ago, and almost 100,000,000 at the beginning of state civilizations, around 5,000 years ago. Today, they predict the world's population will reach 10,000,000,000 by 2050.

The population explosion brought about a few large scale trends. It had impacted our species and our habitat and involved in our own evolution. It drastically enlarged our human talent pool, driving advances in culture, inventions, societies, laws, states, sciences, art, technologies, and brought forth unprecedented prosperity and benefits for our well-being. At the same time, the population had brought us unprecedented destruction and tragedy.

History is a record of activities driven by humans, either faithfully or tinted with prejudice. We see that accompanying the population explosion is the drive for perpetual economic growth dictated by wisdom, or folly, from statesmen and economists. We are in a rat race between drastic population growth and economic prosperity. One wonders how this perpetual growth, exponentially if unimpeded, can be sustained with the limited resources of our habitat on earth.

There is a flip side to the rosy picture of our species' success in numbers: 7.8 billion and counting. We had to organize ourselves along the path to our large numbers, so the growth did not trample upon itself, but in most cases, larger organizations have fostered wars, always in the name of the greater good for one faction of humans against another. History is rife with interesting, heroic, glorious, and intriguing stories, all having something to do with war. Although there are a few bright moments in written history—for example, the Enlightenment movement in the 18th century—the world always seems too quick to find excuses to go to war instead of working out their differences.

Reading through history, we cannot help but wonder whether we are intrinsically good or evil from an evolutionary standpoint. Has the population explosion exacerbated our duality of benevolence and malevolence? If I got anything out of history other than recorded facts and information, it is our urgent need to find out how we should direct our evolution for our good. Yes, we do have the ability to influence our evolution at this stage of our existence.

Philosophy directly impacts how we view ourselves relative to the world around us. A part of philosophy focuses on the origin of organizing cognition and intelligence into logic, science, art, and the technology that has benefited us physically or even mentally. The other part focuses on the meaning of our existence, evolution, surroundings, and place with respect to the universe. In other words, human existence has to mean something to people and the universe they occupy. This concerns the eventual relationship between humankind and the universe we make our home.

Through critical thinking, there may be a solution to our existing paradox. On the one hand, we want to continue our species' longevity driven by evolution while balancing good and evil. On the other, we want to find meaning in it all. In the end, it is not how well we understand the philosophy, the history of philosophy, the argument of existence, reasoning, epistemology, empiricism, and even the famed philosophers. Rather, philosophy with respect to the meaning of life from a physical and mental evolutionary point of view should be the critical thinking in which we should engage.

EVOLUTIONARY PRINCIPLES PRIMER

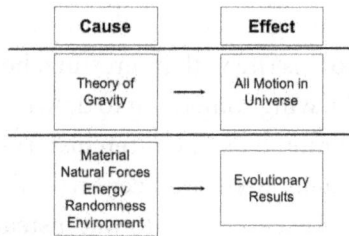

Cause	Effect
Theory of Gravity	All Motion in Universe
Material Natural Forces Energy Randomness Environment	Evolutionary Results

Figure 1. Comparison of cause and effect in gravity and evolution.

If I were to find a principle in evolution I would want it to be simple so it could be described in very few statements. It should also be inclusive or universal, such that anything in evolution is explainable by that simple principle. I would like the principle behind evolution to resemble how the theory of gravity governs all motion in the universe and have a mental picture of a logical analogy between this evolutionary principle and the theory of gravity and motion. The upper half of Figure 1 shows the "cause" and "effect" of gravity. The cause is the gravity that is describable in a single formulation on the left, whereas the "effect" is all of the motion in the universe on the right. The lower part of the graph parallels the causal relationship between the "cause" and "effect" of all evolution activities. It is the cause box in which I have been the most intrigued and have spent most of my efforts to establish that specific evolutionary principle.

A few venerable evolutionists may have a similar concept of simplicity and universality on evolution, but they have yet to crystallize it succinctly. Ernst Mayr said, "The theory of evolution is quite rightly called the greatest unifying theory in biology." This statement implies there is a driving principle behind evolution and its universality is a given.

I am a graphic person who likes to represent ideas in block diagrams. I have theorized that the cause box in evolution should entail (1) raw materials, (2) natural forces, (3) energy, (4) randomness, and (5) environment, as they interplay with each other. The outcome of this interplay is the evolutionary activity and organisms. The resultant organisms go back into the cycle for further evolutionary actions. We will spend some time exploring the principle next chapter so it may be used as a reference for the following chapters.

BOOK OR RESEARCH

This two-pronged effort to find the answers to "where did we come from?" has taken four years and five big note books. There are also numerous sketches with logical blocks arranged in different orders, a little like arranging appliances and cabinetries for our kitchen remodeling searching the most logical orders. This record-keeping enabled me to look back on my years of effort and recall bittersweet experiences. I believe my search for evolutionary fundamentals generates a fresh perspective that may be worth keeping in some form or another.

Flipping through my voluminous notes, mostly in the form of chicken scratches on paper, I believe I have practically gone through the process of earning an advanced degree in anthropology in four years. The thought of participating in a research project to illuminate some important aspects of human evolution is appealing. I thought that linking genetic evolution to speech articulation would be an important subject. Places like the Broad Institute or the Max Planck Institute should be interested in resolving this intriguing question; however, I did not grow up in the molecular anthropology community, and breaking into the circle may require an effort I cannot muster at this time.

I have published numerous scientific and engineering papers in peer-reviewed professional journals. I figured that it would not take much additional effort to edit my notes into a book to share with people with little time but are interested in the subject. I know I have an advantage—since I am not a trained anthropologist or biologist, my writing cannot be overly academic and does not expect readers to have "pre-requisites." I hope that people unfamiliar with academic jargons can read through this with ease to get a good grasp of the big picture as well as details of our evolution.

I have decided to re-edit all of my records into such a book for now.

THE STORY BEGINS FROM 7,000,000 YEARS AGO

Where should the human evolutionary story begin?

It makes the most sense to start when something vaguely resembling human beings first showed up on this planet. This happened when early forms of chimps and early forms of humans went their separate ways from our common ancestors for the first time. This view presupposes a natural evolutionary process along the hominin's lineage from that time up to the present. As to how we got to that initial point, about 7,000,000 years ago, suffice it to say that it was through the evolutionary processes consistent with Charles Darwin's survival of the fittest doctrine from a lot long time ago.

What makes this time a reasonable starting point? This is the age of the oldest fossil specimen having the earliest identifiable human features. The other reason is the multitude of molecular genetic findings corroborating this 7,000,000-year-old milestone. This is obviously a crucial beginning for our existence, and this short statement does not do justice to the critical event. We will dedicate a chapter specifically for this event. When it comes to answering the question "Where did we come from?" the story of evolution starts from there.

3
_____

BEHIND HUMAN EVOLUTION

Ernst Mayr, one of the 20th century's leading evolutionary biologists, famously said that "The theory of evolution is quite rightly called the greatest unifying theory in biology." This chapter attempts to take that statement further and aims at constructing that very unifying theory.

I expected going back to school or researching would provide some glimpses into the fundamental principles. I was not overly surprised that all the knowledge conveyed in classes did not involve evolution's root causes. I had to develop a viable principle from existing evolutionary observations and literatures. About one year into my study, the principle began to take shape. It eventually became the backbone of this chapter, and this book for that matter.

One of the cornerstones of evolution is randomness, which plays a vital role in initiating evolutionary events. However, that subject has not seen a dedicated treatment of any kind as far as I can tell. We will introduce a first-time quantitative verification that randomness is at the root of microscopic evolution processes.

FROM THE VERY BEGINNING

Let us take a quick look at how we came to existence from the very
beginning. Our world started in a massive, fiery explosion 13.7 billion
years ago from nothing, followed by rapid cooling and many elemen-
tary particles materialized: quarks, leptons, and bosons. In turn, they
clumped together to became the more familiar atomic nuclei and
atoms, the major constituents of our sun. Further cooling brought
together heavier elements, the primary ingredients of the solar
system including planet Earth, and quickly brought us to about 5
billion years ago.

About 4 billion years ago, the Earth happened to have an environment suitable for different elements to run into one another and
bond to form a variety of molecules. Most molecules tend to be a
little lopsided either in shape or electrical charge. Molecules of the
same kind like to cling together because of this asymmetry, however
minute. Smaller molecules like lipids may become more complex by
lining up as strings, sheets, or eventually forming membranes that
envelop other molecules, like amino acids, and DNA that can replicate itself. These enclosures are prone to recreating more of the same,
thus starting the process of replication.

Complex replications turned into reproduction giving rise to
biological organisms as early as 3.7 billion years ago. These early
microorganisms interacted with their surroundings and depending
on whether the evolved features worked well with their surroundings, they either survived or perished. The ones that didn't survive
either disappeared or came back as raw materials for other organisms. The surroundings acted as filters that selected and shaped the
organisms into something best fit to replicate or reproduce in the
existing surroundings. The processes went on nonstop and honed the
organisms' features to react to the surroundings more favorably. The
multitudes of the resulting organisms continued to filter through the
environments, enabling the formation of the world of biologically
diverse living organisms in early seawater. Some of them could move
around by themselves as animals. They migrated from the sea, grew

lungs, legs, wings, and finally evolved into sophisticated land and aerial animals.

Planet Earth had not been kind to living organisms. There have been five mass extinctions due to catastrophes caused by the unstable planet or external factors. From each of these sprung a whole host of new species of organisms different from before the extinctions. Some survivors withstood the harshest environmental challenges to live through billions of years.

The last extinction, around 66,000,000 years ago, caused a significant change in our ecosystem, one that gave primates the chance to survive and flourish in the aftermath. They continued along their evolutionary path to diversify into a few apes, one of which was our ancestors. When it was 7,000,000 years ago, our ancestors split into chimpanzees and humans. Finally, we, the most advanced and curious of the apes, have been wondering about from where we have come and trying to make sense of the evolutionary process.

EVOLUTION'S CAUSE AND EFFECT

One can not help but wonder whether there is an underlying driving force behind the evolution that brought us here and now. To me, nothing can arise without cause since, as far as I know, causality continues to be universally true. The essence of causality is the generation and determination of a phenomenon, the effect, by another phenomenon, the cause. In the context of evolution, the "effect" is the collective evolutionary activities and the "cause" is what is behind the effect and what makes it happen.

If the above short summary on our evolution was valid, the cause must have been functioning 4 billion years ago, and it must continue to function in modern times. We will leave the effects (i.e., the happenings in evolution) for the rest of the book. This chapter focuses on building up the principle so we will have an idea about the hidden, driving force behind our evolution: the cause.

LAYING THE GROUNDWORK

Figure 1 in chapter 2 briefly highlighted the cause-and-effect relationship in evolution juxtaposed alongside gravity-motion relationship. We have Isaac Newton to thank for gravity and for making the cause-box so simple, universal, and elegant. The task at hand for evolution is to sort out what factors should be in the cause-box and how these factors interact with one another that can lead to the evolution.

Short of any existing theories to which to refer, the first step is to ensure that all indispensable elements are all there, in the cause-box. The most important criterion for an indispensable element is that evolution would stop if that element is taken away.

The cause-box contains five elements: material, natural forces, energy, randomness, and finally, the environment. Without material, one cannot create anything (except for the very beginning of the universe). When the raw materials come together, they have to follow specific rules to become something more refined. The materials also need the opportunity to meet with each other. They have to be in motion—they carry energy—to have the chance to meet other materials, such that the natural force can exert its influences. However, the movements enabled by energy does not provide a roadmap for the materials to search for their interacting partners. This random encounter between materials happens non-stop and creates organisms. The organisms wander around without purpose or boundary until the environment puts on the constraints, which act like filters weeding out the creations that do not work well with the surroundings. The outcomes of this cycle become the raw material for the next cycle. As such numerous species materialize resulting in the action and outcome of evolution.

RAW MATERIAL—THE FEEDSTOCK

Strictly speaking, the raw materials of our existence—atoms and molecules—are the results of elemental particles that come together according to the rules of the standard model of fundamental particles. We will skip the first nine billion years and start with atoms and molecules when the Earth formed five billion years ago. By interacting with other elements in the cause-box, they become increasingly complex—as complex as our DNA and chromosomes—as the evolutionary process moves along. As we move beyond the raw materials through the evolutionary process, the outcomes could become the next evolutionary cycle's raw materials. Raw material acts as a feedstock in the evolutionary process.

NATURAL FORCE—RULES OF THE GAME

The atoms and molecules do not just bond together willy-nilly and become organic molecules; they have to follow certain rules.

Of nature's four fundamental forces, the strong force governs the atoms' nuclei to stay together and split apart. This is responsible for the formation of all elements we know of on earth and generating nuclear power from fission and fusion. It does not concern us on the evolutionary level since it is not involved with how atoms and molecules interact with one another.

The weak force gives rise to beta decay (e.g., a radioactive, carbon-14 isotope atom would decay into a nitrogen-14 atom). It does not directly participate in our evolution, except to enable us to determine the age of animal fossils or some geological activity.

Gravitational force is too weak to act directly on atoms and molecules; thus, it does not participate in the interplay between the triad of material, force, and energy. It does, however, work as a part of the environment. It is the most ubiquitous environmental filter for evolution happening on earth. For example, gravity dictates all animals' movements on earth; our bipedalism is the result of gravity among other environmental factors.

The fourth force, the electromagnetic force, happens to have the right strength and range for atoms and molecules to feel each other, bond, and initiate chemical reactions. Without it, the materials just ignore each other, and nothing happens even if they are in close proximity through motions. This force penetrates through the vacuum, air, liquid, and water, enabling the creation of complicated organic materials in various parts of the Earth. Of course, this force is also responsible for recombination in sexual reproduction that determines the next generations' traits. The stronger of these forces can rip electrons from atoms and molecules, forming highly-electrically-charged ions that can do all sorts of things to each other and their surroundings. For example, calcium ions contribute to the physiology and biochemistry of organisms' cells. They play an essential role in signal transduction pathways in the contraction of all muscle cell types.

ENERGY—THE MOTIVATOR

If we live in a completely still world—say at absolute zero temperature—everything is motionless. Atoms and molecules have little chance to run into each other and feel the presence of other atoms and molecules. What causes them to get close enough to sense one another? Energy. It enables atoms and molecules to move around and dramatically increases the possibility of their running into other materials, allowing electromagnetic force to take over. The higher the energy, or temperature, the more frequent and harder materials run into each other.

According to the rules of natural forces, when the materials run into each other harder, i.e., at hotter temperature, the probability of formation of new materials will be higher. In this sense, energy, or temperature, is the motivator for materials to get close with one another to create new materials.

RANDOMNESS—THE BACKDROP

Energy enables atoms and molecules, or organisms, to be active to meet their potential partners. There is, however, no instruction as to which direction they will go or who they will meet. While they are motivated to move around, the participants are like headless chickens: they are clueless and without predetermined speed and direction. In every meaningful definition, this is randomness in space.

Complete randomness works in both space and time. The best example of a random situation in space is the Brownian Motion we learn in high school physics. I recall in our high school lab, we introduced a tiny amount of chalk dust on a microscope slide. When we focused on a single dust particle under the microscope, we could see that it moved in a completely uncontrolled manner. Molecules are just like that dust particle and knocked around by other molecules in every possible directions. Only when some molecules happen to run into each other at a certain angle or speed do they combine and become something more complicated than the incoming molecules. All of this happens without a script.

The other dimension of randomness is happening in time domain and are referred to as random processes. Randomness here may refer to a series of similar but unconnected events. Real world random processes consist of multiple series of events happening concurrently. We will focus more on this when we relate the random process with biological mutations later.

One of the most fundamental properties of randomness is that it can only get more random. Just imagine you start with a cup of black coffee, and you want to stir in some cream. Initially, coffee is coffee, and cream is cream. You pour the cream into the coffee, and the cream disperses into the coffee in streams and clumps in the beginning. You stir the mixture thoroughly so it eventually becomes uniform brownish liquid. This is when the randomness of the coffee and the cream is at its maximum.

You cannot un-randomize anything that is already random. Imagine if you try to un-mix the coffee-cream concoction back into coffee and cream—it would be quite impossible, right? As such, we can say that randomization has directionality—it only gets more random as time goes on. It is just like time has the directionality of only moving forward. The impossibility of un-mix the coffee-cream mixture is the same as the impossibility of "time" going backward.

Why is this important for human evolution? If randomness is

involved in any part of evolution, there is no possibility of undoing the evolution, much like there is no possibility of "time" going backward. On the other hand, a do-over is possible if one can scrounge up identical materials and precisely recreate the same environment to prove or disprove a theory. However, due to the random nature of all events, both in time and space, there is no guarantee that the outcomes would be the same every time. This is why, after each mass extinction, organisms are likely to be drastically different from before the disastrous event. Our presence here and now is such a serendipitous event.

ENVIRONMENT: THE UMPIRE

The interplay of the four elements stated above creates new organisms with various characteristics. They are then involuntarily thrown into the surrounding environment to either sink or swim. The environment acts as an umpire calling ball or strike—any organism that cannot work well with its surroundings will sink and not participate in the replication or reproduction process. Since there are various environmental conditions for randomly generated organisms, surviving organisms take on different forms in different environments. Diverse species are, then, the natural outcome of a filtering process.

Not only are there many different surroundings influencing the organisms, but they can also change randomly. For example, there are changing climate conditions in which organisms have to contend with. The mass extinctions mentioned above are examples of changing environments on a global scale.

CONSTRUCTING THE EVOLUTIONARY PRINCIPLE

Having set the stage by introducing these five elements in the CAUSE box, the evolutionary principle begins to take shape. The rest of the task is to organize these five indispensable elements into their logical positions to exercise their functions, producing all the "effects" of evolution. The simple flow chart, Figure 2, results from long deliberation and discussion with my anthropology professor and crystallizes evolution succinctly and inclusively; in other words, simple and universal.

BASIC OPERATIONS

For every evolutionary event there is a fundamental operation requiring the first four elements—material, force, energy, and randomness—working together to initiate the process. The microscopic nature is evident in the preceding introduction of the four elements. In particular, the materials are atoms and molecules initially; the natural force is the electromagnetic force acting upon them; and the energy is the root cause of the random motion. These four elements have to be in operation concurrently, and there is no beginning or end to any sequences. Together, we refer it as the basic operation unit (BOU), enclosed in a dashed-line box in Figure 2, always at work, ceaselessly participated in all aspects of evolution.

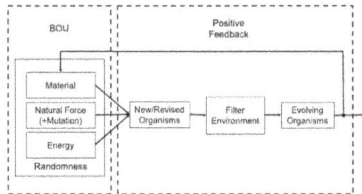

Figure 2. The innerworkings inside the CAUSE box in Figure 1.

The raw materials in our earliest evolutionary cycles would most likely be carbon, oxygen, nitrogen, and hydrogen. They run into each other head-on or in glancing collisions, and in all possible configurations. They come together to form the most rudimentary organic molecules, like lipids and amino acids, when those atoms and molecules see each other favorably. The BOU continues the process numerous times while absorbing new materials until DNA emerges as the earliest form of life.

As soon as new organisms are out of the BOU box, they will encounter the hostile or friendly environments from that point one.

POSITIVE FEEDBACK AND SPECIATION

The outside box encircling the three smaller boxes on the right of Figure 2 entails the positive feedback. New organisms coming out of the BOU now face the surroundings in which they were born. The environment exerts various pass-fail tests on them to see if they can survive. If the organisms cannot survive, they become a part of the raw material and go back into the BOU. If they can, they might also go back to the BOU, come out as a new version and head toward the environment filter again. Assuming the environment has not changed significantly, this filtering process continues undisrupted until an evolving organism is stable enough to be distinctive as a species. We can now identify this repeated environmental filtering with a continuous supply of the organisms, commonly known as "natural selection."

This filtering process is equivalent to positive feedback design with amplification in electrical engineering. A TV receiver is a good analogy for this process in evolution. The receiver acts as a filter, the equivalent of an environmental filter, to pick up one of the multiple TV stations from the air, the equivalent of numerous organisms created by the BOU. With a part of the filtered signal directed back to the receiver's input, the equivalent of the repeated enhancement of evolved features, these organisms' traits become more distinct every time this filter exerts its influence.

A well-designed filter—narrow and clean—filters out unwanted channels better, so you see fewer ghost images from adjacent channels. This sharper filter and purer viewing experience also have an equivalence in evolution. The evolving organisms (there is no fully-evolved organism—even humans are still evolving) or species at this stage will be more specialized if the environment happens to exert harsher or stricter pass-fail decisions on the organisms.

In a TV receiver, if an abundant supply of power works with the well-designed filter, the filtered channel is amplified so more TV sets can view it. This filter and amplifier are how the term "positive feedback" is defined. Equivalently, if there is plenty supply of raw material feeding into the BOU, it results in a successful and prosperous species, just like amplified video channels for multiple viewing.

It is interesting to note the foresight of the famous English ethologist, evolutionary biologist, and author, Richard Dawkins. In his 1986 book, *The Blind Watchmaker,* he declared: "Mutation is random; natural selection is the very opposite of random." In light of the positive feedback part of evolution being choosy and favoring the chosen, natural selection is most definitely not random. We will dive into how to quantitatively describe random mutation later.

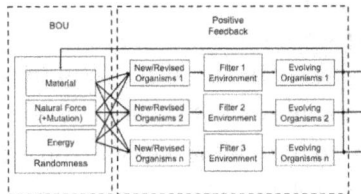

Figure 3. Biological diversification in the evolutionary principle's CAUSE box.

BIOLOGICAL DIVERSIFICATION

Figure 2 brings the OBU and the environment together to form a sequence of events and a positive feedback loop for evolution, complete with cause and effect in causal logic. A single line of this sequence generates a single species. As shown in Figure 3, the environmental filter is not a single-purpose box. The BOU spits out more than one new organism. Each one may be different from the next because of the random nature of the smoldering BOU. At the same time, the environment is a combination of various conditions that could play favorite to more than one organism. So, this positive feedback represents multitudes of parallel lines happening simultaneously.

In the TV receiver analogy, the multiple channels in the air are the numerous organisms. The environments are then multiple TV receivers, tuned to different channels at the same time—you could watch a few channels simultaneously if you had that many TVs. Biological diversification is a natural result from the same principle in Figure 2, except that you simply draw parallel lines, one for each species. In the end, the animal kingdom diversifies into at least 7.8 million species, of which human is one. We have not even included the 250,000 plant species that are part of our food and landscape.

MUTATION

There are two ways an organism's traits can evolve in nature. We will in a later chapter distinguish evolutions by mutation and natural selection. For now, suffice it to know that mutation happens independently of reproduction, although they are not mutually exclusive. Depending on in which part of the genome the mutations happen, they can be inherited and passed down to future generations and possibly shaping a new species.

How does mutation fit into the evolution principle we just established? It sits in the CAUSE box and gives the natural force an additional twist. Rather than needing the organisms to interact with each other on the molecular level, mutations randomly change molecule structure. If mutation is a part of the BOU subjecting to the background of randomness, it should be concluded that mutation is as random as a chance encounter between materials, but over time. Since mutation involves the organisms in the time domain, it can be tracked and quantified if it we can identify what it is in the first place.

CAN RANDOMNESS BE VERIFIED?

Since randomness is such an important cornerstone of evolution, it is paramount to know that it is verifiable from the naturally occurring evolution process of some sort. This section attempts to confirm that mutation, a part of evolution, is indeed a random process in the strictest mathematical and physical sense.

RANDOM PROCESS HAPPENS ON THE MICROSCOPIC LEVEL

One of the central tenets of evolutionary biology is that evolution is blind and it has no foresight or goal. There is no contradiction between this statement and Richard Dawkins's statement that evolution "is the very opposite of random." These two statements represent the two aspects of evolution. On the macroscopic level, evolution seems to be directed by the environment and goaded into a particular direction. As such, the term "very opposite of random" is corroborated. On the microscopic level, the changes in traits are enabled by random molecular rearrangement, generating traits that are neutral to the environment—hence, there is no foresight or goal.

For example, the giraffe's neck lengthened through the generations is a macroscopic change through positive feedback. It is the environment that selected the longer-necked calves—longer necks get access to more foliage. A random molecular process enables the initiation of an equal probability of longer or shorter necks. Their neck lengths, from one generation to the next, can go either way because of molecular randomness in action.

While studying the inner-workings of reproduction may involve keeping track of many molecular parameters in the DNA, this is not impossible with modern science and technology. Mutations have a few obvious and observable characteristics that give science and technology a light working day. First, mutations are simpler to quantify because they do not go through the complex recombination in sexual reproduction. Second, mutations happen a lot less frequently, over a time frame of generations, whereas chromosomal recombination in reproduction happens every generation. Finally, since they occur so infrequently, there are clearly defined parameters to follow. As such, mutations have been widely used in studies of human evolution, migration, and ethnicity. Mutation is, then, the best candidate for a study of randomness.

There have been numerous studies using mutation to decide the ages of biological groups, migrations, medical research, and the like, assuming mutations as being random right off the bat. However, I have not encountered studies specifically on mutations' random nature. How do we know that the mutation process is indeed random? As a physicist, I deal with topics that can be quantified. The question is, then, is there a way to relate mutation and randomness quantitatively? We need two parts for a viable verification: data that signifies mutations and characteristics of randomness.

QUANTIFYING THE RANDOM PROCESSES

In the most fundamental sense, randomness in time is in the manner in which events happen. A random process is a phenomenon that varies unpredictably in time. If we observed an entire time-sequence of the random process under exactly the same conditions, the resulting observed sequences would, in general, not be identical but describable in a statistical manner. That sounds like too much academic gibberish to me. We will use something more practical instead to get to the point.

The nature of the random process can be like the ridership of a city bus. This example can have a practical application for the city's traffic and financial planning. We can characterize the ridership for a specific bus route by an average boarding rate, say, 100 riders per hour. When one counts the actual boarding riders over many hours, it is likely they won't be precisely 100 every hour. Instead, there will be a spread centered around 100. When the frequencies of specific boarding numbers in an hour are recorded, they comprise a distribution. The frequency of boarding rate of 98 is 8, that of boarding 99 is 11, that of boarding 100 is 14, that of boarding 101 is 9, and that of boarding 102 is 7. As you convert this distribution into graphics, it is a histogram. If there is no relation between any two people boarding the bus (riders decide when to board without regard to other riders), it can be considered a random process. The independence between each rider has a fancy name, called "memoryless" by mathematicians. There is a formulation describing this truly random process: Poisson distribution. How random the bus-boarding process is can be numerically judged by how close the actual distribution mimics a Poisson distribution in a mathematical formulation.

A true Poisson distribution would give the probability, P, of k boarders per hour with the average boarding rate x through equation (1).

$$\mathbb{P}(k|x) = \frac{x^{k} \exp(-x)}{k!} \qquad (1)$$

$$\mathbb{P}(k|x) = \exp\left(-\sum_{i=1}^{d} x_i\right)\left(\prod_{i=1}^{d}\frac{x_i^{k_i}}{k_i!}\right)\sum_{k=0}^{max \, k_i}\left(\prod_{i=1}^{d}\binom{k_i}{z}\right)z!\left(\frac{x_0}{\prod_{i} x_i}\right)^{z} \qquad (2)$$

In equation (1), x^{k} represents a quantity of x multiplied by itself k times. exp(-x) is the natural exponential function expressing the natural number exp = 2.71828183 divided by itself x times. k! means k factorial: k*(k-1)*(k-2)...*1. In the bus boarding example, x is 100, and k ranges from 0 to a number far beyond 100. P will peak at 100 and has a value between 0 and 1, as any probability should be.

When the city has a bus network with multiple routes, one can calculate the probability of a specific total boarding number in an hour with a known total average rate through a complete form written as equation (2). d here is the number of route in the bus network. P, again, is the probability of k boarders with the composite average boarding rate of x_0 for the city bus network, where it likely is the sum of the average boarding rates of the individual bus route, x_i's. The symbol sigma denotes the summation and pi the multiplication of numbers for all bus routes. However complicated equation (2) looks, it represents the multiple random boarding processes. Equation (1) is the simplest form of equation (2) when d is 1 for a single bus route.

A human's genetic mutation process is similar to the bus boarding process. Once a mutation happens (one person boarding the bus), we will not know precisely when the next mutation (the next rider boarding the bus) will happen. However, we know with a known average mutation rate (average bus boarding rate), the next mutation event will occur according to the probability described by equation (1). For multiple mutations, the probability of a specific set of mutations happens according to equation (2) if these mutations events are truly random.

These two equations will appear only once here, although equation (1) is used a few times to actually calculate human mtDNA mutation and determine modern humans' age. Equation (2) will see little use except for conceptual illustration when necessary.

It is interesting to note that this distribution saw the first practical application in 1898 when it became necessary to investigate the number of soldiers in the Prussian army killed accidentally by random horse kicks for recruiting and financial planning purposes.

MUTATION DATA

As an amateur learning the general subject of human evolution, I certainly do not have the laboratories, expertise, teams, and finances to gather new data, even if I knew where to look for mutation processes and how to design experiments. Luckily, they do exist in a scientific publication by Cann's group in January 1987. The data—analyzed in a histogram—determines how many mutations in human mitochondrial DNA (mtDNA) have accumulated through the years.

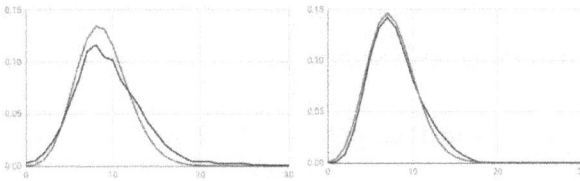

Figure 4. The left-hand side histograms are based on 147 individual mtDNAs and 10,731 pairwise data points (blue) and a calculate Poisson distribution (red) using an average of 8.8. The right-hand side histograms are based on 994 individuals with 493,521 pairwise data points (blue) and a calculated Poisson distribution (red) using an average of 7.5.

The left-hand side of Figure 4 shows the reproduced data (in blue) directly from that publication. It is a histogram of the occurrences of a specific number of mtDNA differences caused by mutations between any two persons. The sample size for this study was a population of 147 individuals producing [147x (147-1)]/2=10,731 possible pairwise data points. Note that the graph shows scaled data since so they can sum up to a 100% probability in total.

If the mutation process is truly random (memoryless) at an average rate (like 100 boarders in an hour), the histogram of how often specific numbers versus mutated differences should follow a Poisson distribution or equation (1).

COMPARISON

The blue (data) curve is the scaled data with a weighted average of 9.47. This means that out of the 147 people, the average difference in the mutated mtDNAs between any two people is 9.47 mutations. The spread around this number indicates that the mutations' divergence is not exactly 9.47 but with some uncertainty or spread. The skew in the histogram should be the first clue that the histogram is likely a Poisson process and not a familiar normal distribution. What is fortuitous is that the weighted average is as low as 9.47. If it were any higher—say, 20 or 30—the skewness characteristic of a Poisson process, and the data's random nature would not be evident and likely disregarded.

The red curve is an attempt to match a Poisson distribution model, equation (1), with data. The first obvious observation would be a remarkable similarity to the blue data curve if we used an average number of 8.8 in the Poisson distribution calculation. In addition to the apparent similarity, there are two key observations. First, by adjusting x in equation (1), we can make the the Poisson calculation look very similar to the measured human DNA mutation histogram (blue curve). Second, the implication that a mutation process is so close to random must have significant importance in evolution. I almost jumped out of my seat four years ago, the first time I realized the similarity was so uncanny, and I knew that I was onto something significant.

I was not completely satisfied with the consistency between the data and calculation in a single case. A different set of data for a similar evolutionary study had surfaced in publication a few years later in Germany. That study had amassed a total of 994 modern humans for the experimentation. The number of data points was a lot higher: [994x (994-1)]/2=493,521. As can be seen on the right-hand side of Figure 4, the close fit of the calculated Poisson distribution (red) and the data (blue) was also very encouraging. The average number in this Poisson distribution calculation is 7.5.

We can conclude that there is a chance that a part of evolution, the mutation in this case, that is presumed random is indeed random. If I were not a physicist and a perfectionist, I would say that these two examples pointed to both qualitative and quantitative verifications.

MUTATIONS, TO BE CONTINUED

More careful readers will notice that there are a few subtle differences between the data and calculated Poisson distributions in

Figure 4. The data curve has slightly higher occurrences either at higher or lower than the weighted average locations. The differences do have some significance that we will explore in more depth in chapter nine, when we introduce the details of the work of this Berkeley group.

PACE OF EVOLUTION—A MATTER OF NUMBERS

Evolution happens in accordance with the evolution principle. But what determines its pace? The changing features of organisms are their adaptation to the environment and takes many generations of adjustments to fit well with their environments. Concurrently, the reproductive recombination randomizes the features rendering them displaying normally distribution characteristics (a real bell-shaped curve) for the "evolved" features.

For example, elephant trunk length have a high probability of being near the average length in a population; super-long and short trunks happen relatively less frequently. The larger the population, the more a trunk length histogram looks like a normal bell-shaped curve. For a smaller elephant population, the very long and very short trunks do not show up often simply because they don't have statistically significant numbers. The larger population have more elephants with long and short necks sitting on the wings of the bell curve. These elephants are the oddballs that smaller populations do not have. This diversity offers more options for elephants to adapt to the changing environments. Simply said, the larger the population, the faster the evolution, a fact Darwin already recognized.

The evolutionary principle does not care whether you have a larger or smaller population of organisms; however, the larger population gives the BOU a different set of initial conditions with which to operate. It is like a positive feedback box designed with a large energy reservoir that potentially provides a higher gain and settles into an optimal operation faster. Thus, a larger population leads to faster evolution when trying to adapt to environments. It is just a matter of numbers.

SUMMARY

We can now put all evolutionary activities and phenomena under the umbrella of this "effect" box whereas the BOU and feedback boxes constitute the "cause." It may not be as simple as the theory of gravity, but evolution is not as fundamental as gravity either. Evolution is messier because it involves materials, the governing electromagnetic natural force, organisms interacting with the environment, and positive feedback. The principle, I believe, is fairly universal to all forms of evolution. As such, the principle introduced here is simultaneously simple and inclusive, relatively speaking. I admit that I am not Isaac Newton, but I take comfort in finding out in 2019 that the discoverer of "Lucy," Donald Johanson, once said that "Evolution is a fact. It is the best explanation of what is known from observations. It's a theory as powerful as the theory of gravity." I welcome constructive and well-thought-through suggestions and critiques to further refine the evolutionary principles introduced here.

A few published studies have addressed the random nature of mutations, but none deals exclusively with its verification. This chapter's attempt—and its partial success—at verification is the first in molecular anthropology. It would be interesting to carry the verification to other elements of evolution, which are supposedly under the influence of the same background randomness any way.

BIBLIOGRAPHY

1. For a similar naturalist view on the origin of life, see, for example, *"The Big Picture: On the Origins of Life, Meaning, and the Universe Itself,"* Sean Carroll, Dutton Publisher, 2016.

2. "Time Dependency of Molecular Rate Estimates and Systematic Overestimation of Recent Divergence Times," Simon Y. W. Ho, Matthew J. Phillips, Alan Cooper, Alexei

J. Drummond, *Molecular Biology and Evolution*, **22**, 1561-1568 (2005).

3. "Biological Diversification and Its Causes," Joel Cracraft, *Annals of the Missouri Botanical Garden*, **72**, 794-822 (1985).

4. In 1953, Miller and Urey attempted to recreate the conditions of primordial earth. They combined ammonia, hydrogen, methane, water vapor, and added electrical sparks (Miller 1953). They found that new molecules formed naturally, and they identified these molecules as 11 standard amino acids.

5. "How Did It All Begin? The Self-Assembly of Organic Molecules and the Origin of Cellular Life," David W. Deamer, *Paleontological Society Special Publication*, **9**, 221-240 (1999).

6. "Mitochondrial DNA and human evolution," Rebecca L. Cann, Mark Stoneking, Allan C. Wilson, *Nature*, **325**, 31-36, (1987).

7. "Neandertal DNA Sequences and the Origin of Modern Humans," Mattias Krings, Ann Stone, Ralf W. Schmitz, Heike Krainitzki, Mark Stoneking and Svante Pääbo, *Cell*, **90**, 19-30, (1997).

8. "A Tutorial of the Poisson Random Field Model in Population Genetics," Praveen Sethupathy and Praveen Sethupathy, *Advances in Bioinformatics*, Article ID 257864, (2008).

9. "New technique delivers complete DNA sequences of chromosomes inherited from mother and father," Loyd Low, *Science Daily*, Mar 7, 2020.

4

WHAT ARE WE?

I believe we now have an overall, albeit oversimplified, answer to "Where did we come from?". However, we have been relatively liberal when using the word "we" in the question. Sometimes we identify ourselves as human beings. We might also include people before modern humans as human beings. There are also a few other confusing names in the public domains, such as Homo *sapiens* or anatomically modern humans. Exactly what and who are we? It would be beneficial to know what "WE" is more definitely before going further. This chapter clarifies a few "official" names, so we have a common language to use when "human" and "we" are the subject of any conversation.

WHAT WE ARE IN A NUTSHELL

Stephen Hawking has a memorable quote on what human beings are: "We are just an advanced breed of monkeys on a minor planet of a very average star, but we can understand the universe. That makes us something very special." Stephen Hawking was a prominent theoretical physicist, widely recognized as the most incisive and perceptive intellect ever. He was the first to propose a theory of cosmology based on the union of relativity theory and quantum mechanics that is still hotly pursued these days. He was a vigorous supporter of the many-world interpretation of quantum mechanics, and his concept has been the basis for many science fiction stories. With these accolades, he is one of the few most visionary people to give a meaningful definition of human beings.

The quote is a serious but lighthearted way to look at us, as it should be. There are three messages in this short statement. First, we are an advanced—probably the most advanced—monkey. Second, our residence is a very average and an insignificant speck of dust in this unimaginably large universe. The third is the most profound one, highlighting the linkage between physical human beings and the meaning of our existence with respect to the universe. It connects our physical presence to the universe in which we reside through our cognition and intelligence. Juxtaposing us against the universe, one cannot help but feel a sense of awe and humility in the tiny time and space we have existed in the expansive universe.

As simple as this quote is, it is a well-thought-out crystallization of what we are, and it should be a pretty good starting point to define us.

WE ARE APES

To be precise, we are not monkeys but apes. Monkeys and apes came from the same ancestors but went their separate ways about 25,000,000 years ago. What are the differences that tell apes apart from monkeys? Tails. Apes do not have them, whereas monkeys do. Tails function as a balancing weight for monkeys' arboreal activities and an extra limb when needed (i.e., prehensile tails). Apes are generally more intelligent than monkeys, and most ape species exhibit some use of tools. While both monkeys and apes can use sounds and gestures to communicate, apes have demonstrated a higher ability of communication.

These differences might not have been very distinct when they split in the early days, but they must have grown more evident as positive feedback evolution process increased the divergence between them. Comparing with our appearances, we look a lot more like apes than monkeys; thus, we are likely descendants of apes rather than monkeys. Today's ape line includes humans, chimpanzees, bonobos, gibbons, orangutans, gorillas, and some smaller types. Of these apes, humans and chimps are most alike and thought to have diverged from each other about 7,000,000 years ago.

A SPECIAL APE WHO CAN THINK, FEEL, AND ORGANIZE

Many of our traits can tell us apart from other apes. We walk upright in a bipedal fashion with the big toe lined up with the other four toes and pointing forward. Other apes have their big toes split from the other four toes so they can grab onto branches for tree-dwelling in addition to it functioning as a part of the foot for quadrupedalism. We have long, opposable thumbs that can fold in the direction of the other fingers, which are relatively shorter for better coordination with the thumb. Together, the fingers and thumb perform complex tasks, whereas other apes cannot manipulate the intricate objects they hold. It could also be that we have shed our fur, earning us the moniker of the naked ape, whereas other apes are still covered with fur. Our nostrils face down, whereas other apes' face the front. Our voice box, larynx, and pharynx have evolved into a different shape and position so that, together with the tongue, throat, mouth, and lip, can make various sounds and vocalize languages that other apes cannot. These comparisons are mostly physical in nature, distinguishing us as an advanced breed of monkeys, in Hawking's view.

There are also other, intangible traits beyond physical features that tell us apart from apes. Nothing is more pronounced than the fact that we can think and have cognition, which inevitably enables us to ponder on our universe. What led to our curiosity about us has its roots in a thinking process able to challenge the environment to survive. As the human species established its footing, thinking became an instinct as much as the desire to eat and mate. The subsequent advance of culture, science, technology, and the arts is due to this ability that is lacking in other apes.

We also have an essential behavioral difference that separates humans from apes. Both humans and apes are social animals that exhibit instinctual empathy toward one another. Chimps use this smartly and often to keep the balance between materialist needs and social cohesiveness for survival. For humans, however, this instinctual empathy has evolved to include a sense of right and wrong toward fellow humans, as well as sympathy, ethics, and morality leading to the necessity of organizing our population. In particular, the organization process is a learned skill through conscious thinking about human behaviors. This ability to operate in large organizations is not evident in the apes.

WHAT IS OUR OFFICIAL NAME?

We can keep making comparisons between human beings and other animals as a way to define us, which is a valid exercise. There exists a scientific methodology to categorize all living organisms into different and distinct compartments that are related structurally and hierarchically. We occupy a specific place in this categorization.

TAXONOMY PUTS US WHERE WE BELONG

We must first have a way to identify ourselves before we can put ourselves in the proper place in the hierarchy. A well-established convention to categorize known biological organisms has been used for a few hundred years. A rudimentary familiarity should help facilitate better communication and help us learn from the cumulative wisdom garnered over the last 300 years.

This convention was established by Swedish botanist Carolus Linnaeus who was considered the father of systematic biology (the scientific method of dividing organisms into larger and smaller groups based on their degree of similarity) in the mid-1700s. He intended to put every organism, including humans, into a well-organized and linked group using his system. His classification of species is similar to the way we classify things in our everyday lives, lumping types together based on physical characteristics that are readily apparent with visual observation, i.e., looks, appearances, and anatomy.

Such a systematic way of naming and classifying the living organisms constitutes the science of taxonomy. It establishes a static picture of existing biological organisms, with no regard to why the picture is the way it is or how it might change with time. The taxonomy also gives every biological organism a unique identification, a name, and eventually becomes a science branch of nomenclature of its own. This science forms the foundation for the study of biological classification today.

WE ARE ONE OF THE ANIMALS

Linnaeus's taxonomy classifies all animals into seven hierarchical ranks and how they are related to each other. Each of these ranks is like a series of nested umbrellas. The top umbrella, the top of the hierarchy, encompasses all animal organisms on earth. Each succeeding lower hierarchy are the smaller umbrellas under the previous umbrella, with distinctions between related organisms becoming increasingly smaller. As it continues to the bottom of the ranks, it constitutes the most natural unit of species. All other higher ranks are a taxonomist's way of making sense of the possible evolutionary past of clusters (under the same umbrella) of related species.

Linnaean Hierarchy				
Linnaean Category Ranks	Human	Human Attributes	Chimpanzee	Tortoise
1. Kingdom	Animalia	Organism able to move on their own	Animalia	Animalia
2. Phylum	Chordata	Animals with a backbone	Chordata	Chordata
3. Class	Mammalia	Vertebrate with fur or hair with milk gland	Mammalia	Reptilia
4. Order	Primate	Mammals with collar bones and grasping fingers	Primate	Testudines
5. Family	Hominidae	Primates with relatively flat faces and 3-D vision	Hominidae (Pongidae)	Testudinidae
6. Genus	Homo	Hominidae with upright postures and large brains	Pan	Manouria
7. Species	Homo sapien	Members of the homo genus with high foreheads and thin skull bones	Pan troglodytes	Manouria emys

We illustrate the hierarchy using examples of humans, chimpanzees, and turtles in the above human-centric taxonomy chart. They include two closely related animals and one distantly related animal, categorized through this seven-rank hierarchy for all living organisms. The top rank is the kingdom, which includes two living kingdoms: plant and animal. The animal kingdom consists of all organisms that can get to places by themselves. These three animals are in the animal kingdom and in the same phylum of vertebrates (*Chordata*), which means they have backbones. Both humans and chimps are in the same class of mammals, whereas tortoises branch off to the class of reptiles. Tortoises are in a different class than their numerous relatives, whereas humans and chimps belong to the same next-rank of primate order. Descending one more rank separates humans and chimpanzees into different families, with humans in the Hominidae family. Chimps are from the other family of Pongidae, which also includes bonobos, gorillas, and orangutans. There is an alternative but more common categorization which considers the Pongidae family as a part of the Hominidae family. Humans are members of the Hominidae family and members of the genus rank of Homo. Finally, humans belong to the species rank of Homo *sapien* below the rank of the Homo genus. It is interesting to note that humans do not have any living fellow species under the Homo genus.

. . .

<u>WE ARE HOMO SAPIENS</u>

Linnaeus first coined the name Homo *sapiens* for us in 1758. The Latin word Homo means "human being," while the participle "sapien" is synonymous with adjectives of "discerning, wise, [and] sensible." The chart implies that Homo *sapiens* is the result of the last step of evolution. As far as species go, modern human is the only extant of the hominin genus and species, as we will see in the next chapter. Our DNA is also the last extant of hominin DNA.

All the categories in the chart have one-word names except for the bottom row, which are the specific IDs for the species. For this most natural unit of species, their names are two-worded, following a binomial system. The first part is the genus name of the organism to which it belongs; the second is the species name, which is usually Latin, printed in italics, although the italics part is not a strict rule. According to Linnaeus, we are officially Homo *sapiens*. Any subspecies (introduced in the next section) names would also be printed in italics.

The taxonomy chart per Linnaeus brings all living organisms under one umbrella, which implicitly includes the evolutionary steps but missing out on now-extinct species. In particular, we have discovered quite a few extinct human relatives not included in the early taxonomy, requiring some refinements to be more complete. We will include them as some other genera and species when we introduce our family tree. Since we are a lot more exposed to the wealth of information of human beings these days, we will likely encounter a few not so well-defined species names and further modifications to the taxonomy are to be expected.

OUR OTHER NAMES

<u>ALL MODERN HUMANS ARE HOMO SAPIENS, BUT NOT ALL HOMO SAPIENS ARE MODERN HUMANS</u>

What are we commonly known as when we are less official? We have habitually and often referred to ourselves as "human beings" so far in this book. According to a definition from the *Encyclopedia*

Britannica, "human beings" are "culture-bearing primates classified in the Homo genus, in particular, the species Homo *sapiens*." It further clarifies that human beings also have a highly developed brain and a resultant capacity for articulate speech and abstract reasoning.

Can we equate human beings with Homo *sapiens*, as listed in the chart? Taxonomy categorizes living organisms according to anatomic similarities, and as far as we know, there are no other animals more similar to us in anatomy than ourselves. Currently living human beings, every one of 7.8 billion people, belong to the same species, that is Homo *sapien*. There is none among us that belongs to any other species. All human beings are Homo *sapiens*.

As it turns out, the classification of Homo *sapiens* is not as well defined as we believe. For example, we have not been able to find Neanderthals a place in this taxonomy, though we know they are another type of human very similar to us. They existed, spread, and roamed over the wide area that is Eurasia for a long time in our past. A part of the reason for not finding Neanderthals a home is because taxonomy does not include extinct organisms, although it alludes to and implicitly advocates evolution. As such, there is a need for categorization with finer grids. If we were to include Neanderthals as Homo *sapiens*, we would have to say that not all Homo *sapiens* are human beings, at least as defined by the *Encyclopedia Britannica*.

On the other hand, if we exclude Neanderthals from the category of human beings, we have to be more specific. We can now define modern humans as Homo *sapiens* directly descended from our MRCA 200,000 years ago. We can then equate modern humans with human beings, again definition per *Encyclopedia Britannica*.

ANATOMICALLY MODERN HUMANS (AMH)

The additional description of modern humans as "anatomic" is a little ambiguous, but this description is used quite frequently. There have been suggestions that Cro-Magnon was the first, true anatomically modern human which is a stretch. We have always had minor differences among ourselves due to local adaptations and accumulated mutations (see chapter 12).

Do we need to create another category of anatomically modern humans? Anatomical modernity is not precise in general, anyway. For example, our wisdom teeth are receding or disappearing—a whopping 35% of us do not even develop them in our lifetimes. It seems like we are still in the middle of an evolution that began about 12,000 years ago and are in the process of obsoleting our wisdom teeth. Other more subtle evolutionary traits going on include our body temperature cooling and our bones lightening. The word "modern," in this sense, is just a matter of degree. 21st century human anatomy is different from that of human beings 12,000 years ago. In this sense, anatomically modern humans should be identical to human beings, and therefore, modern humans.

It is interesting to note that we are the only animal aware of its ongoing evolution, and we are witnessing that happening in front of our eyes. Our evolution is not complete, we are still evolving.

HOMO SAPIEN SAPIENS: A FINER CATEGORIZATION

Our identification as Homo *sapiens* is not 100% clear from Linnaeus's taxonomy either, although our species name of Homo *sapien* is correct. You might have heard people referring to us as Homo *sapien sapiens*, just to underscore our belief that we are not merely wise—we are wiser than wise. Is this our sense of arrogance and narcissism on full display? Is this needed? On many occasions, this double sapien name attempts to utilize an additional rank, subspecies, when Linnaeus's species starts to split into more than one uniform group, something he already recognized in the mid-1770s. Part of the need for the split may be because some other humans, like Neanderthals, also qualify as Homo *sapiens*, but they are still different.

At this time, the subspecies is a commonly accepted standard convention below the species rank. Homo *sapien sapiens* are human beings, modern humans, and anatomically modern humans.

. . .

WE ARE NOT ARCHAIC HOMO SAPIENS

We may also read about the term archaic Homo *sapiens* for some particular purposes. This name is not standardized, but it is a useful reference for people who are Homo *sapiens* but came before modern humans. In that sense, Neanderthals belong to this category. Neanderthals are also assigned the classification of Homo *neanderthalensis* in some cases, meaning they are a species different than human beings.

As we will see later, a large percentage of the 7.8 billion modern humans carry a certain percentage of Neanderthal genes in their DNA, meaning we have undoubtedly crossbred with Neanderthals in the past. Why are modern humans and Neanderthals different species, then? The answer is that we are not. If Homo *sapien sapien* is a legitimate subspecies designation, the subspecies of Homo *sapiens neanderthalensis* should also be reasonable. But we modern humans are not archaic Homo *sapiens*.

HOMININS AND EARLY HUMANS

The above taxonomy chart shows that under the family of Hominidae, there is the genus of Homo, which supposedly includes other Homo members. There should also be a few other species under the genus of Homo. For some targeted discussion, we lump early humans and modern humans under the name of hominin, which comprises all human side members after the split from chimps. In effect, the name hominin combines the rank of genus with at least three genera and all Homo species under them. It refers to the collective group of modern humans and extinct human species, including the genera of Homo, Australopithecus, and Ardipithecus. These names will be become clear in an upcoming chapter.

For some specific discussions, we also use the expression of early humans to represent all hominins except modern humans when we cover our migration throughout the globe in chapter 13.

TAXONOMY, PHYLOGENETIC TREE, AND THE HUMAN FAMILY TREE

The taxonomy chart classifies live animals. It does not contain information on the timing of evolutionary steps. However, the relationship across the ranks implies that evolution was at work to explain morphological similarities and differences. When we include evolutionary steps and milestones in the taxonomy, it becomes the species' family tree, or more adequately, a phylogenetic tree.

A family tree provides family members' details and how they relate in the most traditional sense. Depending on how far back the tree goes, it can range from hundreds of years to as far back as a few thousand years. My short-term family tree goes back 200 years, beginning with my great grandfather (born 1835) at the root of the tree. I can visit his house if I want to because it still stands today. With fewer details and less certainty, I can trace my ancestral line back to around 1050 BCE, when the patriarch was one of the founding fathers of an 800-year-long dynasty. My being a part of royalty is not a surprise since the majority of people would not be living today were they not some royal lines or aristocrats. It is also not a surprise that one of the 2019 *Jeopardy* game show participants, Andrew Kung, was a direct descendant of Confucius. That line of ancestors goes back to about 500 BCE. One thing is definite: our traditional family trees do not include any members that are not Homo *sapien sapiens*.

A phylogenetic tree is a family tree of species, the human phylogenetic tree covers the time since we split from the chimps and became our own species. In this book, "human family tree" and "phylogenetic tree" are synonymous and used interchangeably, depending on the emphasis and context.

SPECIES PRIMER

One cannot help but question what exactly constitutes a species under Linnaeus's categorization system. On its own, the word species is a most confusing term. For the sake of discussion, we will start with the more traditional definition of species for now. We will give "species" and human speciation—the process of humans and chimps going their separate ways—a molecular treatment, as it should, in chapter II.

In general, mammals are considered as the same species if they can successfully interbreed and reproduce offspring. The operative word here is "successful," meaning their offspring can continue to reproduce. Consider the situation in which a male horse (having 32 pairs of chromosomes) and a female donkey (31) mate and produce an offspring: the mule. Wouldn't you say that horse and donkey belong to the same species because they can produce one offspring? For thousands of years—since 3,000 BCE in Egypt—we bred mules for utility purposes because of their hardiness, which we still do in many parts of the world. It is also well known that mules are sterile and thus cannot "successfully" reproduce to perpetuate their lineage. It is still not clear why male and female donkeys produce sterile animals, but it is probable that the offspring of parents with different numbers of chromosomes have trouble deciding what to pass onto the next generation, molecularly speaking. In that sense, animals with a different number of chromosomes do not belong to the same species. As such, horse and donkey are not the same species.

What is the confusion, then? We mentioned that humans and chimps went their separate ways from the same ancestor whereas modern humans have 23 pairs of chromosomes and modern chimps have 24. What happened during this transition time? Both humans and chimps successfully breed by themselves and are their own species, but how many pairs of chromosomes did our common ancestor have? It is not that simple, after all. In reality, the process of becoming the Homo *sapien* species is relatively complicated. The mechanism and duration it takes for "speciation" is another major anthropological topic that will be taken up in chapter II because it is part of the earliest human evolution story from our very beginnings.

THE TIMELINE YARDSTICK: THOUSANDS AND MILLIONS OF YEARS

How is time measured in human evolution? On the taxonomy chart, each umbrella category gives rise to the next level in the hierarchy, demarcating a major categorization and an evolutionary step.

We can start at the top first. Here, there are sequential events of life from the very beginning. First, there is evidence that single-celled organisms appeared four billion years ago. This was followed by multicellular organisms 1.5 billion years ago, the earliest animals 700,000,000 years ago, animal phyla 540,000,000 years ago, dinosaurs 240,000,000 years ago, mammals 200,000,000 years ago, primates 50,000,000 years ago, and finally, early humans 7,000,000 years ago. All of these significant events happened before humans could be demarcated in millions of years.

On the other hand, regular family trees span, at most, in the hundreds to thousands of years. My royal lineage of 3,000 years spans 140 generations. The time of written culture would have started about 7,000 years ago, or about 300 generations ago. While visiting Gobekli Tepe, I saw stone carvings dating back to 12,000 years ago. I believe that would certainly need a convoluted family tree to relate those people to us for the past ~500 generations.

A human family tree, then, would cover changes and members from between 7,000,000 years ago to as recently as 12,000 years ago, covering 300,000 generations. It is no surprise that molecular anthropologists have trouble keeping track of genetic changes that have happened 300,000 times since our beginning, but it is not without hope that we can eventually gain a good handle on that in the future.

Whether it is millions of years, thousands of years, or hundreds of thousands of generations, the timelines give us a sense of awe, considering the immense time scale that measures our evolution from apes to modern humans.

BIBLIOGRAPHY

1. For more detailed information on taxonomy, see, for example, *"Biological anthropology, The natural history of humankind,"* third edition, Craig Stanford, John S. Allen, Susan Anton, third edition, Pearson Education, Inc. Publisher, 2012.

5

THE HUMAN FAMILY TREE

W hen it comes to the human family tree—or phylogenetic tree—we have Neanderthals to thank for getting our human evolution study started. Neanderthal fossils were first discovered in Neander Valley, Germany, in the mid-nineteenth century; thus, the namesake.

The early discoveries created quite a stir because the skeletons were not human and yet so human that scientists did not know what to make of them. Discoveries of Neanderthals at Engis in Belgium followed. They eventually spread over vast areas, spanning Spain, France, Germany, Italy, Romania, Georgia, along the Danube corridor, the Middle East, and as far east as the Altai Mountains, Southern Siberia.

When the proto-human fossil discoveries continued, it turned the scientific world upside down. We believed that nature has endowed us with our birthright as the most superior being in the world without compare. We were entirely different from any other animals and should not even be a part of any taxonomy or evolution. On the other hand, the Neanderthals looked so similar to us—Marcellin Boule's description of their brute appearance notwithstanding—they must be our close relatives. If we put Neanderthals in the taxonomy, why should we not also be a part of it?

How closely were we related? In the years following the initial discoveries, we learned that Neanderthals were almost the same size as us except with more robust build. They also had virtually the same brain capacities, and sometimes even larger. Their artifacts bore evidence of sophisticated thinking and dexterous handiwork. They had similar abstraction abilities and generated artwork as early as we did. They even had throat and voice box structures that could have uttered similar sounds, including communicable languages. Over the last 20 years, we learned that we interbred with Neanderthals, and they left genetic trails in our DNA. There should be no doubt that we modern humans are a part of evolution anymore.

We have been obsessed with Neanderthals for a good part of the last 150 years. They tickle our imagination, and before modern-day science ascertained their specific genetic attributes, we let that run wild because we know that they must fit into our past, we just did not know how. In fantasy and science fiction, we often wonder what it might be like to meet other intelligent species. It's profoundly intriguing to find out that these meetings did happen with evidence left in our genes.

Let's indulge ourselves in some of our fantasy about Neanderthals and how we imagine our relationship could have been. As you will find out, these imaginings are relatively ingenious and often goad us to find how the truth matches our imagination.

NEANDERTHALS INSPIRED OUR IMAGINATION FOR YEARS

I recall reading a science fiction book about 20 years ago with the title of *Neanderthals, A Novel*, during a westbound transatlantic flight. The flight was just about enough to finish the book from cover to cover. I bought the book at the airport bookstore because of the title and a "SOON TO BE A STEVEN SPIELBERG MOVIE" banner on the cover. Steven Spielberg's

DreamWorks SKG studio is said to have purchased the movie rights with a price tag of $1,000,000, which was dirt cheap considering how much money the movie studio would have made if it had become a blockbuster like Jurassic Park. In the end, the movie was never made for some reason.

The book's details have blurred after all these years, and I can only recall that it had a pretty good level of humor, fantasy, pseudo-science, and intrigue in its own right as a fiction book. The writer's imagination was so vivid and realistic that a few significant human issues—psychological and anthropological—are still mainstream in the academic world consuming our brainpower.

The story's premise is that human beings and Neanderthals have been fighting bloody wars for tens of thousands of years that are still ongoing in the present day. These wars are the primary reason for the drastic reduction—but not yet the extinction—of the Neanderthal population. Whether the animosity between the species really happened is unknown, but modern humans and Neanderthals did occupy the same space for at least a few thousand years. One thing is for sure: Neanderthals are all gone, and not a single one of them survived.

In the book, there is constant infighting between the two remaining Neanderthal factions in addition to the conflict with modern humans. One side represents the peace-loving, docile group content with the bare minimum of resources. The others are adventurous, aggressive warmongers who continuously strive for better livelihoods and an abundance of resources. The symbolic messages the writer is trying to convey are unclear; however, they vaguely resemble the two sides of good and evil that characterize humans' internal conflicts. It reminds me of the debates between Hobbes's evil humans and Rousseau's noble savages.

Interestingly, these Neanderthals resided on the Pamir Plateaus of today's Tajikistan Republic. The aggressors lived in a cave that is not too different from the Chauvet Cave in southern France, where cave paintings have been discovered. This middle-Asian location would have been cold and dry, the ideal conditions amenable to preserving DNA. The writer would be pleased to know that Neanderthals had taken residence not too far away from this fictitious location about 40,000 years ago and left traces of their DNA in their fossils. Scientists also discovered a previously unknown Homo species: the Denisovans, who happen to be another of our close relatives.

As a part of the storyline, the writer assumes these modern-day Neanderthals did not have the right anatomy to articulate their thoughts into spoken language; however, they do have extrasensory perception (ESP) abilities, with which they communicate to each other and human beings because they have large cranial capacities. (Although this is accomplished with the help of psychedelic mushrooms. Richard Leakey had a long narration about hallucinations evoked by these mushrooms. There is a revival of academic research on the psychedelic effect for human psychology in the last few years.) However, the writer and the world in the mid-1990s still did not know enough about Neanderthals. Scientists discovered evidence of their speaking abilities from fossil remains dated as early as 60,000 years ago—and possibly a lot earlier—in 2014.

A few episodes of good-natured bantering between the male and female protagonists represent the conflict between the traditional paleoanthropology and molecular anthropology, analogous to a feud between the two academic disciplines. This feud seems to reflect the continuing academic debates that were still raging, even ten years after Cann et al.'s study, which supposedly settled the origins of modern humans once and for all.

This fiction is not the only book leveraging the popularity of Neanderthals to make money. An earlier fiction, The Inheritors (published in 1955), also exploits the general public's obsession on them. It narrates the conflicts between modern humans and Neanderthals from a Neanderthal's point of view. In retrospect, the book was written when we knew little about Neanderthals. There is, of course, the classic series of Earth's Children written by Jean Auel. The first of the series, entitled "The Clan of The Cave Bear", was made into a movie of the same name. It was not a big blockbuster, but I liked the story very much because as early as mid 1980 it had contemplated on mixed relationship between modern humans and Neanderthals.

Neanderthals occupy a good part of what is to come in this book because their physical presence was overlapping in time and location with modern humans. They must be our friends or foes for a few thousand years, after all.

AN ABBREVIATED HUMAN FAMILY TREE

The subject of our family tree deserves an elaborate discussion with concrete evidence leading to comprehensive answers. In addition, we need an educated imagination to bridge obvious gaps in time and in our ancestors' transitions. We have to realize that any rendition of a human family tree will not fully satisfy both purpose and it will never be 100% accurate.

According to the Population Reference Bureau (PRB, a private, nonprofit organization specializing in collecting and supplying statistics necessary for research and academic purposes focused on the environment, health, and structure of human populations), there have been a total of 107 billion individual hominins that have lived on this planet since our split from the chimps. Though it is impossible to include all hominins starting from that fateful time and everything that has happened since, what is definite is that out of the many hominins who represent the collective population since splitting off from the chimps, it is inevitable that one of them was our direct ancestor.

Here, we describe an abbreviated version of our family tree in Figure 5 for a vision of how 7,000,000 years of evolution has played out. The goal here is to outline essential hominin milestones that eventually led to modern humans. It walks through the main branch of a family tree that leads directly back to a common ancestor shared by humans and chimps. We will not dive into complex crossbreeding among the various branches of our ancestors, although there is clear evidence that the family tree would look like a crisscrossing inter-twined bush instead of a single trunk tree. We will address relevant cross-links when we cross that bridge.

This chapter uses the following modern human-centric phylogenetic tree, Figure 5, as a reference. Both fossil records and human genetics have been used to construct this diagram.

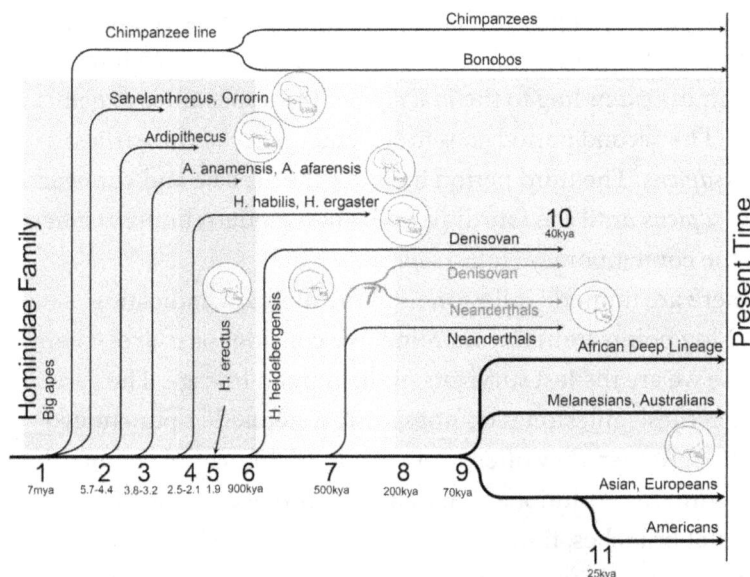

Figure 5. A modern human centric family tree (human phylogenetic tree) covering from 7,000,000 years ago up to the present time.

READING THE DIAGRAM

The diagram reads the timelines from left to right—with a starting point of 7,000,000 years ago—and works its way up to the present to the right, though not to scale for convenience and to include details from the more recent past. The leftmost time represents the starting point of hominins or the split of the Hominidae/great apes family. The thicks line represents the direct ancestral line from which we descended. The arrowheads on the lineage lines denote each organism's final place in time (again, not intended to be accurate). If the arrowheads do not reach the present time, the organisms represented are most likely extinct.

Four Periods And Eleven Milestones

The 7,000,000 years have been divided into four periods, indi-cated by different colors, with the dividing lines representing transi-tions on our evolutionary line. They are divided based on morphological changes, as well as perceived changes in intelligence and behavior. The first period starts at the beginning of a few genera of hominins extending to the first sign of the appearance of genus Homo. The second period goes to the emergence of the earliest Homo *sapiens*. The third period includes the archaic and younger Homo *sapiens* until the fourth period when modern humans emerged from the contemporary Homo *sapiens*.

There are numeral milestones on the diagram, indicating branching points from the mainline. We consider ourselves "main" because we are the last survivors of the human lineage. The gaps between these milestones do not signify a stepped or punctuated evolution. Rather, they often represent available sample points along the continuous evolutionary march. However, we should keep in mind that branches, times, and gaps might have to be modified whenever new, objective, and verifiable evidence surfaces. It is also expected that modifications continue to happen quite often.

THE PRE-HOMO PERIOD: 7,000,000 TO 2,500,000 years ago

The pre-Homo period started 7,000,000 years ago. This starting point is, at best, an estimate based on fossil records and molecular genetics studies. The transition is necessarily long and complicated and happens in the range of a few million years. The chimps and hominins likely simmered in sub-Saharan Africa and built up momentum to transition to the next stage of evolution. In truth, these primates were under the influence of a continuous and relentless positive feedback process at work. The fact that it took a long time to effect species formation may be due to limited population sizes at the time.

. . .

MILESTONE 1: GREAT APES BRANCHING OFF TO THREE LINES

The Split between hominins and chimpanzees

The beginning line at the left represents the common ancestral population for chimps and hominins, great apes in the Hominidae family. While the original divergence between the hominin and "great ape" population could have occurred as early as 13,000,000 years ago, the hybridization speciation process may have been ongoing until as recently as 5,400,000 years ago. From the archaeological and genetic evidence, the commonly accepted rates of gene mutation, and the assumption that there are relatively numerous individuals in the population, speciation between chimps and hominins may have finally taken shape between 6,000,000 and 8,000,000 years ago. We will use the 7,000,000 years ago marker as the first milestone, keeping in mind that the split is complicated. There is a more comprehensive story to this complex process covered in chapter 11. Impatient readers can flip to that chapter for a quick peek if they would like.

The Chimps Went Their Merry Way

After the chimp-hominin divergence, the chimp line must have gone through its evolutionary path over the past 7,000,000 years and taken different forms and morphologies. There is evidence that while hominins became so smart that they dominated their land over the next 7,000,000 years, the chimps—or maybe other great apes—also became smarter, although not as fast. According to a recent study, modern-day chimps may even be more intelligent than our hominin ancestors—such as Australopithecus *afarensis*—at milestone three. Who is to say that they will not become as smart as us in maybe a few more million years, given space and the absence of human intervention?

The chimps' evolutionary path is not well known, but there may have been about four or five subspecies evolving from the chimps of 7,000,000 years ago. Only two have reasonable numbers to qualify as populations surviving in tropical Africa: chimps and bonobos.

A Tale of Two Chimps

Based on genetic studies, the chimpanzee line split into two species: chimps and bonobos around 1,500,000 years ago. This timeline is determined by genetic analysis using a molecular clock technique, the same method used to determine modern humans' age. Long-time geographical isolation between two populations of the same species could be the cause of this speciation.

Today, bonobos live predominantly on the south side of the Congo River's Congo Basin, spanning a few countries in western Africa. By contrast, chimps live mostly on the north side. The Congo River is the fifth-longest river in Africa. It had a lot different riverbed until it settled into its current river geography, about 1,500,000 years ago.

These two events, genetically determined split and geographic isolation, are likely correlated, being so close in time and proximity. Speciation between the chimps and bonobos could happen in the following scenario, starting with a population of the same species, most likely, the common ancestor of both. They were dissected into two bands around 1,500,000 years ago due to geological isolation, caused by the Congo River settling into its current course and becoming a natural barrier. By the way, chimps and bonobos cannot swim.

After 1,500,000 years of independent evolutionary paths, the species are different in a few aspects. Bonobos are female-dominant, with the females forming tight bonds against males through same-sex, socio-sexual contact, thus limiting aggression. In the wild, they do not seem to hunt, use tools, or exhibit lethal aggression cooperatively. These two distinct social behaviors remind me of the more docile Neanderthal band in the science fiction book *Neanderthals*. Chimps, on the other hand, are male-dominant, with intense aggression that can be lethal between different groups. Chimps use tools, cooperatively hunt monkeys, and will even eat the infants of other chimpanzee groups when needed. They are a little like the aggressive Neanderthal band in that science fiction. Morphology wise, whereas bonobos have a slender build, bright pink lips, and a black face, chimps are a robust build with dark lips and whose face color changes with age.

Are Chimps and Bonobos the same species?

Some taxonomies give the name of Pan *troglodytes* (chapter 3) to chimps and Pan *paniscus* to bonobos, treating them as separate species. Irrespective of their morphological and behavioral differences, they can successfully interbreed, albeit only in captivity through human intervention and not in the wild. It is intriguing to note that 1,000,000 to 2,000,000 years of isolation does not fully complete a natural speciation process. According to the "successful interbreeding" definition of species, chimps and bonobos belong to the same species.

The ability to interbreed is crucial because, as we will see later, humans did interbreed with archaic Homo *sapiens*, even though we were genetically 400,000 to 500,000 years apart. It is a testament that nature always finds a way when reproduction is frustrated in the face of phenotypic differences. It also gives more credence that a slow speciation process is the norm rather than the exception.

Of Apes And Men—Sahelanthropus Genus

The first credible evidence of the split between chimps and hominins is the discovery of Sahelanthropus *tchadensis* fossils in which we found the earliest identifiable hominin features, making this possibly the earliest human ancestor.

The fossils—discovered around 2002 Chad Republic, Africa—were dated to about 7,000,000 years ago. Existing fossils include a relatively small cranium, five jaw pieces, and some teeth, making the head a mixture of derived and primitive features. Although the fossils are badly deformed, comparative anatomists are able to assemble them into meaningful body parts. The braincase is small, similar to that of extant chimps, and is considerably less than that of modern humans. Unlike the V-shaped dental arcade for humans, the samples had a U-shaped dental arcade and heavy brow ridges and facial structures, markedly different from those found in today's humans. These are only some of the features that would normally be attributed to the chimp line.

There is, however, anatomical evidence of bipedalism through the position of the hole connecting the spinal cord and the skull base: the foramen magnum. This feature is different from that of chimps, although these people may still squat and slouch while walking. This inference for the beginning of standing upright is what adds the suffix of "thropus" to the full name, indicating a relation to humans. In essence, they are not far from their close relatives at the time, the chimps. Even though we have no idea what the chimps looked like at that time, Sahelanthropus was different from today's chimps.

Using human fossil evidence to determine our family tree depends on openness, objectivity and independent verification. As important as the foramen magnum's anatomic location in the Sahelanthropus skull, the original discoverers never gave access of that skull to any colleagues since 2,001. I debated whether to include Sahelanthropus in our family tree but decided to temporarily accept them as one of our hominin members. Late 2020 had seen evidence in a femur fossil discovered near the original fossil site refuting Sahelanthropus being a hominin. The new evidence is slim, and the supposedly contradicting argument is also weak. For now, the existence of Sahelanthropus will be considered partially true.

A 7,200,000 year-old fossil mandible found near Athens in 1944, given the name of Graecopithecus *freybergi*—named after Bruno von Freyberg who thought the mandible piece was from a monkey—has led to suggestions that it may have belonged to the oldest direct ancestor of humans—excluding the chimp lineage—or the last common ancestor of both humans and chimps. It is not clear as to which line they belonged—the hominin line or the one leading to the hominin line—in the Hominidae family.

Half-Baked Human: Orrorin Genus

Along the lineage a little later is Orrorin *tugenensis*, dated between 6,100,000 and 5,700,000 years ago. We could assign an additional milestone for this genus, but the fossil records are rare and the evidence fairly weak. Morphology-wise, it may or may not be Salelanthropus' direct descendants. Its fossils were discovered in modern-day Kenya and included the rear part of a mandible, some teeth, thigh and arm bones, sections of fingers, and the tip of a thumb.

The comparative anatomy interpretation is a little confusing as it usually overreaches when based on scant fossil evidence. Orrorins are different from chimps and have relatively smaller teeth with thicker enamel, similar to modern humans. They are sometimes bipedal, given anatomical evidence in the thigh bone. Their thumbs have some ability to fold in and grab things with the other fingers, likely used for climbing and grasping things for tool using at the same time. All of these signs suggest they are a continuation of the evolution away from chimps and toward humans. They died away relatively fast since there are no more fossils of this kind soon after 6,000,000 years ago, and there are no other links between us in the time after their existence. Instead, there are other organisms with less similarity to us, at least in early times, filling linkage gaps. These rare fossils have not given traditional anthropologists enough to dig deeper into their lineages.

MILESTONE 2: ARDIPITHECUS GENUS

As human evolution progressed grudgingly but assuredly, it came to Ardipithecus, indicated by milestone two. As you will see later, the suffix "pithecus" appears quite frequently because it means "ape" in Greek. Most fossils akin to the hominins discovered are attributable to multiple apes-like species. The "Ardi" prefix means "ground floor" in the Afar language (a region in Ethiopia, Africa). The "Afar" name has worked its way into the naming of another of our ancestors, albeit not a direct one: the iconic Lucy who captured public interest and became a part of the pop culture in the 1970s.

Ardipithecus fossils consist of fragments of skulls, mandible, pelvis, arm bones, hands, feet, and some teeth from a few locations, discovered in the 1930s through to 2010. One of the most complete Ardipithecus fossils discovered was Ardipithecus *ramidus* by Tim White in 1994. Generally accepted dating puts Ardipithecus as living between 4,400,000 and 5,700,000 years ago. A few key facts inferred from an anatomic analysis include: a protruding mandible and maxilla, retaining the primitive feature of chimps; a still relatively small brain; and a splayed big toe, functioning for facultative (i.e., taking place under some conditions but not others) bipedal walking and quadrupedal climbing when necessary. It is particularly revealing that this splayed big toe lines up in a direction for walking. As such, they were, at times, upright and bipedal—which is generally referred to as abductive—although they also retained their tree-dwelling and quadrupedal nature.

They also possessed canine-shearing complex where utility canines and first premolar teeth form a self-sharpening apparatus similar to that of chimps. It looks as if Ardipithecus is a mishmash of half-baked organisms sitting between humans and chimps. The follow-up evolution continues their divergence, moving toward full bipedalism, freeing up the hands for toolmaking.

Since bipedalism is a critical differentiation between chimps and humans, it is reasonable to ponder the necessity for an organism to evolve gradually toward walking upright. For a long time, the origin of our lineage's bipedalism was postulated to have its roots in the expanding savannas of the period, starting from 5,300,000 years ago, when the Earth experienced cooler and dryer climates. A further examination of the geological records, considering the locales and times in which Sahelanthropus, Orrorin, and Ardipithecus lived, does not fully support this supposition. Alternatively, the geological change resulting in Eastern Africa's turning from lush to barren land might have more to do with this bipedalism.

MILESTONE 3: THE EMERGENCE OF AUSTRALOPITHECUS GENUS

There was a flourish of other less primitive apes found over east-, south-, and north-central Africa in the 2,000,000 years after Ardip-ithecus. We collectively referred to them as the Australopithecus genus, so-named by Australian anatomist Raymond Dart in 1925 after finding a type of this specimen in South Africa. Hence, the word is a combination of australis (south) and pithecus. The time of this genus's emergence is still uncertain, but a general time frame should be between 4,000,000 to 3,200,000 years ago. In an alternative categorization, a "subtribe" of Australopithecine includes both Ardipithecus and Australopithecus. Although Ardipithecus is more primitive than the generic Australopithecus, they are almost contemporary, with Ardipithecus barely predating Australopithecus (by 200,000 years), and they lived near each other. As for the various Australopithecine species, with some distinct differences, the species names represent the fossils' discovery locations, consistent with biological naming conventions.

Milestone 3 roughly dates to around 3,800,000-3,200,000 years ago, referring to the earliest of the Australopithecines (the subtribe of Australopithecus genera), Australopithecus *anamensis*. The word "*anam*" means "lake" in the Turkana language since the specimen was discovered in the region of West Lake Turkana in northern Kenya. The fossil specimen includes a humerus (arm bone), upper and lower jawbone, cranial fragments, tibia parts, and a femur, found in Kenya and eastern Ethiopia.

Comparative anatomy has determined a few Australopithecine features. They are habitually bipedal, although they retained some primitive features of the chimps' upper limbs, implying that they often climbed trees. Such arboreal dwelling was one behavior retained by early hominins until the first Homo genus's appearance about 2,500,000 years ago, when these qualities totally disappeared.

A. *afarensis* shares a fair number of traits with A. *anamensis*, but it shows up a little later in the fossil records. This is one of the longest-lived and best-known early human species. Paleoanthropologists have uncovered the remains of more than 300 individuals. Found between 3,850,000 and 2,950,000 years ago in Eastern Africa (Ethiopia, Kenya, Tanzania), this species survived for more than 900,000 years, which is over four times as long as our subspecies has been around.

A. *afarensis* is best known for specimens from sites in Ethiopia— "Lucy," the "First Family," the "first child"—and the oldest docu-

mented bipedal footprint trails at Laetoli, Tanzania. All of these locations are within the Afar Triangle Region, or the Afar Depression,
named this due to its low altitude, which is also one of the most critical areas for the study of paleoanthropology.

Located in East Africa, the Afar Triangle is a part of the Great Rift
Valley. The area sits on top of a junction where three continental
plates meet, called a triple rift junction. At this rift junction, there is a
continually widening rift (referred to as rift valley) in the Earth's
crust. The rift consists of nearly 200 meters of strata—rock layers of
sediment—that span a significant geological period of time. The sediment is fossil-rich and often preserved partial animal skeletons, and
the researchers could potentially recover well-preserved and more
complete fossils from the environment. Furthermore, the area had
feldspars and volcanic glass valuable for chronometric dating.

Lucy In The Sky With Diamonds

Out of these 300-plus Australopithecus *afarensis* individuals, Lucy
is the rock star, named after The Beatles' song, "Lucy in the Sky with
Diamonds." The specimen is one of the most complete hominin
skeletons ever found. It is dated to about 3,200,000 years ago and was
discovered by Donald Johanson. The skeleton is a female, 12 years of
age, and has a small skull similar to that of apes, and evidence of a
walking, bipedal, upright gait close to that of humans. This combination supports the view of human evolution that bipedalism preceded
an increase in brain size. She must have been more upright and
bipedal than tree-dwellers, judging by the fact that her big toe had
merged with the rest of the toes and was arched and stiff, much like
ours, handicapping the quadrupedalism needed for climbing.

In addition to her significant discovery, Lucy captured much
public interest and attained an iconic status in the 1970s. Her popularity was buoyed by her association with the song by The Beatles.
The music was played loudly and repeatedly in the expedition camp
in the evening after the excavation team's first day of work on the
recovery site. The Lucy discovery has raised public awareness of the
complex evolutionary processes through which humans have gone
through to become what they are today.

The aftermath of Lucy's discovery created some long-lasting feuds between newer and older crops of paleoanthropologists in the later 1970s. With the popularity of Lucy's fame, the rivalry was prominently played out in public. A supposedly friendly TV discussion between the newer and older groups, moderated by none other than Walter Cronkite (A 1960 to 1970 TV news anchorman once enjoyed the reputation of the most trusted man in America), devolved into snide remarks and ridicule. I thought I had seen a few vehement disagreements in the physics world, but the disdain displayed between these parties is the worst I have witnessed. No one can afford to be authoritarian in physics and we don't vote on physics, neither can we afford to be one in anthropology. Authoritarianism in anthropology might just put us in the position creationists occupy today.

The "First Family"

The "First Family" was the first discovery of multiple hominins in a single setting that represents either a family or a small social group. That they belong to the same family or social group indicates that A. *afarensis* must have been relatively populous, and consequently, pretty successful as a species. The discovery was made in 1975 by Donald Johanson's team in Ethiopia, and they are dated to about 3,200,000 years old. The subsequent recovery of a total of 216 individuals nearby provides further evidence of the species' abundance, its fecundity, and its active social networks.

The Laetoli FootprintS—Imagination Running Wild

Another intriguing discovery attributed to A. *afarensis* is a 75-foot-long trail of bipedal footprints, believed to have been left behind by three individuals walking on wet volcano ash. This discovery was made by Mary Leakey—of Leakey family fame—in 1976. The footprints demonstrate that hominins walked habitually upright as there are no knuckle-impressions present. Besides, the feet do not have the mobile big toe of apes. Instead, they have an arch (the bending of the sole), typical of modern humans. Together with other studies, the footprints support the theory of a human-like gait. We are not exactly sure as to whom these footprints belong, although they are likely that of A. *afarensis*.

Fossil records require an imagination and solid, comparative anatomy to make inferences about the morphology of ancient hominins. Once in a while, a creative imagination can inject some fun into the boring daily digs in the field, typical of early paleoanthropologists. Some analysts have noted in their interpretations that the smaller trail—left by a female due to apparent sexual dimorphism—bears "telltale signs" that suggest whoever left the prints was burdened on one side. This imbalance may suggest a female carrying an infant on her hip, but there is no definitive proof. Conjecturing is fun, but weaving a story based on nothing more than footprints might go a little too far.

A quick summary of A. *afarensis*: they had both ape and human characteristics—apelike facial proportions (a flatter nose, a strongly projecting lower jaw), small braincases (with the brain about 1/3 the size of a modern human brain), and strong, long arms with curved fingers, adapted for climbing trees. They also had small canine teeth like all other early humans and a body that stood on two legs and walked upright regularly. Their adaptations for living both on the ground, and less frequently, in trees helped them survive for 1,000,000 years while the climate and environment continued to change.

Contemporaneous Australopithecus

Potential contemporaneous Hominins			
Age (Mya)	West Africa	East Africa	South Africa
7.0-7.5	Sahelanthropus tchadensis	Orrorin tugenensis	
3.9		Au. afarensis, Au. anamensis	
3.6	Au. bahrelghazali	Au. afarensis, Au. kenyanthropus, Au. platyops	Au. africanus
2.6		Au. garhi, Au. aethiopicus	Au. africanus
2.5-2		Au. boisei, Au. garhi	Au. africanus, Au. robustus
2.1-5		Au. boisei	Au. sediba Au. robustus

The abundance of Australopithecus fossils indicates a diverse morphology, ages, and locations. The table on the right summarizes contemporary organisms belonging to the Australopithecus genus along with their approximate ages. One apparent observation is that they are present in a broad region, spanning at least half of Africa.

There is even some evidence that Australopithecus had reached as far as Eastern Asia.

THE HOMO PERIOD: 2,500,000 TO 900,000 YEARS AGO

With so many Australopithecines existing simultaneously, there must have been large populations for many species. I would pay anything to ride a time machine back to 3,000,000 years ago to see how they all behaved and interacted with each other. The African forest and savanna must have teemed with hominins and their activities. It must have felt like there was pent-up energy behind a dam ready to break out of the positive feedback process. The outcome of differentiated organisms better suited for survival is almost a sure thing.

MILESTONE 4: WE ARE GETTING SMARTER—HOMO GENUS

The dividing line between the genera Australopithecus and Homo is a rough brain capacity of around 600 cubic centimeters. Brain capacity is a part of physical evolution that we discuss in the next chapter. Hominins with larger brain capacities belong to the Homo genus. Some other criteria resort to toolmaking as a specific characteristic of the Homo genus, one the Australopithecus genus does not demonstrate (before discoveries in 1990 placing toolmaking as early as 3,400,000 years ago). Although there is no one-to-one correspondence between brainy hominins and toolmaking, a higher brain power or intelligence is needed for toolmaking. Another criterion to distinguish the two genera is based on the manner in which they walk. Whereas the Homo genus is obligate bipedal, Australopithecus is still facultative quadrupedal, based on the foot anatomy.

Early H. Habilis

About a million years elapsed from Australopithecus's emergence to the genus of Homo, marked as Milestone Four around 2,500,000 years ago. A fossilized jawbone fragment discovered in 2013, dated 2,800,000 years ago, was considered to be from the first Homo genus, recognized as early Homo *habilis*, sitting between the Australopithecus genus and Homo *habilis*. They are the first species for which we have positive evidence of the use of stone tools, having developed the Oldowan lithic industry—named after Olduvai Gorge, the same location where the first Homo must have lived. The fossil was perhaps the earliest evidence of the genus Homo known to date.

The designation of habilis is because toolmaking required some level of hand-eye coordination and skill specialization required to find, use, and fabricate tools from surrounding stones. The word habilis means the ability to be handy and skillful in some activities. The naming of the genus of Homo and species habilis follows the Linnaeus naming convention.

H. Habilis

The more distinct Homo *habilis* came around 1,750,000 years ago, according to discoveries by the famous Leakey family around 1960 in Olduvai Gorge, Tanzania. Homo *habilis* is an intermediate between Australopithecus and the somewhat younger Homo *erectus,* following its appearance and morphology. Homo *habilis* was short and had disproportionately long arms compared to modern humans; however, it had a less protruding face (maxilla) than Australopithecus, from which the habilis may have descended. They had a cranial size slightly less than half of modern humans, yet a marked increase from Australopithecus. Despite the apelike morphology of its body, Homo *habilis* remains are often accompanied by primitive stone tools (e.g., Olduvai Gorge, Tanzania, and Lake Turkana, Kenya). The main argument for its classification as the first Homo ("human") species centers around its use of flaked stone tools; however, there was evidence discovered in the 1990s for earlier tool use (3,390,000 years ago) by undisputed Australopithecenes. This discovery pushes the Homo *habilis* back another million years, although it is still too speculative to create a separate species called Australopithecus *habilis*.

MILESTONE 5—THE RISE OF HOMO ERECTUS

By 1,900,000 years ago, some early transitional humans had evolved into a new, fully-human species in Africa. Most paleoanthropologists refer to them as Homo *erectus*, literally "upright human." A few researchers split them into two species: Homo *ergaster* ("working human") and Homo *erectus*. The Homo *ergaster* fossils were found somewhat earlier and in Africa.

Homo *erectus* discoveries are widespread in Africa, Asia, and Europe. In practice, we can treat them both erectus and ergaster as Homo *erectus* based on morphology, their ability to use tools, and the beginning of the use of fire.

Early African Homo *erectus* fossils—or Homo *ergaster*—are the oldest-known early hominins to have possessed modern human-like body proportions with relatively elongated legs and shorter arms relative to torso size. These features are considered adaptations to a life lived on the ground, indicating the loss of earlier tree-climbing adaptations and the ability to walk and possibly run long distances. Compared to earlier human fossils, it had an expanded braincase relative to the size of the face. There is fossil evidence that this species also cared for old and weak individuals.

Early fossil discoveries from Indonesia—"Java Man" in China in the 1890s, "Peking Man" in the 1920s, and Homo *erectus georgicus* in Georgia—comprise classic examples of this species. H. *erectus* has generally been considered the first species to have expanded beyond Africa. They are a highly variable species, spread over Eurasia, and possibly the longest-lived early human species. They existed for about 2,000,000 years or ten times as long as modern humans have been around. This is significant for the temporal span because it is the first fossil ancestor to modern humans that, in many ways, shares a lot of its ecology.

As a note in passing, all evidence since 2,100,000 years ago points to Homo *habilis* preceding Homo *erectus*. This indicates that humans were capable with their hands before they were exclusively upright and completely abandoned tree-dwelling. In a similar vein, the evolution of brain size comes after upright walking as the last evolutionary step for evolving toward modern man. This just shows that evolution is logical (though it may not be perfect) in retrospect, although it is slow, circuitous, and completely random when it begins.

THE ARCHAIC HOMO SAPIENS PERIOD: 900,000 to 40,000 YEARS AGO

MILESTONE 6: THEY ARE ALMOST US

Archaic Homo *sapiens* had a brain size averaging 1,200 to 1,400 cubic centimeters, which overlaps within the range of modern humans. They are different from anatomically modern humans, with a thicker skull, more prominent supraorbital ridges, more massive brow ridges, and the lack of a prominent chin. More importantly, their foreheads slope more, although their brain sizes grew beyond that of other contemporary Homo *species*.

A more specific H. *erectus*—Homo *heidelbergensis*—arose around 9,000,000 years ago. Homo *heidelbergensis* was found in 1908 near Heidelberg, Germany. Since then, more fossils were found throughout the Old World (The term "Old World" is commonly used in the West to refer to Africa, Asia, and Europe.) Although it is named after a European location, evidence shows that Homo *heidelbergensis* showed up 900,000 years ago in Africa and spread out to Asia and Europe.

This early human species also had a massive brow ridge, larger braincase, and flatter face than earlier human species. It was the first early human species to live in colder climates; their short, wide bodies were likely an adaptation to conserving heat. It lived with definite control of fire and the use of wooden spears, and it was the first early human species to hunt large animals routinely.

This early human broke new ground and was the first species to build shelters, creating simple dwellings out of wood and rock. It was also the first species to use flake-sharpened, stone Acheulean tools for butchering their game. These widespread populations show regional variations in physical appearance, but the extent of interaction between these diverse and widely-distributed populations is not clear.

Before the advent of molecular anthropology, scientists thought Homo *heidelbergensis* was the direct ancestor of all modern humans springing up in the different areas of the Old World, but the narrow genetic lines and uniformity of modern humans is a strong argument against the theory of multiregionalism. This is particularly true when we consider the contrast between the anatomically diverse and mosaic features of this late Homo *erectus* and uniform modern human traits.

When naming the Homo *heidelbergensis* species, scientists were in the habit of referring to early humans showing traits similar to both Homo *erectus* and modern humans as "archaic" Homo *sapiens*, rather than simply Homo *sapiens*. As a species goes, for Homo *sapiens*, we are not entirely a distinctly separate species from Homo *heidelbergensis*, as we will see in later discussions. The adjective of "archaic" added to Homo *sapiens* for Homo *heidelbergensis* seems appropriate.

MILESTONES 7 AND 7[1]: HOMO NEANDERTHALENSIS, NEANDERTHALS

Next come the most well-known specimens and our closest extinct relatives: the Neanderthals. From mtDNA genetic studies, it was discovered that they could be direct descendants from the same mainline that eventually gave birth to modern man. The black line that splits off from the mainline, Milestone 7, indicates the rise of Neanderthals dated around 500,000 years ago. For the full genomic analysis, there exists a possibility that Neanderthals split off from H. *erectus* or Homo *heidelbergensis* slightly later on the red lines indicated as milestone 7[1]. This ambiguity will be further clarified in chapter 10.

The Neanderthals are very well-studied, including their morphology, populated areas, technology, culture, demise or extinction, and the time and space they overlap with modern humans. They are an extinct species of archaic humans in the genus of Homo that may have been born in Europe around 500,000 years ago and lived in Eurasia from circa 400,000 years ago to 40,000 years ago. Currently, the earliest fossils of Neanderthals in Europe are between 450,000 and 430,000 years old. After that, Neanderthals expanded into Southwest and Central Asia as far east as the modern-day Altai Mountains. The type specimen was found in

the Neander Valley in German Rhineland in 1856, and given a name
of H. *neanderthalensis*.

Compared to modern humans, Neanderthals were stockier with
shorter legs and bigger bodies, likely an adaptation to preserve heat
in cold climates. They had cranial capacities averaging in the upper-
range of values for anatomically modern humans. Their physical size
is also similar to that of modern humans. Compared to modern
humans, Neanderthals were better suited for sprinting and pouncing
activities than endurance running, which would have been adaptive
in the forests and woodlands that seem to have been their preferred
environment.

They were sophisticated enough to make stone tools, use fire,
speak, create art, and be efficient hunters. An analysis of a Neanderthal's fossilized hyoid bone—a horseshoe-shaped structure in
the neck—suggests the species could speak, and this consequently
led to high levels of culture. The ability to speak must have lent
itself to language, consciousness, symbolic thinking, and the
abstract, like creating art as early as 110,000 years ago in the form of
seashell art in Spain. This ability to speak will be taken up in more
detail later.

We draw lines with uncertain endpoints along the phylogeny tree
since it is unclear as to how the species went extinct and was replaced
with a more advanced, new species. Because of their abundance in
the fossil record and due to the improvement in dating sensitivity and
accuracy, we now know that Neanderthals went extinct no later than
40,000 years ago except in regions at modern humans' farthest
reaches. In those areas, 37,000 years ago is suggested as their last
appearance. Either they went extinct 40,000 or 37,000 years ago, they
overlapped with human beings in both time and space; they could
have even been neighbors. We will see later that they were, at times,
more than just neighbors.

The Genetic Who Dunnit: Denisovans

Up to Milestone 7 on the phylogenetic tree, our knowledge of the
human species is from our understanding of fossils. They tell the
story of the emergence and demise of species through accurate

dating and comparative anatomy. We essentially need a physical specimen for the discovery of a human species.

There was, however, one species discovered differently, although its starting point is still human remains, and it is from a bone fragment preserved in cold, dry conditions for 50,000 years. During the complete mapping of the Neanderthal genome, a research group in a lab also discovered that there was a contemporary species that may have coexisted with them in Central Asia. Comparing the genome from that bone remnant sample to the Neanderthals, the scientists decided that this species' genetic composition was similar to that of the Neanderthals but different enough to warrant the species name of H. *denisovan*.

In addition to having resided in South Siberia, there is evidence that they roamed in the general area of Central Asia, South East Asia, and the high mountains of Tibet about 160,000 years ago. As far as their proper place in the family tree is concerned, H. *denisovan* comes into the phylogenetic tree through two scenarios. They are likely the direct descendants of Homo *heidelbergensis*, based on one type of molecular clock study; however, based on a complete nuclear DNA genome analysis, they are closer cousins to the Neanderthals. Milestone 7[1], at a little later than 500,000 years ago, indicates the second scenario, colored red.

THE MODERN HUMAN PERIOD: FROM 200,000 YEARS AGO

MILESTONE 8: HOMO SAPIENs SAPIENS

Aided by pioneering research work in molecular anthropology, we can now pin down Milestone 8 to around 200,000 years ago, indicating the rise of modern humans descended from either Homo *heidelbergensis* or a closer lineage. This 200,000 years ago number has an inherent uncertainty of 30% due to the lack of the molecular clock's precise calibration. It should not be surprising if fossils of modern humans dated to as early as 260,000 years ago in Greece. The presence of modern humans in Greece suggests that these people, early Homo *sapiens sapiens*, spread wide in and out of Africa very early. This early exit from Africa must not have been very successful since the next modern human presence in the Middle East was around 110,000 years ago.

MILESTONE 9: OUT OF AFRICA

The population of the ancestral Homo *sapiens* line did not stay put in Africa. They moved around from Africa to other places, most likely following food and game. They tried to expand beyond Africa through available thoroughfares a few times, much like their Homo *erectus* ancestors did. Some of the excursions succeeded, and some failed.

The populations staying back in Africa continued their spread into east, west, and South Africa. We call them the deep African lineage.

There are two primary routes out of Africa for the more adventurous among them. One group followed the southern route, starting from East Africa, hugging the South Asia shore, and ending up in Australia and Melanesia 70,000 or 60,000 years ago. The second group went first through East Africa and the Middle East and then farther eastbound toward Asia and northwest-bound for Europe. This second group became the common ancestors of our population, occupying the continents of Asia and Europe today. We take up the migration story in more detail in chapter 13.

MILESTONE 10: WE ARE ALONE NOW

Milestone 10, at 40,000 years ago, signifies a time when Neanderthals and Denisovans disappeared from the face of the Earth—at least, from the physical world we know. A few faraway spots may have evidence that they lingered later than 40,000 years ago, but these may have been isolated remnants. Starting from this point on, we become the only remaining species to carry Homo DNA.

. . .

MILESTONE 11: WE CAME TO THE AMERICAS

One branch of Asian Homo *sapiens* continued their trek to central Asia and eventually the Americas. Their expeditions included going across a land bridge—Beringia between Asia and the Americas—about 25,000 years ago on foot when sea levels were substantially lower than today. The emphasis of "on foot" may not be exclusive—since some have speculated about seafaring modern humans, this conjecture is still under debate. Again, the details will be a part of chapter 13.

SUMMARY

The human phylogenetic tree is a drastically truncated version of the more elaborate ones in other publications, leaving out a few minor branch lines. Continuous modifications or changes to this tree should be the norm as discoveries are continuously providing our stories with new blood.

There have been two apparent themes running through this chapter: the first is our ability to determine how fossils fit into the larger human evolutionary picture; the second is that we can pin down when these periods and milestones occurred. Obviously, fossils play a crucial role in how we understand ourselves. The next two chapters will focus on how we began studying fossils and how we brought about our phylogenetic tree. A little further down, we will dive into the molecular anthropology that helps us fill in the phylogenetic tree's genetic parts that do not come directly from fossils.

BIBLIOGRAPHY

1. "Cerebral blood flow rates in recent great apes are greater than in Australopithecus species that had equal or larger brains," Roger S. Seymour, Vanya Bosiocic, Edward P. Snelling, Prince C. Chikezie, Qiaohui Hu, Thomas J.

Nelson, Bernhard Zipfel and Case V. Miller, *Proceedings of the Royal Society B: Biological Sciences*, Nov. 2019.

2. "Nature and relationships of Sahelanthropus *tchadensis*", Roberto Macchiarelli, Aude Bergeret-Madina, Damiano Marchi, and Bernard Wood, *Journal of Human Evolution*, 149, Dec. 2020.

3. *"Lucy, The Beginning of Humankind"*, Donald Johanson and Maitland Edey, Simon and Schuster Publisher, 1981.

6

HUMAN FOSSILS

T he construction of our phylogenetic tree relies heavily on human fossils. They generally come with their attributes, ages, and locations. Fossils not only got our evolutionary study started, they are also the richest of treasure troves. We have been studying them for 150 years and have learned a lot about our ancestors and ourselves from them.

First, the fossils' appearances—or morphology—have given us a tremendous amount of knowledge of their owners. They can tell us how our ancestors looked—how tall, wide, husky, robust, etc.; they can tell us how they moved around—walking or crawling; they can tell us how smart our ancient relatives were by the size of their brain-cases; they can even tell us if the ancient humans were left- or right-hand dominant. A successful interpretation of their anatomy—by way of comparative anatomy—helped fit the owners into the proper stage of our evolutionary progression.

Second, not only do fossils retain the shapes of the people that owned them, but they also contain crucial organic material relevant to their existence. They can keep the DNA for a long time, albeit not all of it intact, but with the capabilities of modern science, the full genomes of certain ancient people can be reassembled from DNA remnants found in fossils. A comparison with modern human genomes can fill in some of the phylogenetic gaps not possible otherwise. Case in point is the discovery of the Denisovans, which would not have been possible if it were not for genome analyses.

Fossils of human teeth are also incredibly rich in information. Not only can they, on occasion, reveal a genetic history older than what DNA can, they can also infer the livelihood of ancient people through the wear and tear of their teeth. For example, tearing marks on molars have revealed a person's diet or even their handedness.

One of the most important revelations is the age of the fossils. This is the time at which these humans last lived. A part of the fossils contains information in their organic constituents, DNA that has in turn become a meter stick in time.

This chapter gives fossils a proper treatment in two aspects. First, it is interesting to find out how we got involved in studying our evolution through fossils, a little historical perception, per se. Second, we explore various techniques of finding out their ages, which, together with morphology, improved the accuracy of our family tree.

LEARNING ABOUT HUMAN FOSSILS

My early interest in fossils was for those of the dinosaurs. I used to know the names of many dinosaur species without giving a thought as to when they appeared on earth and how they related to each other during the vast 180,000,000 years of their existence, and of course, how they disappeared. As we now know from chapter 3, all dinosaurs had to have gone through the same evolutionary processes, resulting in a diversified dinosaur family. Their emergence, existence, evolution, and demise follow the same principle of the positive feedback process. Yes, even the catastrophe caused by the killer asteroid hitting the Earth 65,000,000 years ago is merely a change of the environmental filter in this feedback loop.

When I started to get serious about evolution, the most useful shortcut for learning about human fossils was to learn from the experts by taking paleoanthropology courses. Since paleoanthropology's scope does not warrant an independent subject or study, I took the next best thing I thought reasonable; that is, archaeology. As it turned out, I learned a lot more than about ancient human fossils.

ARCHAEOLOGY EXPERIENCE

I started to attend archaeology classes in 2015 after finishing a biological anthropology course the prior year. I recall that I had to take some extra initiative to focus on the human evolutionary principle while flooded with the sheer influx of information. I expected similarly structured lectures on definitions, facts, dates, and charts for archaeology. Little did I know that archaeology, or the teaching and learning thereof, would be so fascinating that it did not take any effort to learn the subject.

The Real-Life Professor Indiana Jones

One of the high points for this course came from knowing and interacting with the colorful and dynamic archaeology professor named Robert Cartier. First of all, the world owes him big time for his contribution to the movie industry. During his early career—in the late 70s, I believe—Professor Cartier went to Nepal for his early fieldwork. Local people warned him that working at the high altitude required a good sunshade to block out the unhealthily high UV radiation. In his haste, he purchased a dirt-cheap fedora from a street vendor at a small border village in Tibet, China, before entry to Nepal. He also added a durable leather jacket, able to withstand the expected wear-and-tear from fieldwork.

He kept wearing the same fedora for subsequent fieldwork, including an archaeology and cultural resource management outing (ARM, a practical archaeology career path unlike Indiana Jones's) in the Los Angeles area. A fellow archaeologist from UCLA working as a consultant to a film director in Hollywood approached him for his fedora. The movie director was interested in the typical archaeologist's attire for his "secret project." Upon seeing dashing Professor Cartier wearing his beat-up, dusty fedora, the film consultant strongly recommended to Steven Spielberg that the fedora should be part of an archaeologist's costume. The rest, as they say, is history.

Professor Cartier was not allowed to wear the hat for a while for trademark reasons, again, according to him. I know this might be how copyright works, but where do you draw the line of real ownership?

<u>Native American Archaeological Discoveries</u>

Besides contributing to the movie industry, Professor Cartier is a hardcore and well-respected archaeologist of Native American history and continues to this day. Near his residence in Yellowstone National Park was a wide swath of land belonging to his neighbor, who was puzzled by some rock formations/arrangements in his back-yard, and he made sure to investigate before his neighbor's plan to plow the field a few days later. He took a quick look and realized that it was a giant geoglyph left behind by some ancient culture. Although it was not apparent initially, the geoglyph was a rendering of a human figure with a rectangular head, a long, skinny body, and a pair of short, squat legs. It was huge and measured about 1,300 feet from head to legs.

Professor Cartier correctly identified it as a part of the Avonlea culture, well known for its innovative, effective, but cruel bison hunt-ing, which was invented long before Avonlea came to existence, ~ 11,700BCE. The Avonlea people were early tribes that migrated south-ward to the Wyoming/Minnesota/Idaho area from Canada in the 800 CE time frame.

Shown here is an aerial photograph of the geoglyph and detailed hand-drawn documentation of the discovery (Figure 6). It took a pair of keen eyes and a wealth of experience to recognize the artifact left behind by Native Americans before it was lost for good.

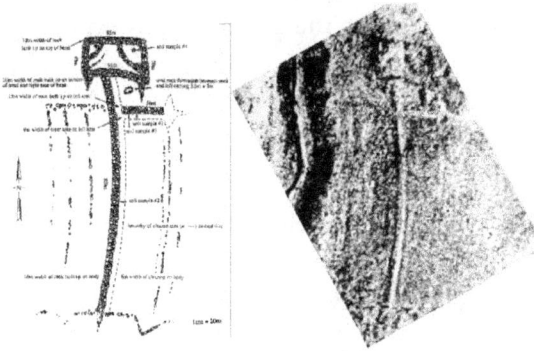

Figure 6. Professor Robert Cartier's discovery near Yellowstone
state park. A hand-drawn documentation of the discovery on the
left and an aerial photograph of the geoglyph.

There is a side story of bison-hunting, or more specifically the
bison/buffalo jump, by the native Americans. Professor Cartier
showed a dirt path lined by two rows of prearranged pebbles/stone
piles, or cairns. He explained that the path was used to corral the
bison by shouting loudly on both sides from behind the stone piles
on the way to a high cliff and presumably killed the bison by scaring
them off the cliff. There were thousands of bison skeletons found at
the bottom of the cliff. This hunting skill is very effective indeed, but
it is unnecessary overkill because that much bison meat would be
enough to feed a lot more than the Avonlea population. Was the
hunting only for food, or was it for the thrill of the sport, too?

Eight Hundred Miles Away And 1,200 Years Later

On a trip I took to Powell Lake, Utah, in the USA a year later, I ran
into a $3,000 hand-loomed piece of art at a souvenir shop featuring a
few human figures with rectangular heads, elongated bodies, and
short legs. Before I could lay my hands on it, one of my traveling
companions bought it on the spot and had it ready to be wrapped for
shipping back to her hometown in New Jersey. Bargaining with this
companion was futile because she loved it so much and wouldn't
trade it for another artwork, so I had to settle for an iPhone photo
here.

Upon seeing the artwork, shown as Figure 7, I immediately recognized the similarity between the artwork figure and the geoglyph near Yellowstone Park. I asked the store owner about the artwork's origin and found that the local Navajo people had loomed it based on an old mental image of humans. I did not have the time to visit the artist to enquire about his possible connection to Avonlea, but I believed there must be some connection to the geoglyph.

Figure 7. Photograph of a hand-loomed artwork weaved by Navajo people in south Utah, USA. The human caricatures are similar to the geoglyph in Figure 6.

It was no surprise that later, after some research, I found out that Navajo/Apache and Avonlea shared a linguistic lineage originating from the Athabaskan language system from Canada. I also found out that the Navajo did not initially live in the Southwest US, but they moved from the general Minnesota area to the Southwest US around 1,400 CE. I might have found some more connections between the Navajo and Avonlea independently, and I felt as if I was no longer just a bystander in the field of archaeology!

There is still some controversy as to the connection between the Avonlea people and Canada's Athabaskan language system as of today, but this does not diminish my excitement for this discovery. I got back to Professor Cartier, who was also understandably excited. This microscopic migration of Indian tribes is part of a larger human migration story, the focus of Chapter 13.

Professor Cartier is a resident consultant for the local government's cultural resource management effort making sure major constructions do not destroy native Americans' ancient residences and artifacts. He is also a master diver with many pearly abalone shells hanging on his property's fence in California. Professor Cartier leads a fulfilling life, indeed. Other than the bullwhip and teaching at Marshall College, he is a real-life Indiana Jones.

Archaeology Classes And Human Evolution Presentations

There is close relation between archaeology and biological anthropology. Just like in the biological anthropology course, I worked my way up to give two lectures on the topic of the human phylogenetic tree we shared in chapter 5. The presentation now included pioneering work on mtDNA Eve's age and her homeland in chapter 9 and the evolutionary principle introduced in chapter 3. Using similar mtDNA molecular clock analyses, I also included a study that determined when humans started to wear clothing (i.e., pelts and hides), which is around 170,000 years ago.

It must be my talkative nature that impressed Professor Cartier. He introduced me as Professor Kelly for these lectures. I had taught some graduate telecommunication courses at reputable universities with my professional experience and association, but it was most satisfying to be recognized as an anthropology professor, considering that I had been a total novice only the year before.

THE WELL-RESPECTED ARCHAEOLOGY PROFESSIONALS

A significant part of the archaeology course was devoted to paleoanthropology, which deals with ancient human fossils and artifacts made and/or manufactured by our ancient ancestors. It was the major cornerstone laying the foundation for the study of human evolution. Behind the discoveries and studies are dedicated people with an in-depth knowledge of human anatomy and a solid anthropological background, prospecting landscapes for likely fossil sites, working in dusty, arid, and desiccated lands under the scorching sun. What is most amazing is that they are able to sort through the massive, fragmented, yet somehow intertwined information to reveal one puzzle piece at a time and put the complete puzzles together without knowing what the finished picture should be. You have to admire and respect these anthropologists' dedication and professionalism they exhibited in the past and continue to do so today.

CHALLENGES IN HUMAN FOSSIL DISCOVERIES

In addition to the obvious academic challenge of piecing together our history from fossils, there are a few mundane challenges that have—and may still—hinder paleoanthropologists' tasks. Most of the problems have become less severe these days, though it has taken a while, and there was a lot of wasted effort to overcome.

MISSED DISCOVERY OPPORTUNITIES

A lot of archaeological discoveries happen while construction and excavation is going on near possible ancient human dwellings. Any archaeological or paleoanthropological discoveries invariably destroy records that can never be restored, although they have helped us learn about our past. Institutions are set up to manage these cultural resources in most conscientious nations and with local governments, setting a mandate that archaeological evaluation is included in geological studies for large construction projects. Of course, the purpose is to make sure that people do not accidentally throw away valuable ancient artifacts that may contain important scientific or historical information about our ancestors.

For example, a set of high throughput aqueducts were to go through a rural area south of San Jose, California, USA, to feed water to the city. The local government requested Professor Cartier do a geological survey before starting the project. Upon investigation, he found a Native Ohlone (a Native American tribe) tribal dwelling with many circles of low stone walls, supposedly to be the foundation of ancient tepees. All of the smaller circles were on the perimeter of a larger circle. Together, they are called a circle of circles. He was able to find artifacts as well as midden, proving human inhabitation, dated to around 5,000 years ago. As a result, the aqueduct construction had to be rerouted at additional cost and time.

The discovery of the first Australopithecus fossils almost did not happen. If it were not for Raymond Dart's comparative anatomy training and the sheer luck of being exposed to it, we might still think that modern humans arose from Asia or somewhere other than Africa.

Another example is the discovery of Peking Man. Somewhere near Beijing (the modern spelling of Peking) was a mountain named Dragon Bone Hill, famous for its easy access to "dragon bones," which are the most expensive ingredients in traditional herbal medicine. People kept going back to caves in Zhoukoudian to retrieve fossils of ancient humans and animals, sold as herbal medicine, to be ground up into a powder as a part of a remedy for anxiety and dizziness. These fossils—and an important piece of our evolutionary story —would have been lost forever if it were not for an observant geologist and paleontologist in the 1920s. Working together, they concluded there must have been human beings in the neighborhood able to transport foreign materials to these locations from far away. The subsequent excavation unearthed Homo *erectus*, with an antiquity ranging from 750,000 to 300,000 years ago.

ULTERIOR MOTIVES

Some paleoanthropologists had ulterior motives, too. It often happened that discoverers would hog their finds, refuse third-party examinations, or defend their academic positions and territories for personal pride, legend, and ego. It got to the point where they even forged for fossils to serve their agenda, like the Piltdown Man hoax, putting up barriers to obstruct the construction of our family tree.

DIGITAL FOSSIL AND OPEN COMMUNICATION

There have been cases when academicians hoarded fossil samples in the name of preserving their integrity, and such acts were detrimental to advances in our understanding. Fortunately, the situation is a lot better due to the open communication between fellow scientists. The casts of the fossil discoveries have now been replaced by digital files providing 3-D external shapes and forms of specimens. They can also look deep into a specimen's inner-structures with tomography. Also, we have digital technologies and 3-D imaging that people can share without holding physical samples in their hands for detailed examinations except when we need the original sample/specimen for molecular genetic analysis. These digital or virtual fossils have become the basis for a collaborative effort to openly and objectively study our history.

FROM FOSSILS TO HUMAN EVOLUTION

Fossils and evolutionary stories have been joined at the hip from the very beginning. Evolutionary thinking has its roots in antiquity in the form of fossils, according to ideas from the ancient Greeks, Romans, and Chinese, and medieval Islamic science. With the beginnings of modern biological taxonomy in the late 17th century and as the Enlightenment progressed, evolutionary philosophy spread from fossils to natural history. The first concrete thoughts about evolution were proposed by early 19th century Jean-Baptiste Lamarck (1744–1829) as the transmutation of species, the first fully-formed theory of evolution. The following is a brief account of what we thought of fossils from ancient Greece to the present. The years since Lamarck bear the most consequential importance regarding theories of human evolution.

GREEK ROOTS

There is a long history behind the effort to understand lives on earth by studying fossils left behind by once-living organisms. Starting as early as the 6th century BCE, a few philosophers, scientists, and thinkers from Greece—the birthplace of philosophy—were already curious about the rocks resembling existing marine organisms, giving rise to reasonable speculation that part or all of the land had once been underwater.

The general study of organisms through these ancient rocks are collectively called paleontology, ancient (*paleo*, the same as in the Paleo diet) beings (*-onto*), and study (*-logy*). This lies on the border between biology and geology. Still, its historical development has been closely tied to geology, and it is the first effort to understand the Earth's history. There was not a lot of follow-up after the ancient Greeks' interest in Western culture through the dark ages. When dinosaurs' fossils showed up in the 18th century, it revived fossil studies.

INTEREST IN FOSSILS THROUGH THE AGES

The curiosity surrounding fossils is not confined to Western culture, at least in the early days. According to British science historian Joseph Lee, Shen Kuo (1031-1095) was the most influential scientist and mathematician in China in the 11th century. Shen proposed a hypothesis concerning a gradual yet massive climate change after finding ancient, petrified bamboo preserved in a dry, northern Chinese habitat underground, that would not have supported bamboo growth in his time. Incidentally, Shen was also well-versed in mathematics, and he invented the precursor of integration, a part of calculus.

During the Middle Ages, fossils were also discussed by Persian naturalist Abu Ali Ibn Sina in *The Book of Healing* (1027), which proposes a theory for petrifying fluids, right in the middle of the Islamic Golden Age. Ibn Sina made the following observation on theories held on fossils and the petrification of plants and animals at the time:

"If what is said concerning the petrifaction of animals and plants is true, the cause of this phenomenon is a powerful mineralizing and petrifying virtue which arises in certain stony spots or emanates suddenly from the Earth during earthquake and subsidence and petrifies whatever comes into contact with it. The petrifaction of the bodies of plants and animals is not more extraordinary than the transformation of waters."

Albert of Saxony would elaborate further in the 14th century, and Abu Ali Ibn Sina's hypothesis of fossil formation was accepted in some form by most naturalists by the 16th century. Although the theory of petrifying fluids is incorrect, based on what we know today, there was nevertheless a curiosity about how fossils came into existence as early as the 11th century.

THE BEGINNING OF PALEOANTHROPOLOGY

After Charles Darwin published *The Origin of Species* in 1859, much of the paleontology's focus shifted toward understanding evolutionary paths—including those of humans—and evolutionary theory. Paleoanthropology is the part of paleontology that focuses exclusively on human beings. It becomes an entity by itself as an academic branch, although not a wide-reaching one in the early days.

HUMAN FOSSIL DISCOVERIES

FIRST HUMAN FOSSILS DISCOVERED IN EUROPE

As early as 1823, William Buckland, a paleontology expert famous for studying dinosaur fossils, found a human skeleton in Wales enveloped in red ochre. As knowledgeable as he was as an expert on the human frame, he misjudged both its age and gender due to his lack of academic objectivity. Buckland believed that human remains could not be older than the biblical flood, thought to have occurred 4,300 years ago; thus, he underestimated its actual age wildly, dating the skeleton to the Roman era. He believed the skeleton to be female primarily because there was ochre tinting on the bones (ochre is a red pigment consisting mainly of oxidized iron, used for cosmetics and artwork in ancient times and still used for rouge today). Also accompanying the discovery were a few decorative items. These two items caused Buckland to mistakenly speculate that the remains belonged to a Roman prostitute or witch.

We now know that the skeleton was of the Homo genus, around 40,000 thousand years old, and most likely Homo *neanderthalensis*. In 1829, he discovered more fossils in a cave in Engis, Belgium. Although unidentified at the time, these remains also belonged to Neanderthals and dated between 40,000-80,000 years old.

These discoveries inspired the interest in human fossils when people started to realize that modern humans had come from earlier forms of humans. This was the idea once named as the transmutation of species by Lamarck in defiance of religious orthodoxy. However, the same thinking was welcomed by people seeking to widen democracy and freedom to overturn the aristocratic hierarchy as part of the European enlightenment movement.

Evolutionism Versus Creationism

Following a famous heated debate on evolution in Oxford in 1860 between Thomas Huxley—a staunch supporter of Charles Darwin and evolution—and Bishop Samuel Wilberforce—a creationist— Darwinism and evolution came out victorious. Irrespective of this, the debate did not settle the subject once and for all. Although there are no written accounts of the debate, it is most memorable for the exchange in which Wilberforce supposedly asked Huxley whether it was through his grandfather or his grandmother that he claimed his descent from a monkey. Huxley is said to have replied that he would not be ashamed to have a monkey for his ancestor, but he would be ashamed to be connected with a man who used his great oratory gifts to obscure the truth, obviously referring to the Bishop. The subsequent discovery of more Neanderthal fossils in Europe only served to solidify Darwinism further.

Who Is The Smartest European?

Early Darwinists, including Darwin himself, were hesitant to accept the evolution of human beings in fear of the backlash from religious orthodoxy, even though evolution in every other living thing was considered okay. By the late 19th and early 20th centuries, human evolution was a more accepted doctrine, but underlying this acceptance was inherent competition from major European powers for dominance in the age of imperialism and colonialism. These powers all claimed superiority in every aspect, including intelligence. The purported justification is that a more intelligent group of people deserved to dominate the world because they were more evolved. This political agenda spurred a race to find more European fossils to give more credence to their claim of being the self-professed superior race. As a result, there were more concerted efforts in archaeological digging in European locations sponsored by states, whether directly or indirectly. Engis, Belgium, is a famous site because of its history of finding Neanderthals there in the early efforts.

The frenzy certainly bore some significant fruit, but it also gave rise to endless and senseless feuds between major institutions, competing to be the first to find discoveries of the most evolved or the smartest. This desire to claim the title of being a superior race or ethnicity set the stage for racism, fraud, and even hoaxes in early paleoanthropology. The racism that has spawned so many atrocities in our recent history is completely senseless in light of modern-day molecular anthropology. One hoax was so bizarre and scandalous that it steered the study of human evolution in the wrong direction, and it was not entirely resolved until 1949 when better dating technologies became available and objective and clear heads prevailed.

THE ASIAN CONNECTION, JAVA MAN, PEKING MAN, AND DENISOVANs

The next significant discovery happened in Asia in the late 19th century, when Eugene Dubois dug up fossils of human ancestors in Indonesia. Dubois was a Dutch paleoanthropologist and geologist, a medically trained professional, and well-versed in comparative anatomy. He was personally involved in some Neanderthal digging efforts in Engis Belgium as the location has been historically rich in human fossils. He believed that humans had evolved in the tropics because of the perceived easy access to food and resources. Considering that we might be somehow related to monkeys and apes, Dubois thought humans were closely related to gibbons in particular, which are plenty in Indonesia. A fossil ape found in India was another reason for his belief that Asia would be an excellent place to look for human ancestors and hominin fossils. As a Dutchman, a Dutch colony like Indonesia was a convenient place for him to live and work.

Although hominin fossils had been found and studied before, Dubois was the first anthropologist to embark upon a purposeful search for them. He used his Dutch West Indie connection and explored the islands of Sumatra Java in Indonesia. In 1891, Dubois described his fossils finds as "a species in between humans and apes," a description enabled by his expertise in comparative anatomy. He called his finds Pithecanthropus *erectus* (ape-human that stands upright) or Java Man, dated to 850,000 years ago, now classified as Homo *erectus*.

A few other significant fossil discoveries in Asia include Peking Man, discovered in 1930, and belonging to H. *erectus*, dating to 700,000 years ago. The other is the Hobbit, H. *floresiensis*, discovered in 2004 and believed to have lived around 50,000 years ago, categorized as archaic Homo *sapiens*. One of the more recent ones is the discovery of Denisovans in China (the fossil was discovered in 1980 but identified as Denisovan in 2019), dated 160,000 years ago. It is the first discovery of fossils from the Denisovan east of the Altai Mountains, in the Xiahe region in the middle of China.

FIRST AFRICAN FOSSIL DISCOVERY AND RAYMOND DART

Raymond Dart pioneered the study of human fossils in Africa in 1924. He was a trained scientist, a medical specialist, and most importantly, a professional anatomist. He became aware of a supposed baboon skull, brought to his attention by one of his students while an anatomy professor at the University of the Witwatersrand in Johannesburg, South Africa, but Dart discovered that the baboon skull was so much more. It was the first evidence of our ancestors in Africa. This started a chain of events in motion that led to the discovery of the "child skull of Taung," later dated to 2,500,000 years ago, and identified as belonging to the genus Australopithecus. As mentioned before, Dart was the one to coin the genus as the southern ape, the literal meaning of Australopithecus. It was a significant event because it was the first human fossil discovery outside of Europe, debunking the myth that early humans evolved in Europe. His findings were initially dismissed because he was not a part of the European scientific establishment. It was also because he had found the fossil in Africa and not Europe or Asia, where the establishment supposed man's origin at the time.

In fact, there was quite a lot of animosity between Dart and the most eminent human study organization—Sir Authur Keith, to be more specific—in Europe that lasted more than 20 years. Dart's discovery of a hominin fossil was finally getting its recognition, 25 years after the discovery.

GLOBAL HUMAN FOSSIL PRESENCE

Once the floodgate of fossil discoveries had opened, it seemed there was one significant discovery after the next over the last 150 years, and from all over the world. Other than the fossils being on or close to the direct modern human lineage, we will not dwell on the less relevant details in this book. There is a complete list of human fossils in *Wikipedia* under the title of "List of Human Evolution Fossils" for the interested readers.

Human fossils are almost everywhere you can think of, even in places barely habitable. Starting in West Europe, fossil sites extend through Europe, Africa, Asia, India, Siberia, Tibet, Indonesia, Taiwan, Philippines, Vietnam, and the Americas. In terms of their antiquity, they span from 7,000,000 years ago to as recent as 5,000 years ago.

The Earth has been our backyard for the last 7,000,000 years. Chapter 13 discusses how hominins started with a local boy in Africa and wound up taking over the globe as their residence.

By now, there is no doubt that that fossils and human evolution are closely linked. The rest of this chapter plans to lay the groundwork for how their antiquity is determined.

FOSSIL FORMATION

The most common fossil formation begins when a plant or animal dies in a watery environment and is buried in mud and silt. Soft tissues quickly decompose, leaving membranes, bones, and/or shells behind. Over time, sediment builds on top of them and hardens into rock. As the encased materials decay, minerals seep in, replacing the organic material cell by cell in a process called "petrification." Alternatively, the membranes or bones may partly or entirely decay away, leaving behind a cast of the organism. The void left behind may then fill with a mineral solution—either calcium carbonate or silica—making a rigid replica of the organism. These rocks may be different from their rocky surroundings in color, hardness, or content, but they retain shapes easily identifiable by archaeologists and anthropologists. This process is called "permineralization," which is predominantly how human and most animal fossils are formed. The degree of fossilization depends on the material burying the bones, but the bones are considered fossilized if they are 10,000 years old or older.

Very few animals are fossilized, fewer are preserved, and even fewer are discovered. To become fossilized, an animal must die in a watery environment and be buried in the mud and silt. Because of this requirement, most land creatures never have the chance to fossilize unless they die next to a lake or stream by chance. Indeed, there may be a whole species of land animals for which there is no fossil record, let alone those not yet discovered. We may never know how many animals there were or their degree of diversity. The same argument is valid for human beings. We may never know how many human beings there were in our past or how varied, but because of their rarity, any human fossils found are precious since they are rich in information.

There are other ways an organism's remains can become fossils. For example, chemistry can play a role when fish bones are carbonized. Alternately, seashells can become fossilized when their molecular structure is rearranged in a process known as "recrystallization."

DATING THE FOSSILS

Once human fossils are discovered, they are subject to crucial scrutiny. However, it is most important to determine when the human remains were left behind using one or a few dating techniques. There are two categories for dating techniques: direct and indirect. Direct dating analyzes the age using the material in the biological remains; indirect dating equates the fossil's age by analyzing nearby materials that presumably have the same age as the fossils.

DIRECT DATING
Radiocarbon Dating

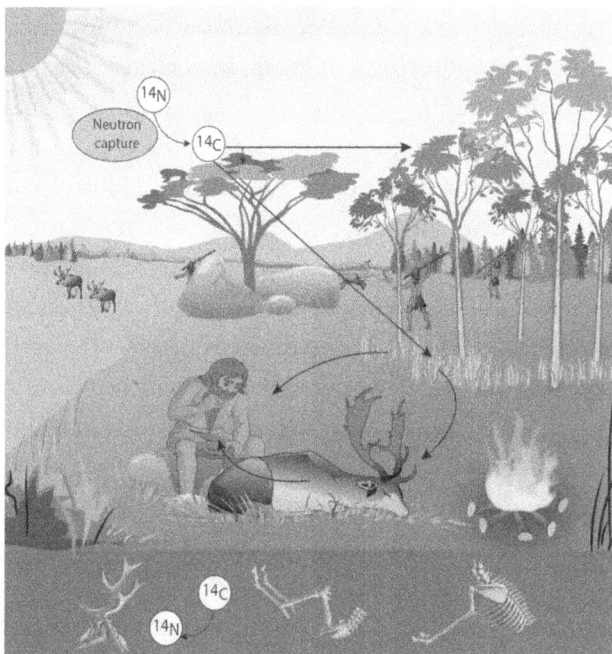

Figure 8. Radiocarbon atoms come to existence when the upper
atmospheric nitrogen atoms capture thermal neutrons and spit
out a proton turning N-14 into C-14. Biological cycles then
embed C-14 into animals while they ingest organic foods
resulting in a known amount of C-14 in their bodies while alive.
The somewhat constant C-14 amount starts to dissipate at a
fixed rate once the animals stop ingesting organic foods or die.
Radiocarbon dating simply measures how much C-14 is lost and
back calculate when the animals die, thus their ages.

Willard Frank Libby was an American physical chemist noted for
his role in the 1949 development of radiocarbon dating. This technique drastically revolutionized archaeology and paleontology. For
his contributions, Libby was awarded the Nobel Prize in Chemistry in
1960.

Figure 8 briefly describes the radiocarbon formation and dating
principle. It measures the loss of radioactive C-14 from biological
organisms to estimate the time since their deaths. C-14 contains six
protons and eight neutrons in its atomic nucleus. It is unstable in its
natural occurrence. One of its protons is turned into a neutron and
changes the atom from carbon to nitrogen, or N-14.

C-14 is naturally present at a known amount in the atmosphere, resulting from N-14 capturing a neutron, which is generated by the presumed constant cosmic ray flux, while spitting out a proton. Having the same chemical properties as C-12, the C-14 embeds itself as C-12 in the process, which can be absorbed by living organisms— such as plants—during photosynthesis. Animals ingest the C-14 from plants on which they graze. Carnivores, like humans, absorb C-14 by eating plants and animals that consume the plants. When an animal dies, it no longer absorbs C-14. The time of death sets the radio-carbon clock to zero. The dead organism can only lose C-14, through beta decay back to N-14, at a rate characterized by its half-life, which is 5,730 years. A measure of how much C-14 is lost through radioactive decay can be used to back-calculate how many half-lives have passed since the organism's death. This is the sample's age—or the age of the proxy samples—in which we are interested.

In a practical implementation, scientists determine the change of the ratio of C-14 to its dominant isotope, C-12, from its nominal quantity in the atmosphere. This nominal ratio, C-14/C-12, has a value of about one part in a trillion. If a sample has an expected age of about ten times the half-lives—or 57,300 years—the C-14/C-12 ratio will be 1/1024 of the initial ratio, making it extremely small to be reliably determined. Since the C-14 content in the sample could be minuscule, samples can be easily contaminated by inadvertently letting the atmosphere seep into the sample. The additional C-14 in the contaminated sample will give a false reading of a much higher C-14/C-12 ratio. This erroneously high number may lead us to believe that it hasn't been that long since the organism's death, and thus it is a younger age than the actual age. At the same time, the tiny amount of C-14 left in the samples needs to be accurately determined even without contamination. Using accelerator mass spectrometry— adopted for archaeological dating over the last 20 years—has drastically improved the dating of human fossils.

Keeping the sample isolated from any possible contamination has become a general practice for radiocarbon dating. The same approach is the norm for any dating technique nowadays. This significance of sample contamination and handling is not lost in re-dating the abundant Neanderthal specimens.

Re-dating The Neanderthals' Demise

While making sure that contamination does not happen when using this sensitive technique, Thomas Higham and his group have undertaken a large-scale re-dating of Neanderthal specimens from Western Europe to Russia, beginning in 2010. This extensive effort has narrowed the timing of Neanderthal's extinction to between 39,000 and 41,000 years ago.

INDIRECT DATING: PROXY DATING AND STRATIGRAPHY

Radiocarbon dating becomes ineffective when the ratio of C-14/C-12 can no longer be determined accurately. Modern technologies can push the limit further, but they reached a rigid wall around 60,000-70,000 years ago. For these fossils, we resort to indirect dating to find the ages of materials contemporary with the fossils. Of course, the burden is now on the dating of these materials using various dating techniques. Two steps need to happen: one, establishing contemporaneity of the proxy materials with the fossils; and two, determining the ages of these materials.

Human fossils—or any fossils for that matter—continue to be buried deeper and deeper by later sediments after their formation. As the Earth progresses through its own life, tectonic movement, earthquakes, volcanic activity, rainfall, floods, the remnants of micro- and macro-organisms, minerals, and rocks all constitute sediments that pile on top of the fossils with layer after horizontal layer. Naturally, earlier layers are covered with more recent layers in succession. All layers have their signatures, reflecting the geological, biological ecology, and living things making up the geological structure of the foundation of stratigraphy, the study of these geological layers.

These successive layers tell the floral and faunal changes along the time defined by the accumulated layers. Older fauna occurs lower in the layers, where species have deposited their fossils and left their traces for the record. If they do not appear in newer layers, they most likely become extinct. If the never-before-seen species show up in more recent layers, they might have either migrated from somewhere else or evolved locally from something yet unknown. Stratigraphy, then, lends itself to being the fossils' proxy. Now, the remaining task is to establish the age of the layers.

Proxy Material Dating Using Radioactive Elements

There are similar techniques used to determine the ages of proxy materials like radiocarbon dating, but using different elements for different ranges of ages. The appropriate time ranges vary drastically depending on specific atomic elements' half-lives, including rubidium/strontium, thorium/lead, potassium/argon, argon/argon, and uranium/lead. They have longer half-lives, ranging from 0.7 to 48.6 billion years, and are thus used for dating times beyond what radiocarbon dating can adequately do.

Volcanic Rock Dating

Volcanic rock dating is a variation of radioactivity dating. Volcanic rocks typically contain naturally radioactive minerals. We can date these minerals using techniques based on the radioactive decay of isotopes, which occurs at known rates. Measuring isotopes typically involves lasers, mass spectrometers, and sometimes even nuclear reactors. We calculate the age using decay rates and measurements of isotopes, which gives us the time elapsed since the beginning.

In 2013, scientists discovered a fossil from the genus Homo dated between 2,800,000 and 2,750,000 years ago using the naturally radioactive mineral feldspar, making this the oldest known fossil from our genus. This may move the milestone of the emergence of the Homo genus back by 200,000 years, marked as Milestone 4 on our phylogenetic tree in chapter 5. That time accounts for 8,000 generations of human evolutionary activity and change. This may seem insignificant given our long evolutionary history, but just imagine—we modern humans have been in existence for around the same range of time.

Optical Luminescence Dating

Luminescence dating refers to a group of techniques used to determine how long ago mineral grains were last exposed to sunlight or sufficient heating. The basic concept still relies upon radioactive isotopes. All sediments and soils contain trace amounts of radioactive isotopes of elements such as potassium, uranium, thorium, and rubidium. These elements decay over time, and the ionizing radiation they produce is absorbed by mineral grains in sediments such as quartz. The radiation causes a charge to remain in the grains in structurally unstable "electron traps." The trapped charge accumulates at a rate determined by the decay process at the location of the sample. By measuring the luminescence released through stimulation, scientists can back-calculate when quartz was buried at sites, and thus the age of fossils sitting next to the minerals.

There are a few ways to induce the luminescence released from samples, including optically stimulated luminescence (OSL), infrared stimulated luminescence (IRSL), and thermoluminescence (TL). The range of applicability is between 100,000 to 350,000 years.

Rigorous Dating and Multiple Techniques Corroboration

As paleoanthropology gets more critical in understanding our evolution, reliable dating has to come from more than one method and be corroborated with other evidence. In return, the information is a lot more than just the age of the samples. Proximate fossils other than human can also provide indirect evidence of how and when organisms—or more specifically, human beings—lived. Archaeologists sometimes resort to fossils of animals and plants in close location and time with the discovered human fossils to infer how we lived and the state of contemporary surrounding ecologies.

For example, the Dmanisi, Georgia, archaeological site has been rigorously dated through multiple methods to approximately 1,800,000 -1,700,000 years ago. The initial publication of this discovery provided five dating methods to support this date: (1) K-Ar dating on the Masavera Basalt, (2) Paleomagnetic correlation with the Olduvai Geomagnetic Subchron, (3) Late-Plio-Pleistocene vertebrate fauna, (4) Hominin morphology similar to early African H. *erectus* (Homo *ergaster*) and (5) Oldowan stone tools. The research scientists did not want their reputations tarnished by not being thorough.

Sleepless in Dmanisi

The discovery of human fossils in Dmanisi, Georgia, is accompanied by fossils from sabretooth cats, proving that the big cats were hunted and butchered. Also, the fossil of a human skull was discovered nearby with two oval punctures in the back that neatly fit a young sabretooth cat's upper canines. We can infer that around 1,800,000 years ago, big games must have roamed in current-day Georgia. Humans hunted the big game for food, but they were also food for the big games. It is very likely that our ancestors lived in considerable danger a lot of the time.

This primal fear of danger and having to stay alert may have resulted in changes in our genetic disposition. For example, I tend to sleep lightly, according to my *23andme* portfolio. Indeed, I am a light sleeper, upon reflection of how I have slept throughout my life. There is the possibility that my branch of ancestors lived in areas populated with big games or perceived danger. Thus, the necessity for remaining alert was gradually built into my DNA after, say, thousands of generations. My ancestors became a group who always slept lightly.

It is believed that the DEC2 gene on chromosome 12 experiences a mutation in some population that may have increase the production of orexin hormone, which promotes wakefulness. It would be interesting to find out when this mutation happened and how that seeped into modern humans' genes.

Other Proxies

Other indirect fossils can also shed light on the organisms under study, in addition to collocated human and animal fossils. For example, molds and casts, tracks and trails, burrows and borings, pollen, and coprolites (fossilized dung from humans and other animals) can all be helpful in fitting together the puzzles of various knowledge bases. In particular, stone tools and the subsequent artifacts manufactured by the stone tools can be a reference to the hominins' abilities and intelligence. Even DNA remnants in dirt trotted upon by ancient beings can indicate the age and species once located at some discovery sites.

When accurately determined for specific fossils, whether direct or indirect, the ages can serve as a foundation for a molecular genetic clock since they are used to calibrate the speed of molecular evolution and mutations. This, in turn, helps us to establish a better phylo-genetic tree using molecular genetics.

NATURAL RADIOACTIVE DECAYS

I cannot let this chapter wrap without injecting a little physics into fossils. As it turns out, almost every technique mentioned here involves the physics-oriented process of one isotope decaying into another. Although we frequently use radioactive decay for dating, working behind the scenes is the weak force, one of four funda-mental forces in the universe.

It is the weak field theory under quantum mechanical formula-tion that governs the behavior of the decays. Quantum mechanics is involved because the decay process is probabilistic and random. Recall that a random process consists of a probability of the Poisson process. Indeed, if you count the decay events in a unit timeframe—a second, a minute, or longer—they follow a Poisson distribution, just like human mutations, or the ridership of a city bus. It is interesting to note that the disparate subjects of evolution and natural decay follow the same general random concept and the same mathematical formulation.

PHYSICAL EVOLUTION IN CONTINUUM

It is worth noting that even with the abundance of human fossil collection today—and it continues to increase—there are gaping holes between discoveries. We don't know what we don't know when there are no fossils available. Our human phylogenetic tree will likely be forever handicapped by these gaps.

Fortunately, scientists have not been deterred or discouraged. They have helped fill in some of the gaps through creativity based on Charles Darwin's long-held gradualism principle and the wealth of comparative anatomy. We can bridge the gaps and imagine the morphing of one form into another. The next chapter intends to illuminate steps of human physical evolution, bearing in mind that they happen in the continuum that nature has intended.

BIBLIOGRAPHY

1. "Revised age of late Neanderthal occupation and the end of the Middle Paleolithic in the northern Caucasus," Ron Pinhasi, Thomas F. G. Higham, Liubov V. Golovanova, and Vladimir B. Doronichev, *Proceedings of the National Academy of Science of the United States of America,* **108**, 8611-8616 (2011).
2. For an exhaustive list of human evolutionary fossils since 1850 to the present, see, for example, https://en.wikipedia.org/wiki/List_of_human_evolution_fossils.

7

OUR PHYSICAL EVOLUTION THROUGH TIME

L ast chapter tells the story of fossils, it is time we learn about ourselves from them. This chapter explores how we have physically changed or evolved from the early days, based on the fossils that are been left behind, or in some cases, what are missing. It would enliven our physical evolution if we could visualize the features change through time from one form and morph smoothly into another. In the ideal situation, we would need fossils from every few generations and every species to facilitate a continuously moving picture. As is evident from the phylogenetic tree, there are gaps in time and discontinuities in physical characteristics between milestones. A smooth visual of our progression seems infeasible despite the effort over the past 150 years since we just do not have enough fossils to cover the time through our evolution.

We do not expect this fossil scarcity to improve dramatically any time soon. Nevertheless, through scientists' creativity and logical reasoning, we can bridge the gaps between eras to provide educated guesses of intermediate steps. These guesses are the missing links in two senses: they indicate one, a viable evolutionary path; and two, a roadmap or guideline for continued fossil searches.

There are, however, gaps that may be wider than others, both in time and morphology, that make speculating on missing links seem a stretch. In those cases, we may have to realize that a simplified interpretation of the long-held concept of Darwin's "gradualism" may not be a universal concept. Instead, an alternative theory of stepwise evolution is at play resulting in these perceived time and morphological gaps. This concept has the fancy name of "punctuated equilibrium" in an attempt to explain away our seemingly staccato evolutionary rhythm.

To bring together the train of human morphological changes, the differences between continuous changes and wider gaps that seem to indicate stepwise changes must be reconciled. Gradualism is an outcome of natural selection in evolution that happens continuously from generation to generation. Punctuated equilibrium results from less frequent but more drastic changes to genomes initiated by mutation. They both contribute to our evolution significantly and affect physical changes and other parts beyond the physical.

As to precisely how gradualism or punctuated equilibrium influences changes, it is ultimately governed by the interaction of both processes, gradual and abrupt, with environments subjected to the positive feedback loop elaborated in chapter 3.

The first half of this chapter describes how we can make sense of the fossils, which are inherently scarce, fragmented, and incomplete. We will also outline how to weave together a moving picture by filling in the gaps where no physical evidence exists to prove them right or wrong. The second half narrates through the changes in our morphology. They include the changes to our heads, our upright postures and bipedalism, hands and arms, and throats and voice boxes. Also, there are some subtle differences between the Neanderthals and us that illustrate how gravity has caused the anatomy of our upper bodies to diverge slightly in different environments in as short a time as 500,000 years.

Human fossils also provide information beyond the physical appearances—they contain DNA and proteins that connect us to other hominins and each other genetically. The ancient DNA and proteins have been the primary focus of research over the last 15 years. We will touch on this in the next two chapters, but for now, let's look at our physical changes.

MAKING SENSE OUT OF HUMAN FOSSILS

COMPARATIVE ANATOMY

Through the years of the history of paleoanthropology since the discover of the first Neanderthals in the 1860s (although there was an earlier Neanderthal discovery in the 1820s, but it was not recognized as such until much later), we have collected the fossils of 6,000 hominin individuals, spanning 7,000,000 years and a wide geographic range extending over Africa, Europe, Asia, Polynesia, Australia, and the Americas.

Out of the thousands of fossil fragments and samples, most are not identifiable as existing animals or organisms, or in this case, modern human beings. How does one know that they belonged to hominins in the first place, let alone how to reconstruct these hominin bodies? What gives fossil researchers the ability to find them, study them, and conclude where they fit into our family tree? The most basic requirement is anatomy, and more specifically, comparative anatomy, to make sense out of the whole fossil mess.

Comparative anatomy is the study of the similarities and differences in the anatomy of different yet somehow connected species. It is closely related to evolutionary biology but based primarily on the anatomy of living organisms that aims to help construct the biological taxonomy of living animals. It tries to bridge and connect physical and anatomic discontinuities between distantly or closely related species, genera, families, or higher taxonomic levels. At times, it also helps to verify, supplement, or correct taxonomic mis-assignments. Comparative anatomists are good at connecting seemingly unrelated animals anatomically. For example, they conclude that humans and horses are descendants of a common ancestor with five digits on each limb. As horses evolved to live on the open grassland, their anatomy required a more compact design to enable movement across the firm and stony plains, and the five digits subsequently morphed into a single hoof. The ability to give a different perspective on body parts and functions is the exact expertise needed to sort out the human fossil mess.

Comparative anatomy expertise being the necessary skill notwithstanding, there still need some ground rules to piece together the fossils and the stories behind them. One intuitive and widely accepted practice is gradualism, but the possibility of punctuated equilibrium should not be discounted.

GRADUALISM AND PUNCTUATED EQUILIBRIUM

Considering that there is a vast period of 7,000,000 years from the beginning of the hominin population to their numbers reaching the billions, we have discovered very few hominin individuals: the remains of 30 different species. It is not surprising that the gaps in time and morphology are significant. We don't know what we don't know when there are no fossils available. This has certainly frustrated academicians for a long time, but it has not stopped us from using our imagination and intellect to bridge these gaps.

If there is a direct lineage from us to our earliest ancestors, all of these gaps can be filled by simply drawing lines between adjacent points. If the length of the thumbs of two distant relatives is different by 50%, it should be reasonable to conclude that the species between them would feature a thumb length 25% different from the long and short ones. This interpolation is the intuitive concept behind Charles Darwin's gradualism.

Darwin believed that evolution was a slow and gradual process. By "gradual," Darwin did not mean "perfectly smooth," but rather, "stepwise," with a species or features evolving and accumulating small variations over a long period of time until a new species or feature was born. He did not assume that the pace of change was constant, however, and he recognized that many species retained the same forms over long periods.

Still, if evolution is gradual, there should be fossilized records of small, incremental, and intermediate changes along the way to a new species and/or feature, but in many cases, scientists have been unable to find these intermediate forms. Darwin himself was surprised by their absence. He concluded that the fossil record lacked these transitional stages because the fossil record was so incomplete that the transitional fossils had not been discovered yet. This is undoubtedly true in many cases because the chance of finding each and every intermediate change in the form of fossils is small. This argument is logical; I tend to agree with Darwin.

In 1972, evolutionary scientists Stephen Jay Gould and Niles Eldredge proposed another proposal, which they called "punctuated equilibrium." That is, species are generally stable and change little over millions of years. This steady situation can be "punctuated", or disrupted, by a rapid burst of changes, resulting in new species. The new species equilibrates to a stagnant state until the next punctuated changes happen after a long time. These sudden changes would leave few fossils behind because the changes did not take very long to happen. As such, only the fossils in an apparent state of equilibrium would exhibit themselves in the fossil record. The original concept of punctuated equilibrium specifically refers to the formation of new species. I believe this can be generalized to cover any abrupt change in features and/or traits. This alternative explanation for pauses in fossil changes, whether real or perceived, is unnecessary, as it does not satisfactorily explain that most physical changes are gradual.

Physical evolution is molecular action manifested in morphological variation. Inherent in molecular evolution is that two different mechanisms bring about change—one slow and the other abrupt. These slow but persistent changes are caused primarily by environmental influence on a species through natural selection evolution. Mutations initiate the more abrupt changes to the DNA for which the environmental impact is minimal. Whatever the changes are, the resultant feature or species still needs to survive the environmental filtering to continue through to following generations per the evolutionary principle in chapter 3.

Changes initiated by mutation are rarely drastic since any significant feature changes will have resulted from collaborative expressions by numerous genes thus moderate the drastic genetic changes. However, they could be still more drastic relative to what is brought about by natural selection. Even then, there would still be transitional stages before a new feature or species finally exhibits as being clearly distinguished from previous forms. Using gradualism to bridge the gaps should be a good practice, even in the cases of punctuated equilibrium.

In sum, for gradualism, the slow and gradual changes occur in constant, minuscule changes from generation to generation, whenever chromosomes go through crossovers and sexual reproduction in mammals. In the end, however, this long-term natural selective change is determined by the influence of the environment. In a punctuated equilibrium process, evolution occurs in spurts of relatively rapid changes initiated by rare episodes of mutation. Once the spurts pass, the species is subject to the same natural selection evolution and proceeds with their lives. These are two different evolutionary mechanisms and there is no need to pit one against the other.

INCOMPLETE JIGSAW PUZZLE PIECES FOR UNKNOWN PICTURES

The task of reconstructing our forms and shapes from fragmented human fossils, as well as figuring out how they fit into the existing family tree, is very daunting. This intellectually challenging exercise reminds me of a party game we used to play in graduate school, invented by John A. Wheeler. Professor Wheeler should have trademarked his initials—JAW—so Steven Spielberg might have had to have used something other than *JAWS* for his claim to fame movie or pay Professor Wheeler for it. He is the same physicist who coined the moniker "black hole" in 1967, which is used so liberally by everyone today, it is as if it were second nature. This party game is usually played by a group of people with one player—the guesser—correctly guessing an item agreed upon by other players—the gamers. The guesser has to ask the appropriate questions from each gamer to get the right answer and win, a familiar game to most of us.

The Wheeler twist is that the gamers agree to nothing except that everyone has to come up with answers consistent with all previous answers. This game is more interesting because it gets everyone's brains cranking instead of just the guesser having all the fun. The best way to play the game is that when the guesser is sent out of the room, assuming the game will be played just as usual, the guesser does not know of the rule change. I recall that I once hosted a Christmas party and played this game with my family and friends. The perplexed look on the guesser's face was so precious, as was his delight, once he had figured out about the rule change. One problem of the game is that once the change of the rule is known and everyone is let in on it, it is not as much fun, although it still intellectually challenging for the participants.

Studying human evolution based on fossils, or on certain aspects of fossils, is a little like playing this game. The challenges paleoanthropologists face is in having to piece together incomplete fossils, not only in an attempt to complete the individuals but also for the betterment of the human family tree. To further complicate the task at hand is that this feat must be accomplished without reference as to how the finished product should look. Other than not knowing a heck of a lot about the finished look, the game rules may change without them knowing it.

Investigators or scientists are the guessers in this game, trying to reach a consensus of an evolutionary story consistent with their cumulative answers. It would be very satisfying if any of the discoveries turn out to be a missing link able to bridge discontinuity, but I thought it might be even more exciting if the guessers came up with revolutionary discoveries and concepts that upset the status quo of evolutionary theory. Given the overwhelming odds that they will come away with little in their daily activities most of the time, you have to admire the faith, knowledge base, and cumulative efforts exhibited by all brilliant paleoanthropologists.

To change or evolve from an ape to a human, we have undergone drastic modifications to significant parts of our bodies. The most noticeable physical changes happened to at least five body parts: the head, our posture for bipedalism, the hands and arms, the voice box in our throats, and the upper body. They are categorized this way for convenience and should not be treated as independent, exhaustive characteristics.

THE CHANGING HEADS

The first of the most dramatic changes to the human body is the head. This change is not a stand-alone affair. There are usually other collaborative changes in other parts of our bodies. We occasionally include body parts associated with head changes when necessary.

BRAINCASE SIZES

A general trend for the change in braincase is that it got bigger as it evolved from its ancestor to modern human. What must be obvious is that modern humans have (almost) the largest braincases among all animals. We have even used brain capacity to define the dividing line between the genera of Australopithecus and Homo, as mentioned in chapter 5, which is around 600 cubic centimeters (cc). Figure 9 shows the progression of braincase increase through time.

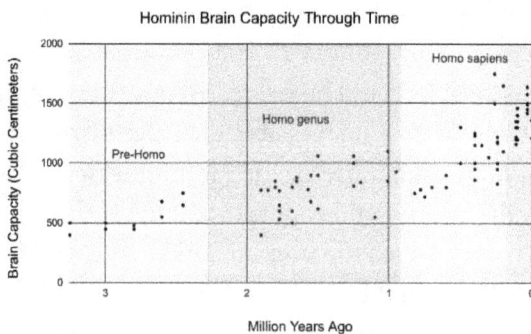

Figure 9. Progression of brain capacity through the last 3,200,000 years. Note that four periods in this chart are the same as shown in Figure 5.

Since our brain cases are a lot larger than our early ancestors', it is reasonable to conclude that larger brain cases accommodate larger brain capacities. Thus the owners of the larger brain cases are smarter animals. The chart shows hominin braincase sizes from early 3,200,000 years ago to the present, based on fossils accumulated to date. Brain capacities fit roughly into four groups. The first is the early hominin/Australopithecus group, with a braincase capacity of around 500 cc., about 20% larger than modern chimps. This group continues through 2,000,000 years ago until there seems to be a gradual rise beyond this, forming the second group. This was when the Homo genus came onto the scene, including Homo *habilis* and Homo *erectus*, with brain sizes ranging from 600 to 1,200 cc. In the third group, the capacity rises steadily, beginning 900,000 years ago. Finally, the last group coincides with the rise of modern humans 200,000 years ago. This group has brain capacities ranging from 1,200 to 1,750 cc.

These groups coincide with the four periods on our phylogenetic tree in chapter 5. The increase in brain size is a part of the reason behind the assignment of various genera. It has been successful to mark the time according to braincase size until we get to modern humans and Neanderthals; the largest braincase size belongs to the Neanderthals rather than modern humans.

IS BRAIN SIZE EQUIVALENT TO INTELLIGENCE?

It is worth noting that the braincase of our most recently lost relative, the Neanderthals, have even larger braincases than ours in some cases. Were they smarter, more intelligent, better at vocalization, better thinkers, and/or better artists? We probably will never know. In reality, simple size may not tell the whole intelligence and/or smartness story, which may not be an absolute measure. Male gorillas have a huge brain size, but they are stuck on a different evolutionary path, fairly remote from human lines, and we would not consider them very intelligent. Perhaps a gorilla's large brain is due to its sheer body size. There have been various attempts to better quantify intelligence based on the braincase size. Maybe we need to scale brain size relative to an organism's body size as a measure.

There is a branch of neurological study for a figure of merit for intelligence, called the "encephalization quotient." This figure of merit is modeled by an unnecessarily complicated and sophisticated-sounding multiple variable regression, taking the brain size of most mammals into account. This algorithm works well and concludes that humans are the smartest animal/mammal on earth. Would you expect anything different? Was this even worthwhile "research" in the first place?

In the end, the most straightforward, sensible, size to weight ratio is scientific and convincing enough that anything beyond this has failed to make a believer out of me.

It might be interesting to get back to the size of a Neanderthal's brain from another angle. Even though we cannot tell if they were smarter than we are, we know, through a series of studies, that they were a lot smarter than that for which we give them credit. A recent discovery of plant fibers twisted into strings and ropes in Southeast France, dated to 50,000 years ago, was most likely made by Neanderthals. We believe that, 50,000 years ago, modern humans may have also had the same capability, but they did not arrive in Europe until later. Neanderthals have been on an equal level of intelligence with modern humans, at least where rope-making is concerned.

A physical attribute of brain size or the ratio of brain to body size is not the only measure of our intelligence, in light of a recent anatomic study. The flow of blood into and out of the braincase also factors into an organism's intelligence. The study published in late November of 2019 reported that despite having a similar-sized brain to modern gorillas, chimps, and orangutans, Australopithecus had a lower blood flow rate to its brain. The research suggests that the window-like openings between the braincase and spine are larger in modern apes than in Australopithecus. This larger, "big hole," or *foramen magnum*, allows as much as double the blood to flow through than in Australopithecus. Our Australopithecus ancestors may not have been as smart as the great apes of today. A figure of merit for intelligence could then include braincase size, body weight, and foramen magnum size, all of which are related to each other in a simple formulation.

SKULL SHAPE

Accompanying the change of braincase size is a progression of various skull features along our evolutionary path. The following list is but a few of the most apparent changes in our skulls.

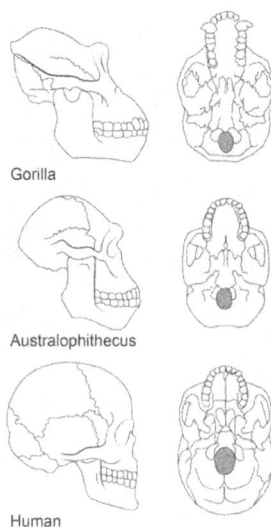

Gorilla

Australophithecus

Human

Figure 10. The skulls and the changing positions of the great hole for gorillas, Australopithecus, and modern humans.

The first is the great hole placement. The great hole sits at the base of the skull through which the spinal cord and main arteries enter and exit the braincase. The position of the great hole in apes and early ancestors reflects habitual body posture and mode of loco-motion. The forward placement (anterior position) of the great hole in modern humans is due to an adaptation for maintaining the balance of the head atop the cervical vertebral column for bipedal-ism. It is also due to the required upright upper body posture. Accordingly, the relative placement of the great hole on the base of the skull explains bipedal locomotion and the hominin progression over several fossils, dated between 5,000,000 to 2,500,000 years ago. These skull features are shown quite prominently in Figure 10 showing the skulls and the positions of the great hole of gorillas, Australopithecus, and human beings.

Human skulls have evolved toward a rounder shape with a reduced site above the mandible (the lower jawbone, or the zygomatic bone) for muscle attachment on the sides, especially those used for chewing. Most likely, this is due to a diet rich in meat and cooked food.

The skull's forehead rises sharply from a slope and has smaller eyebrow ridges as we evolve. The sharply rising forehead might come from the need to accommodate the expanded braincase volume for a continuously enlarging brain. The smaller eyebrow ridge might be because faces do not need such strong mechanical muscular support for chewing hard food, much like the site for jawbone muscle attachment near the ears. The rising forehead poses difficulties in childbirth for modern humans due to our upright posture, which facilitates bipedalism.

According to one theory, modern human developed prominent chins to support and compensate for the structurally thin, slender mandibles. Another idea postulates that our prominent chin is the result of a shrinking lower jaw; a larger jaw was our ancestors' signature. There is also speculation that the chin is a sexual attraction, much like the peacock's massive plumes—attractive but not practical. On the other hand, maybe sexual attraction is its useful utility.

POSTURE: FULLY BIPEDAL ADAPTATION

WE ARE THE ONLY OBLIGATE BIPEDALs

As far as bipedalism is concerned, there are partially upright and bipedal mammals, like baboons, bonobos, chimps, and gibbons. There are also marsupials we consider bipedal some of the time, like kangaroos and wallabies. Modern human beings stand upright whenever they have to move from place to place on two feet/legs, either by walking or running. This type of bipedalism became habitual and necessary during the last stage of our evolution, toward Homo *erectus*. Bipedalism is a feature enabled by more than a few physical changes. We have already alluded to a few of them in our discussion of skull evolution. The following are additional features enabling our bipedalism.

A pair of bony knobs facilitating the connection between cervical vertebrae and the great hole (*occipital condyle*) moved toward the center of the braincase in concert with the great hole's forward position. This movement keeps the head—the braincase carrying the brain material—above the braincase's center of the gravity. Modern humans suffer from this critical alignment because even a slight habitual misalignment can create chronic back problems in all ages.

Our rib cages are flattened from front to back, which moves the center of gravity closer to the spine. This movement improves the balance of the upper body in an upright posture, but the balance is now more critically aligned since our spines are not entirely straight. Our spine has evolved into an "S-shape," allowing the chest's weight to sit above the pelvis rather than further forward. The S-shaped spine also helps us absorb the shock from prolonged upright walking.

Our pelvis shape has changed from high and narrow to a low and wide bowl shape—a larger valgus angle—for better balance and upper body support. This pelvis shape better facilitates childbearing to accommodate the enlarged head and high human forehead. Our femurs have become longer and more robust, angled more outward with a longer femoral neck to accommodate a larger valgus angle.

Our big toes are in line with other toes such that the feet act as a platform, but they have lost the ability to grasp things for tree-dwelling. The feet have also developed an arch to give the feet a springy feel while walking or running. By the way, it should not come as a surprise that our relatives, the Neanderthals, also had similar foot structures even though they may not have been built as runners.

HANDS AND ARMS

Other changes have an equal impact and are related to bipedalism, but only indirectly, such as the hands and arms. Human hands serve many purposes. They carry objects while traversing large terrains, make tools, fight, hunt, and make art, among other things. There is enough evidence from the fossil record to suggest that the hand changed gradually toward its modern functions. Oldowan tools (thus names because they were first discovered at Olduvai Gorge), dates to as early as 2,600,000 years ago, and Acheulean stone hand tools (named after the site of St. Acheul on the Somme River in France), dated to as early as 1,600,000 years ago, indicates dexterous hand use. These tools were manufactured and used in broad geological areas, spreading over South Africa, Europe, India, and Asia, most likely by H. *erectus*. They were made by repeatedly knapping a flint, using a hammerstone to shape it into a sharp flake for meat cutting or hunting. This technology and industry took a long time to master and flourish to such ubiquity in the Old World. It is hard to imagine that our evolved hands are not the source of these advances.

The changes in the hand started pretty early. The most illustrative difference is in a long-fingered fossil of an Ardipithecus from Ethiopia (4,400,000 years ago, see chapter 5). The hand structure from that of Homo *habilis* (1,700,000 years ago) already shows longer thumbs accompanied by a shortening of other fingers for toolmaking (because the stone tools and hand fossils appeared together.) The physical evolution of our hands, the emergence of hand tools, and the jump in brain capacity happened at almost the same time, serving as convincing evidence that these features did not change sequentially. Instead, evolution happens to collaboratively adapt to the environment according to collective needs in what is probably the most expedient manner.

Two levels of arm evolution are most apparent. The first is the shortening of the arm, both the upper and lower parts. This shortening may have been partly due to bipedalism since there is no longer a need for quadrupedal motion. Besides, fully upright locomotion is more efficient when the arms are shorter as they are not needed to push the body forward, causing a "drag" in upright walkers. There are plenty of other examples showing that shorter upper limbs are beneficial for upright posture and bipedalism. Chickens and kangaroos are two good examples.

The second is the handedness of hand use. Neanderthals have handedness tendencies similar to modern humans because they had unusually strong right arms based on fossil studies. A cross-section view of these upper arm bones reveals that whereas the human humerus has a rounder shape, the Neanderthal humerus was more oval-shaped. This might be because this oval shape has better strength along the length, needed for the Neanderthals' spear-throwing for hunting. The asymmetric strength of the oval shape is similar to the concept of I-beams in architecture. An I-beam can also withstand a lot more mechanical stress along its length.

Further, it was determined that Neanderthals exhibited strong handedness, just like the people that predated them a few million years before. Evidence shows that most of the stone tools showing up started approximately 2,000,000 years ago were made by and for right-handed users. The subject of handedness will be a part of a discussion on genetics in a later chapter.

THROAT AND VOICE BOX

The ability of modern human to speak has a lot, but is not exclusively due, to do with our throat and voice box anatomy. First of all, we are able to create sounds and tunes with multiple octaves. We can also manipulate our tongues, lips, jaws, and teeth to make many more sounds, like vowels, consonants, and tones. Also, we need something a lot more than the physical—we need the brainpower to formulate ideas into language, articulate this in the brain, give commands to our nervous systems, and activate proper muscles and bones in concert to *talk*. It is a pretty involved and complex sequence of events.

.   .   .

VOCAL CAPABILITY

The morphological changes to our throats and voice boxes are an essential and necessary reason behind why we talk. This evolution toward speaking continues to be shrouded in mystery since most of the voice box consists of cartilage and does not fossilize to leave any evidence behind. The exceptions are rare hyoid bone fossils obtained from a Neanderthal and a Homo *heidelbergensis* specimen.

This mysterious transition from wordless communication to speech is excellent material for science fiction books or movies. One of the better science fiction movies that I like is *Rise of the Planet of the Apes*, released in 2011. This movie is the prequel to *Planet of the Apes* in the 1970s. The newer movie explains why apes are the masters of the earth instead of humans, for box office reasons, of course.

CAN A CHIMP TALK?

The demotion of humans to slaves for apes begins with a very smart chimp, according to the 2011 movie. This chimp, Caesar, inherits a genetic boost toward intelligence and cognition from his mother. The mother acquires these qualities by taking an experimental drug that repairs brain cells, increases mental acuity, and is intended for human consumption. The drug is developed to treat generic dementia, supposedly for older humans, to restore their mental acuity. The backdrop of the drug's development is that a mega-pharmaceutical company in San Francisco will rake in tremendous profit if the drug works. Hollywood is always trying to convey some messages, justified or not.

Of course, things don't work out as planned, and baby chimp Caesar ends up growing up with humans. He is subsequently sent to a primate shelter since the animal control agency will not allow him to live in residential areas. This city or local ordinance is reasonable, considering that people keep tigers as pets in urban homes.

Because Caesar is a lot smarter than other primates, he quickly establishes supremacy among apes of all sizes due to his intelligence even without a physically intimidating stature. There is a scene in which Caesar stands in the middle of the shelter center, demanding subjugation from the other apes to solidify his alpha-male dominance. When the shelter's caretaker approaches and commands him to go back into his suffocating cage, Caesar refuses. The caretaker uses an electric cattle prod to zap him repeatedly and beat him to obey, but Caesar—who is still a youngster but certainly much more robust than regular humans—cannot be quickly subdued by electric shocks and the beating from the human.

The standoff continues for a few moments, and Caesar's anger builds until it reaches a breaking point. He grabs the cattle prod and won't let go. When the caretaker commands, "Take your stinking paws off me, you damn dirty ape," there is a momentary pause between them. Some of you might recall that this is the exact phrase Charlton Heston yelled at one of the apes as he held him with a manacle around his neck in the original *Planet of the Apes* movie. Caesar puffs heavily a few times, then utters a loud, guttural, and gravely, "NO." I still remember when the theater audience gasped and then went quiet. My hair raised, and goosebumps popped up all over my neck. I would say that this moment is the climax and the whole point of the movie. The build-up of the mood and the display of Caesar's anger in human words is the most dramatic and powerful scene I have seen in science fiction movies—credit to the movie's director.

Even with the close genetic relationship between humans and chimps, Caesar should not have been able to talk. The chimp just did not have the anatomy for it, even if the "smart drug" improved his intelligence.

WHY CHIMPS CANNOT SPEAK

There are two reasons that chimps cannot speak: the physical or anatomical and the genetic. Further, these two factors are interdependent—both have to work together to properly enable speech.

Not In Anatomy

Modern human voice boxes—and maybe Neanderthals'—are

situated a lot lower in the throat than that of the chimps. The two
vocal cords in the voice box vibrate like the double reed in an oboe.
They vibrate to produce a buzzing sound when air flows past the
vocal cords, either through exhaling or inhaling (for ventriloquists).
Finally, the buzzing sound resonates within the cavity enclosed by
the voice box and the back of the throat, the resonator.

This buzzing is similar to the vibrations that come from rubbing
the rim of a wine glass. The wine glass acts with the wine as the
resonator, determining the pitch. The lowered voice box allows for a
wide audio frequency range and higher octaves that only humans can
produce. You can try to feel how your Adam's apple moves up and
down when you change your tone.

Through the coordinated action of the tongue, lips, teeth, vocal
cords, and throat, we can make any sound as well as have a voice with
which to speak. A chimp's voice box is situated at a much higher position, shrinking the size of the cavity, producing only higher-pitched
sounds. This is why chimps can only make the shrieks you hear in
zoos.

Not In Intelligence

The other thing responsible for speech comes from the intelligence to formulate speech and utilize the motor skills to complete the
talking. The critical gene responsible for speech development in our
DNA is FOXP2 on chromosome 7. This gene works in coordination
with many other genes (at least 40 and not necessarily on the same
chromosome) for the physical and mental ability to speak, as well as
other related behaviors (like hand gestures and facial expressions).
Although FOXP2 is highly invariable across most mammals, humans
differ at two functional amino acid substitutions from chimps, bonobos, and gorillas, and an additional fixed substitution found in orangutans. If Caesar's FOXP2 gene were identical to a human's PLUS the
other associated genes were simultaneously transplanted into
Caesar's molecular construct in every cell, he might have the chance
to speak.

At this time, we still do not know how the other associated genes
work collaboratively with FOXP2 in totality for speech. Would phar-

maceutical companies know more about FOXP2 and the link to speech than the collective wisdom of hardcore scientists who have been in the field for many years? Even if Caesar somehow inherited the cognitive ability to formulate ideas to transmit to other individuals, the hardware—the anatomy—of talking is simply not there.

CHIMPS CANNOT TALK, BUT NEANDERTHALS MIGHT

At what stage of our evolution did we begin to speak? It was common to believe that complex language did not evolve until about 100,000 years ago and that modern humans were the only ones capable of complex speech, but a 1989 discovery of the hyoid bone of a Neanderthal fossil in Kebara, Israel, may have changed that. An analysis of the 60,000 years old hyoid bone suggests the Neanderthals could speak since the hyoid bone looks (and would act) just like that of modern humans. The hyoid bone is a U-shaped bone situated at the root of the tongue, between the lower jaw and the top of the larynx, or voice box. The hyoid bone's primary function is to act as a structure anchoring the tongue, which serves the purpose of speaking, chewing, and swallowing in concert with other movements of the mouth.

Not only does the Neanderthal's hyoid bone look very similar to humans, but a computer modeling of how it would work has shown that this bone would function in a way similar to that in humans. It suggests that Neanderthals could have been as sophisticated speakers as modern human beings, assuming that Neanderthals' vocal cords were similar to that of modern humans. The depiction of Neanderthals uttering nonsensical grunts for communication may just be our narcissistic belief that we are the only primates who can speak. If Neanderthals can talk, they must be able to hear. In a research published in March 2021, it is determined that they can hear just fine. Their ear drums are as sensitive to high pitch voice as ours.

A much older hyoid fossil recently discovered is attributed to another relative of ours: Homo *heidelbergensis*. The site of this discovery, which is over 500,000 years old, is Spain. This new finding has yet to be computer-modeled, but it was, at first glance, similar to those of modern humans and Neanderthals. This could push the origins of speech further back in time. It would be interesting to determine whether a full Neanderthal genome (the entire Neanderthal genomes have been reconstructed since the 2010s) might shed some light on their ability to speak.

At this time, we have not found hyoid bones as the missing links to bridge Homo *heidelbergensis* to its ancestors older than 500,000 years. We are not exactly sure how the hyoid bone transitioned from chimp form to human form. It would be interesting to do a computer model of how an intermediate hyoid bone might look and sound, following the practice of gradualism.

However, the physical anatomy of current chimps does not have the right voice box structure to articulate human sounds, so enjoy the fiction for now.

UPPER BODY: MODERN HUMANS VS. NEANDERTHALS

Neanderthals are often depicted as barrel-chested, hunched-over cavemen, thanks to Marcellin Boule, the renowned French paleontologist, who declared that Neanderthals weren't able to stand up straight. His study of the "Old Man" in the early 1900s cast Neanderthals as unintelligent brutes. More than anyone else, he is responsible for the gross misconception of Neanderthals that persists to this day in everything from literature and movies to cartoons.

Later Neanderthal fossil evidence tells a different story. Somewhere along the evolutionary path, Neanderthals took on a different spinal shape from that of modern humans, as mentioned before. An effort to reconstruct the rib cage and upper spine of a Neanderthal man who died roughly 60,000 years ago reveals that they might have had straight spines with a slight curve shaped like a flattened letter C instead of an S-shaped spine like ours and a similar-sized chest to modern humans. If someone cannot stand up straight, it is the modern humans having problems straightening his S-shaped spine.

The difference in the upper body between modern human and

Neanderthals is in the thorax as a whole, including the rib cage, spine, and the cavity housing the heart and lungs. This region is of particular interest because it tells us about breathing and balance. Compared with modern humans, Neanderthals' ribs are more horizontally oriented. The rib cage is more robust and flares out at the lower end to form a bell-shape, indicating an enlarged diaphragm. This structure suggests that Neanderthals relied more on their diaphragms for breathing, whereas modern humans rely on both the diaphragm and the expansion and contraction of the lungs.

The upper body difference between modern humans and Neanderthals reminds me of a requirement in executing the art of Tai Chi. For a proper Tai Chi fighting stance, one needs to keep the lower crook of the spine's S shape filled in at all times, equivalent to straightening up the backbone. Besides, Tai Chi requires practicing breathing from the lower abdomen (i.e., using the lower diaphragm to expand or contract the lungs). It is the simultaneous action of a stabilized stance with a straight lower spine and more efficient lower abdomen breathing that makes a good foundation in Tai Chi, according to my master. This posture facilitates better stability through a lower center of gravity and smoother tangential deflection of incoming forces enabled by a straighter back, serving as the center of a cylinder. Neanderthals are better on both accounts by anatomic design—maybe they were more natural Tai Chi practitioners than modern humans. A proper Tai Chi stance is anatomically optimum for everyone. In particular, an anteverted (backward) pelvis position better preserves the wedge-shaped L5-S1 disc in your spine. It is the same as filling in the lower crook of our S-shaped spines.

Modern man's upper body anatomy—as they are svelter and more gracile—has its evolutionary advantage over Neanderthals for long-distance running. Their slightly bell-shaped rib cage might have given Neanderthals a potbelly that would hinder flexibility and the motion needed for running. As well, modern humans' S-shaped spine serves as a springy shock absorber for the continuous pounding, giving an additional advantage to modern man for long-distance running over Neanderthals. On the other hand, the modern human's

S-shaped spine may not be our proudest evolutionary outcome, considering that pain in our lower backs has inflicted upon so many of us, unless, of course, we continually and consciously strike that proper Tai Chi pose.

PACE OF PHYSICAL EVOLUTION

We have always wondered how long our evolution has taken to get to our current shape and form. We can use hand adaptation as an illustration point. The two views of an Ardipithecus hand in Figure 11 are a reconstruction by Ray Matternes, based on Ardipithecus *ramidus* fossils.

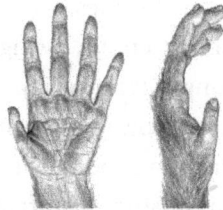

Figure 11. Artist rendition of Ardipithecus hand based on fossils by Ray Matternes. Ardipithecus are believed to live more than 4,400,000 years ago (See Figure 5).

The straightforward shortening of the fingers and lengthening of the thumb from Ardipithecus to ours has taken, conservatively, at least 2,000,000 years to achieve, assuming our Homo *erectus* ancestors evolved with our present hand form; a span of 2,000,000 years and approximately 80,000 generations. This is such a long time to comprehend, considering our written culture needed only about 300 generations—or 7,500 years—to the point where I can now write about this.

Through these 80,000 generations, the positive feedback process —consciously or unconsciously—selects offspring with shorter fingers to continue the lineage. One can imagine that hominins awkward with their hands may not be as popular as ones who can use them effectively, making them slightly less desirable as mating partners. For every successful offspring, there must be more with the wrong finger lengths which were left behind.

This positive feedback is similar to hearing a screeching noise when you put a microphone too close to the speaker in any public speaking setting. The audio voice is amplified, just like the adaptation for finger characteristics, and the audio frequency or pitch creating the screeching is the selection of hominins with longer thumbs and shorter fingers.

How long did it take for all other adaptations, like feet, pelvis, arms, and legs, that transformed us from apes to humans? These changes may or may not have happened concurrently with the finger length change, but the sheer amount of needed changes is more dramatic than just the finger length change. The 7,000,000 years of evolution that completely transformed us from apes to modern man seem fast enough. Along the slow transformation paths, there may be spurts of changes that could have made more drastic changes to speed up the evolutionary process. However, these events are few and far between, and we know that the 7,000,000 years of evolution already includes these moments.

SUMMARY

This chapter set out to follow our physical changes through the ages, in particular, the head, posture, hands, voice box, and upper body. These changes were not independent acts. Instead, they worked continuously together to ensure the end product to be as optimal as possible. Wherever there are gaps, we imagine filling them by common senses and Darwin's gradualism principle. This practice does not rule out the influence of mutation to account for more abrupt transitions, except that they might just be gradualism on steroids.

The influence of gravity accounts for a substantial portion of our evolution. Besides braincase size, almost every change was made to deal with gravity pulling us down toward the ground. Although gravity is not the driver of evolution, per se, our movements and reflexes are fine-tuned to accommodate a gravity of 9.807m/sec^2. It took us at least a few million years of swimming in this gravity to get used to it fully. I am always amused at so many science fictions on TV and in the movies about how humans act utterly normal under the simulated gravity of spaceships or on other planets. Fiction is what it is; it does not have to reflect reality.

Although the possibility of finding every critical piece of our missing fossil record is slim, it should not stop us from searching for them and continuing to fill in the missing links. We have to recognize that insufficient fossil samples and missing links will always handicap us.

It is an amazing feat that a team at Max Planck Institute, led by Svante Pääbo, has reconstructed ancient DNA from fragmented fossil segments. We have learned tremendously from them. Imagine how much more we could learn if the genomes of our extinct ancestors were also available. In fact, some very old DNA, as old as a few million years, is readily available from living apes. There is an attempt to unravel the process of our speciation using modern human DNA and that from living apes. The next two chapters will explore DNA and genomes and how they drive evolution behind the scenes, resulting in the physical changes we describe in this chapter and a lot more beyond that.

BIBLIOGRAPHY

1. "Direct evidence of Neanderthal fiber technology and its cognitive and behavioral implications," B. L. Hardy, M.-H. Moncel, C. Kerfant, M. Lebon, L. Bellot-Gurlet & N. Mélard, *Scientific Reports*, **10**, Article number: 4889 (2020).
2. "New technique delivers complete DNA sequences of chromosomes inherited from mother and father," Loyd Low, *Science Daily*, Mar 7, 2020.
3. "Genetic evidence for complex speciation of humans and

chimpanzees," Nick Patterson, Daniel J. Richter, Sante Gnerre, Eric S. Lander, and David Reich, *Nature,* 441, 1103–1108 (2006).

4. As for an estimate of the total number of people ever living on earth, please see "How Many People Have Ever Lived on Earth?" Toshiko Kaneda and Carl Haub, *Population Reference Bureau Planet,* Jan. 2020.

8

DNA AND EVOLUTION

P revious chapters have identified our place in the animal kingdom, established our family tree, and sketched physical changes through time using fossils. They focus human beings' evolution from a macroscopic point of view. We also explored the evolutionary principle, highlighting that evolutionary activities are initiated by molecular actions from a microscopic perspective. Obviously the two aspects of us have to connect.

CONNECTING OUR MICROSCOPIC AND MACROSCOPIC ASPECTS

The connection between the two elements is the linkage between DNA and evolution, the main subjects of this chapter. As a physicist, and an experimental one at that, I am usually not at ease taking what I read as the truth unless there is credible and indisputable evidence or robust logical justification. I always want to have hands-on experience, either macroscopic or microscopic, to feel at ease with any subjects. I have no real feel for anthropology because my life experience has been somewhere else. It took me a long-time to finally feel comfortable in how anthropology research is conducted and reported. Part of the reason I am more at ease now is because most of the microscopic anthropological knowledge is consistent with the evolutionary principle I developed in chapter 3 linking the two aspects together. The question is, then, whether the microscopically-driven aspect of evolution can be experimentally tested resulting in macroscopic aspect of ourselves.

NATURE'S EXPERIMENT

We are the outcome of nature's evolutionary experiment. It took close to four billion years from organic molecules to complex organisms, such as ourselves. There must be an abundance of concrete examples of easily observable macroscopic features related to microscopic parameters. A sensible process would be to collect relevant macroscopic and microscopic data and analyze it to determine whether and how they correlate with each other.

Prominent examples linking our mundane features to microscopic differences abound, but my earwax comes to mind. I happen to have a gooey, yellowish, wet type, whereas other people might have a grayish, dry type. As it turns out, with thorough gene study and comprehensive statistics, our earwax type is related to a gene on chromosome 16. The two types of earwax are distinguished by a single permutation of the molecular arrangement of ABCC11. To me, this correlation is such a convincing example of the micro to macro connection. There are also other well-known examples: our adaptivity to high-altitude living, our tolerance for lactose ingestion, and even the shape of our earlobes. Nature certainly provides a wealth of evidence when it comes to the micro to macro connection.

CONTROLLED DNA EXPERIMENTS

There are also controlled DNA experiments linking microscopic constructs to macroscopic features. A scientific experiment requires a series of actions: hypothesis, experimental design, data collection, data analysis with significant statistics, and confirmation or voiding of the hypothesis. Finally, the processes and results have to be independently verifiable by a third party.

Such an experiment has actually been performed, proving that some genes modify corresponding traits. The FOXP2 gene on human chromosome 7 is similar to that of most mammals. The difference of two amino acids between humans and chimps profoundly impacts our ability to speech. Their similarity in mammals makes possible the replacement of the gene of one species from another species. This hypothesis states that replacing the FOXP2 in a mouse with a human's would result in changes in the mouse's vocal characteristics. It will establish a cause and effect association if this happens. The outcome of the experiment would then affirm the hypothesis.

In a presentation by Svante Pääbo, the lead investigator of the work, I heard an audio recording of the sound uttered by a regular mouse and a mouse with the modified FOXP2. Whereas the regular mouse made a lower, chirping tone, the genetically modified mouse uttered a high-pitched squeal. This stark difference would have taken at least a change in the vocal cords or the throat or mouth anatomy to become noticeable. As to how many other associated changes happened, it would require a thorough analysis of the mouse's full new genome and anatomy. This gene by gene to feature by feature correspondence has not been—and may never be—established, but the cause and effect connection is unmistakable.

CONTROLLED HUMAN EVOLUTIONARY EXPERIMENT?

One might ask whether we can take the next step to design and perform an experiment to verify the whole evolution. Further, it might be convincing to make this connection not only for biological organisms but specifically for human beings, just to make believers out of everyone. Following the teaching of the evolutionary principle, making molecular changes and translating to macroscopic changes is the first step. The experiment would also need to mimic the environmental influence on the organisms to render apple-to-apple comparisons. It would not be complete without imposing a realistic environmental ordeal on the organisms being tested.

There are a few additional considerations that make doing an evolutionary experiment directly on an organism problematic. First, we still do not have the full scope of correlation between genes and traits. We do not know how many genes control one specific trait or how many characteristics are affected by one particular gene. These experiments most likely cannot have a set of definite observables and would thus be ill-defined.

Second, we simply do not have that much time to wait for the experiment's outcome, even if we know precisely which microscopic parameters to tweak. Take the evolution of the human hand as an example. We know for a fact that it takes at least 2,000,000 years to evolve from grasping tree branches to the dexterity needed for stone tool making. A prolonged experiment needing that much time is simply not feasible. Third, we cannot recreate the identical environmental conditions for an actual test of their influence on the outcome of the experiment.

Finally, there is the subject of how to judge the success or failure of the experiments. Nature is probably is the only one that should wield that ultimate power. More importantly, if the experiment is on humans, what do we do with the failed outcomes, who are still human beings, after all? There lies the intricate ethical and moral propriety of using human beings as guinea pigs, not to mention the possible political and legal issues.

THIS CHAPTER

I have had the pleasure of working with a few great minds in physics and engineering. These people's common characteristics include honesty, transparency, objectivity, and openness with each other and colleagues in the same field. These are the qualities of professional integrity I look for in their work, either published or through personal communication. I have not had the pleasure to interface directly with well-respected scientists in anthropology, molecular genetics, and molecular anthropology, but judging by their peer-reviewed publication systems like those in physics and their reputations having withstood intense scrutiny and longevity, I believe I can put a lot of trust in their integrity and collective academic wisdom. In particular, when modern-day molecular anthropologists have implicitly embraced the cause and effect of evolution causality, I know I was on the right track in putting together the evolutionary principle in chapter 3.

The discussion on connecting microscopic to macroscopic evolution requires us to know a little more about DNA. This chapter will first briefly walk through the history of the discovery, isolation, analysis, and understanding of DNA up to the present. Next are the DNA molecules themselves and how DNA is involved with evolution. Finally, we introduce a particular DNA (i.e., mtDNA) that was the major player propelling us into the era of molecular anthropology's early days.

A BRIEF HISTORY OF DNA DISCOVERY

GREGOR MENDEL, FATHER OF GENETICS, THE 1860s

In the beginning, the discovery of DNA had nothing to do with human evolution. Instead, it was due to the curiosity of whether fundamental constituents in biological organisms—be they animals or plants—passed from generation to generation. The original purpose of the interest was for practicality. For example, selective breeding is essential for both plants and animals. Selective breeding for Belgium Blue cows for leaner meat was intended to increase farmers' profits. Selective breeding of higher yield teosinte resulted in maize. There was also the desire to keep the breeding results so the right breed will continue to bear fruit for the breeder. These age-old practices were art forms or trade secrets until they became the rule of science to accelerate repeatable breeding, mass production, and profit.

There was also an interest in finding out how the animals on the Galapagos changed from generation to generation, following Charles

Darwin's publication of *The Origin of Species* in 1859. What proved to be the breakthrough was when Gregor Mendel spent eight years performing his experiments and documenting his findings with peas. It began with an attempt to crossbreed true line peas (the word "true line" is relative) in various combinations to gauge diversity and understand inheritance.

Among a few obvious characteristics of pea plants, the most obvious trait to observe was the color of the unripe pea pods. These pods observed while unripe on the same pea plant were uniformly yellow or green. Mendel found the ratio of yellow pods plants to green pods plants was mysteriously close to 3:1. In one case, when a yellow pea plant and a green pea plant are cross pollinated, their offspring was yellow. However, in the next generation of the pea plants, the plants with yellow to green pods returned to that mysterious ratio of 3:1. To explain the "experimental outcome," he had to propose that some messengers were inherent in the plants that determined the pod color. The $64,000 question was what that messengers were.

The ratio of 3:1 must be due to these messengers in operation, Mendel speculated. The simplest possible scenario was that there are two messengers, one carrying yellow, Y, message, and the other carrying green, G, message, both working together to determine the pod colors. The combination of these two messengers in cross pollination would have the following possibilities: YY, YG, GY, and GG. When one of the two messengers had an upper hand—meaning it was stronger influence on the pod color—then there was a possible ratio of 3:1 favoring the color carried by the stronger messenger. Now we can understand that a yellow pea pod plant can reproduce plants, through multiple generations of cross pollination, with the ratio of 3:1 favoring the yellow. The messengers having stronger and weaker influence on the pea pod color were coined by Mendel as dominant (Y) and recessive (G).

This hidden messengers, Y and G that eventually determined the outcome of the pod color, is what we know as genes today. More specifically, it is known as two versions of the same gene. More precisely, these two genes—one from each parent plant—that worked together to produce the resultant color were two alleles of the pea pod color gene. Mendel is recognized as the father of genetics for the discovery and theorization of this. Incidentally, the word "gene" was later coined in 1905 by Danish scientist Wilhelm Ludvig Johannsen. It originally came from Greek *genera,* meaning generation or race. This term is generally used as the word root for "gene," representing the meaning of "giving birth and begetting." The word "generation" comes from the same etymology.

The next logical question is, then: where do genes take residence in an organism? As well, whatever the gene is, it must be fundamental, robust, not easy to destroy, hard to reduce further, not easily altered, and present in a majority of all organisms.

FRIEDRICH MIESCHER, FUNDAMENTAL MATERIALS IN US, THE 1870s

In a study done in 1869, Swiss physiological chemist Friedrich Miescher was trying to characterize the protein part of white blood cells when he came across a substance different than the protein for which he was searching. Instead, the substance had resistance to protein digestion, prompting him to believe he had discovered something new and fundamental. He named the substance in the nuclei of human white blood cells "nuclein," indicating it was the cell nucleus's basic substance. He immediately sensed correctly that these nucleins must be something fundamental and vital. We now know that what he called nuclein was DNA. Despite its significance, it took more than 50 years for the broad scientific community to appreciate his work.

ARCHIBALD EDWARD GARROD, GENES AND INHERITANCE, THE 1900s

We didn't connect genes and inheritance until Sir Archibald Edward Garrod associated Mendel's theories with human disease in the 1900s. This might have been the first time they made this connection to the disorder being predetermined. These discoveries were some of the first milestones in scientists' developing an understanding of the molecular basis of inheritance.

DNA IDENTIFIED AS LIVE'S TRANSFORMING MATERIAL, THE 1940s

By the 1940s, genes were considered discrete units of heredity corresponding to traits for biological organisms and humans. However, it wasn't until 1944 that deoxyribonucleic acid (DNA) was identified as the material of the "transforming principle." The person making this breakthrough was Oswald Avery, an immunochemist at the Hospital of the Rockefeller Institute for Medical Research. Following clues provided by Avery, Erwin Chargaff discovered that DNA composition is species-specific. DNA is not only an identification of species, but it also carries genes that determine species' traits. The connection between DNA to genes was finally evident, and genes are a part of DNA.

JAMES WATSON AND FRANCIS CRICK, the 1950s

Using X-ray diffraction techniques in the early 1950s, Rosalind Franklin obtained diffraction patterns of purified DNA crystals. She was well on her way to analyze and model their molecular structure. X-ray diffraction patterns are like shadows of crystal structures on the atomic level as shone by the X-ray. The patterns are deciphered by the process of Reverse Fourier Analysis to reveal the molecular arrangement, atom by atom. Eventually, James Watson and Francis Crick solved the puzzle that had baffled scientists for decades and reconstructed the molecular structures of DNA. They published the now-famous paper in *Nature* in April 1953 and won the Nobel Prize for Medicine along with Maurice Wilkins in 1962.

· · ·

LINKING GENES WITH BIRTH DEFECTs, THE 1950s

These days, scientists routinely use a growing understanding of genetics for disease diagnosis similar to the approach used by Archibald Edward Garrod (i.e., using genes to identify the inheritance of diseases). One of the most important milestones of DNA and chromosomes was the discovery of an additional copy of chromosome 21 linked to Down's syndrome in 1959. The irregularity of chromosomal behavior demonstrated the random nature of microscopic randomness despite an organism's attempts to keep everything under control.

BREAKTHROUGH IN DECODING DNA, THE 1970s

Starting with small chunks of DNA, research scientists—most notably Fredrick Sanger—were able to devise techniques to quickly decode them into the sequential order of how base pairs were arranged on the molecular level. Since mid-1970, his rapid DNA sequencing technique ushered in widespread research activities linking DNA, genes, nucleotide sequences, and almost everything we want to know about life.

By the way, Sanger is one of the very few scientists who have won the Nobel Prize twice. One of his Nobel awards is for his contribution to the decoding of the X-ray diffraction of DNA with Rosalind Franklin. The well-respected Wellcome Sanger Institute 60 km north of London where Sanger is named after Fredrick Sanger.

LINKAGE BETWEEN GENETIC MARKERS AND DISEASES, THE 1980s

Scientists anticipated close links between genes and diseases as early as the 1900s. It was finally possible to identify and map genes connected to specific diseases in the 1980s when a genetic marker on chromosome 4 was linked to Huntington's disease and was later isolated in the 1990s. Also, around the 1980s, a gene was found to be associated with increased susceptibility to familial cancers, indicating that some cancers are heritable from generation to generation.

THE HUMAN GENOME PROJECT, 1988-2003

Realizing the importance of human DNA to medicine, heredity, and health, The National Research Council of the USA recommended the Human Genome program in 1988 at the behest of private research institutes and academic organizations. It officially started in 1990, when the US Department of Energy (DOE) and the National Institutes of Health (NIH) published a plan for the first five years of the anticipated 15-year project. The goals were to determine the arrangement of base pairs making up human DNA and identifying and mapping all genes in the human genome from a physical and a functional standpoint. The project lasted through 2003, when it was declared complete on April 14. It has successfully mapped the complete human genome and made it available to all interested parties, but the connection between the genome and its physical and functional parts still have a long way to go to claim completion.

OPEN HUMAN GENOME ACCESSIBILITY, 2000

There was a race between government-sponsored research and private companies to see who could sequence the human genome the fastest. The private sector, specifically Celera Genomics, moved a lot quicker, started to file various patents on the means to decode the genomes, and tried to take ownership of the human genes. There were some fears that any company in the private sector might hoard the information, thwarting promising genetic research by academics, as well as competitors. These fears were laid to rest in March 2000, when the then-president Bill Clinton announced that the genome sequence should be made freely available to all researchers and could not be patented. A couple of months later, five years ahead of schedule, the public and private projects jointly published the draft of the human genome sequence, an event featuring a joint announcement by Bill Clinton and the then-UK prime minister, Tony Blair. The success of the sequencing was possible with contributions from institutes and research centers throughout the United States and the UK. There was also some contribution from sites in France, Germany, Japan, and China.

SEQUENCING OF NEANDERTHAL AND DENISOVAN GENOMES, 2010-2012

The human genome is relatively easy to access since every one of us has 30 trillion copies of them. Offering DNA for the genome project entails a very involved process with multitudes of legal and ethical consequences. Prehistoric DNA is, on the other hand, very rare and hard to come by. Irrespectively, through innovation and hard work, Svante Pääbo and his group at the Max Planck Institute for Evolutionary Anthropology was able to accomplish this feat, and we are beginning to understand our relation to archaic Homo *sapiens* on the molecular level with this success.

The same research group achieved something else important. Their study of fragmented DNA allowed them to fully sequence the genome of a then unidentified human species in a publication dated 2012. Not only did it help us find a related species we did not know of, but it opened up the possibility that there may be more unidentified relatives that have left traces of their existence in our DNA.

ANCIENT DNA RESEARCH, 2012 AND ON

The ability of sequencing the full genomes of Neanderthals and Denisovans ushered in a new field of research specifically focusing on the ancient DNAs from fossils and remains of ancient hominins. Thus far, scientists have recovered DNAs from about 4,000 ancient human individuals, in particular, those of modern humans. We are able to understand major modern humans' migration history through our haplogroups (chapter 13), these ancient DNAs tell our migration and dispersal history with much finer details. The migrations history of our more recent past, 5,000 to 20,000 years ago, can now corroborate with the study of origins of various languages.

That pretty much brings us up to date on DNA, genes, chromosomes, and genomes. There is, however, a continued effort throughout the scientific world for more detailed research linking DNA and genes to traits, appearances, medicine, health, minds, evolution, and all facets of life. Moving forward, with this much focus and effort, it is our responsibility to ensure the research is relevant and meaningful and that we are not just doing it for research's sake.

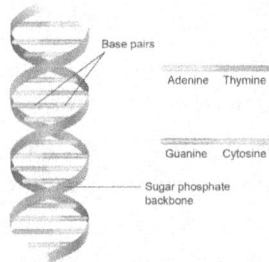

Figure 12. A simplified DNA structure.

Advanced in DNA has happened at a dizzying pace over the past 70 years, with each milestone becoming the impetus for the next milestone, continuously adding to our knowledge of DNA. The implication of this ever-increasing knowledge base has far-reaching consequences with respect to our very existence. We must get our minds around the ethical and moral ramifications of this on humanity before we inadvertently use it for unseemly purposes.

DNA PRIMER

DNA MOLECULES

For illustration purposes, a simplified picture of DNA construction is shown in Figure 12. DNA (DeoxyriboNucleic Acid) is a large molecule composed of two chains that coil around each other to form a double helix, carrying genetic instructions for the development, function, growth, and reproduction of all known organisms and many viruses. This double helix is like a long, skinny, twisted, spiraling ladder with rungs and rails. When the molecules unwind entirely, they can be as long as two to three meters per copy. Another type of DNA is not a double helix, yet it has a similar tendency to replicate itself.

Each rail of the twisted ladder consists of smaller molecules that can string together to form large molecules (i.e., the DNA). The rungs of the twisted ladder keep the two rails together. Each of the rungs comprises a connector from one rail, reaching the other through another connector. There are four connector types: adenine (A), cytosine (C), guanine (G), and thymine (T). Each of these four connectors is called the base. The bases link together to form nucleotides as the rungs of the ladder. Each of these has interlocking parts, much like a protruding and a depressed part in jigsaw puzzles. As such, the rails are long strings of these four types of nucleotides connected.

The bases are connected according to pairing rules of C with G and A with U/T. T and U are similar except that U usually exists on a separate, stand-alone rail, or RNA. These pairs are commonly known as base pairs. It is the sequence or order of these four base pairs along the rails that encodes genetic information. In the discussion ahead, we refer to these ladder rungs as base pairs. A complete human genome consists of 3.2 billion base pairs or bps.

In cells with a nucleus, DNA is organized into long structures called chromosome. Before typical cell division, these chromosomes duplicate in DNA replication, providing a complete set of chromosomes for each daughter cell. Organisms with these types of cells (animals, plants, fungi, etc.) store most of their DNA inside the nucleus as nuclear DNA, and some are stored in the mitochondria as mitochondrial DNA. In contrast, cells without a nucleus (like bacteria and archaea) store their DNA in the cell fluid, and mostly in the form of circular DNA.

WE ARE A BOOK OF DNA, GENES, CHROMOSOMES, AND GENOMES

There are four interrelated terms often used that describe similar things but focus on different aspects.

DNA is composed of macromolecules that tend to replicate themselves. All living organisms store genetic information using these molecules. Written within these genetic codes is compelling evidence of the shared ancestry of all living things.

These DNA molecules are the major constituents of our chromosomes, all 23 pairs of them. We have a copy of chromosomes in the nucleus of each of our cells. They carry all the information needed to form the people we are and the offspring we generate. Chromosomes reside inside the nuclei of each of our cells with a few exceptions, but DNA does not necessarily have to be enclosed within the cell membranes.

Genes are sections of chromosomes that provide a blueprint for specific proteins, and eventually, macroscopic traits. For example, they can determine how your ears look. Some people's earlobes are attached to their faces, whereas others—like mine—are detached. I know this for a fact by just looking into a mirror; my *23andme* profile said the same after analyzing my saliva sample. Our genes are what tell us apart, and they are the basic unit of genetics. Human beings have 25,000 genes accounting for about three percent of our DNA. Scientists think the remaining 97% may have something to do with controlling the genes or their expression.

A genome is an organism's complete set of DNA. Most of the time, the term refers to the totality of the 23 chromosomes.

Consider we have a complete manual on building a whole individual, DNA is a set of codes/ideas/instructions organized into paragraphs. These paragraphs are your genes. The paragraphs are, in turn, organized into chapters that are equivalent to chromosomes. There are 23 chapters in all for human beings. The genome is the complete book of you, including the codes, genes, and chromosomes, providing a step by step guide on how to build a whole you.

GENOTYPE AND PHENOTYPE

Since we are connecting our microscopic and macroscopic sides, it is appropriate to formally introduce these commonly used terms. Your <u>genotype</u> is your complete heritable genetic identity. It is your unique genome that would be revealed by personal genome sequencing; however, the word genotype can also refer to a particular gene or set of genes carried by an individual. For example, suppose you carry a mutation linked to diabetes, you may simply refer yourself as having that certain genotype, without regards to any other gene variants you may carry. Of course, you may also refer yourself as a genotype of Huntington's disease in addition to your diabetes.

In contrast, your <u>phenotype</u> is a description of your actual macroscopic physical characteristics. The phenotype includes specific visible attributes like your height and eye color, overall health, disease history, and even your behavior and general disposition. Typical questions concerning the phenotypes could include: Do you gain weight easily? Are you anxious or calm? Do you like dogs? These are all ways in which you present yourself to the world that are supposedly encoded in your genotype. However, not all phenotypes are a direct result of your genotype. Chances are that your disposition to dogs is the result of your life's experience with pets rather than a mutation in a hypothetical dog-lover gene.

Most phenotypes are influenced by both your genotype and the unique circumstances in which you have lived your life, including everything that has ever happened to you. We often refer to these two inputs as "nature"—the unique genome you carry, and "nurture"— the environment in which you have lived your life.

The connection between genotype and phenotype is not necessarily direct and straightforward. That is, there is not a one-to-one correlation between genes and traits. It is not always as simple as one gene controlling one feature. This is due to the complicated relationship between genotype and phenotype. A single gene usually requires multiple collaborative genes to effect a final phenotype. For example, the aforementioned FOXP2 gene is an essential factor for the human ability to speak by positioning the voice box optimally, but it requires at least 40 other genes to place the voice box, form the

throat cavity correctly, formulate words and language, activate the
necessary motor skills, and move the hyoid bone in concert with
other parts of the mouth for language and communication.

DNA's FOUR FUNCTIONS

What does DNA do? To achieve the goal of replication and reproduction, they serve four primary interdependent functions. The
following briefly summarizes these functions: replication, encoding
information, carrying mutation/recombination, and gene expression.

Replication

DNA resides in the nucleus of cells, which are to be replicated or
divided to grow the organisms. When a cell divides, chromosomes
containing DNA strands must replicate or make copies of themselves
so that both daughter cells receive the full set of genetic material.
During replication, the DNA double helix first unwinds, allowing
each strand to act as a template for a newly-synthesized complemen-
tary to form the new double-helix DNA. Along the way, the enzyme
DNA polymerase assists in the process.

Encoding Information

Base pairs group into units called genes along the DNA strand.
An adjacent trio of base pairs is a codon, specifying a particular
amino acid. Therefore, the sequence of bases in genes determines the
sequence of amino acids in proteins, the biochemical units of a cell's
structure and function. RNA, a chemical similar to DNA, is an inter-
mediary in protein synthesis. The DNA first transcribes genes onto
RNA segments using the base-pairing logic that holds the double
helix together. The DNA subsequently translates the RNA strands
into proteins, three bases at a time, or a codon at a time. Proteins are
now duplicated with the intended codes, or blueprints, prescribed by
the DNA.

Mutation and Recombination

DNA plays a central role in the evolution of species. A more
detailed discussion relating to evolution will follow after this brief
introduction. Chromosomal DNA does not usually interact with each

other; however, through the process of genetic recombination, segments of different chromosomes from either parent swap places with one another, creating new sequences of genetic material. If changes—mutations—occur to the DNA sequences of sex cells, the changes are then passed on to the next generation. An inheritable mutation occurs in the sex cells' chromosomes. Mutation and recombination can be beneficial, but it can also create genetic diseases and malformed offspring.

Gene Expression

Each cell contains a full complement of genes, yet cells from different tissues and organs look and behave differently. The reason is that only some of the DNA from each cell is used to make proteins. It also plays the role of traffic cop for the types of proteins made by a cell. It does this through interaction with proteins in the cells that cause specific genes to express themselves. This traffic control is the mechanism through which a single fertilized egg cell differentiates into the many types of cells, tissues, and organs found in complex organisms. The DNA can respond to a particular protein's need by exposing the appropriate genes for transcription while keeping other genes inactive.

DEBUNKING DNA FANTASIES

It looks like we now are capable to know everything about ourselves from a DNA point of view if we have to; however, there has been a general misconception that knowing the full structure of our DNA can lead to the total reconstruction of an organism. At this time, we are, indeed, able to decode 100% of any person's individual genome when given enough resources and time. In an engineering analogy, this is the hardware of our construction. A computer is useless if there is no software or instructions on how to manipulate bits of information. If we don't know the instructions as to how each part of the gene works with other genes, we are just biological computers with all the hardware but no software. Let us take a look at one specific example to debunk some erroneous impressions and fantasies for the time being.

There is a particular subfield of physical anthropology called forensic anthropology. As the name suggests, it utilizes the anatomical analysis of human remains involving body parts, muscles, and skeletons to solve criminal cases. Human remains these days are a far cry from simple bone structures or pieces of skin. Not only does it includes the physical body parts but also the DNA of individuals under investigation, however minute, left behind by either a victim or perpetrator of a crime.

It is well-known that DNA has parts unique to each individual, the same as our fingerprints. The likelihood of two people having identical fingerprints is very rare. DNA fingerprinting can function similarly to identify criminals but with a much higher degree of precision. A statistical modeling of selected DNA items recommended by FBI reveals that the probability of two unrelated Caucasians having identical DNA fingerprints is approximately one in 575 trillion. In real DNA fingerprinting identification, one only needs to cover a small set of items suggested by the FBI to reach a high level of certainty. DNA fingerprinting has helped exonerate many innocent people involved in cold criminal cases and incriminate the real criminals.

As powerful as DNA fingerprinting is to solve crimes, our knowledge is still a long way from being considered a panacea solution to every occasion in modern-day crime-solving. There was a crime story in an episode of the NCIS series on TV wherein the perpetrator of a crime had left nothing physical or tangible behind except for some DNA in the form of a blood smudge. Forensic scientist Abby Sciuto tries to use modern DNA technology to solve the crime. The concept is that every part of the human face—or trait—is an expression, exhibition, representation, or phenotype of correspondent genes, the genotype in the DNA.

The hypothesis is that by knowing the full DNA and the genes, a person's every trait—such as hair color, eye color, nose shape, height, ear lobe, chin size, and other traits—can be faithfully recreated. As the story goes, Abby synthesizes a face purely from the DNA left behind by the criminal. Based on this facial reconstruction, the crime team uses facial-recognition software to identify and apprehend the criminal when he tries to flee the country at the airport, thus solving the crime.

It is worth repeating that there has not been an unambiguous, one-to-one correspondence between genes and features. In fact, the opposite is true. Many genes are needed to determine a feature, and each gene affects more than one feature. As much as we try to apply the logic of cause and effect to reconstruct human parts, Abby Sciuto's ability to solve her crime remains a fantasy.

DNA AND EVOLUTION

Let us expand further on how the four DNA functions work together. In particular, we will zoom in on the specific "mutation and recombination" function that is the core of our evolution. We have stated in various manners that DNA carries the blueprints of our lives and is able to pass along that blueprint to the next generation. It also provides the primary mechanism enabling the variation from generation to generation, moving evolution along.

The most fundamental biological purpose of life is growing and reproducing if we temporarily ignore other more intellectual and conscious goals for our species. DNA fulfills both purposes. Grossly simplifying, growing is a function of DNA replication and maturation while reproduction is mixing the DNA and genomes from parents to provide the offspring the diversity to cope with the environments.

DNA's task is to grow embryos into adult human beings and sustain and reproduce lives with diversity. Two types of cell divisions fuel these purposes.

GROWTH AND MATURATION, NON-REPRODUCTIVE CELL DIVISION
When a cell divides, it must replicate the DNA in its genome so

that the two daughter cells have the same genetic information as their parents. Cell division works only on non-reproductive or chromosomal DNA. These cells make up most of your body's tissues and organs, including skin, muscles, lungs, gut, and hair cells. In this process, the critical thing to remember is that the daughter cells have the same chromosomes and DNA as the parent cell. The two daughter cells have two complete sets of chromosomes from the parent cell. Since the daughter cells have exact copies of their parent cell's DNA, this mitosis process in normal, healthy cells does not create genetic diversity.

In reality, cell division is a little more complicated than making copies of parent cells. We have different types of cells—muscle cells, skin cells, heart cells, and the like—how does the embryo know which kinds of cells should be divided? This feat happens through a process called gene expression, the combination of genes that are turned on or off (expressed or repressed), dictating why a cell might function as, for example, a bone cell but not a muscle cell.

Not only does cell division grow the number of cells, but it also decides which specialized cells the daughter cells should be. This process continues through to adulthood and maintains the necessary replenishment of all cells after that.

REPRODUCTION, REPRODUCTIVE CELL DIVISION, AND RECOMBINATION

Reproductive cell division is responsible for diversity before organisms enter the environmental filter to complete one of the many steps of the evolutionary cycle. This type of cell division, called meiosis, creates four sex cells like female egg cells or male sperm cells, or gametes, each has 23 chromosomes, half of that of the chromosomal cells. At the end of the process, each new cell contains a unique set of genetic information. After meiosis, the sperm and egg cells join to create a new organism during fertilization.

Reproductive cell division is why we have genetic diversity in all sexually reproducing organisms. During this process, the chromosomes from one parent break off and reattach to the other parent's chromosomes. This process is called "crossing over" or "genetic recombination." The resultant chromosomes now carry a mixture of genes from both parents. Recombination on the molecular level is random and produces new genomes, different from their parents'. No two combinations from the same gametes are the same. This is also why siblings from the same two parents can look very different from one another.

In the end, the offspring are a random combination of features that falls into position as a normal distribution. Some offspring bear exceptional talent in certain areas, whereas some need special attention to bring out the best in them. With the broad intrinsic spectrum of abilities and probabilistic outcomes, these variations create the diversity with which the population has benefited tremendously through the ages.

EVOLUTION BY RECOMBINATION

Recombination allows chromosomes to exchange genetic information to produce new genomes that eventually guide an adult organism's growth and maturation. The new organism carries the majority of features from its parents. Organisms from this newly-generated genome, of which half is from each parent, are slightly different from their parents. These differences may give them an advantage or a disadvantage when coping with the environments they experience.

For example, Ardipithecus parents may have offspring with longer, shorter, or the same length fingers due to this diversity. The organism may live in environments that favor offspring with shorter fingers and pick them to survive (See Chapter 7). Gradually, 2,000,000 years or 80,000 generations later, and this favoritism eventually creates the hands of Homo *erectus*. We, the modern humans, inherited our general hand structure from them. The same mechanisms are also responsible for lengthening giraffe necks to pick off foliage high up in trees or lengthening elephant trunks for breathing, smelling, touching, grasping, and producing sound. The type and pace of change is the evolution by natural selection in a nutshell.

At least two other factors can also influence the natural selection processes. First, the environment has changed, and this could accelerate or slow the pace or even change the direction of evolution. Second, there is the possibility that the size of a group is small and isolated, with some individuals not reproducing for one reason or another. Either or both may quickly limit diversity and change the pace and direction of evolution.

EVOLUTION BY MUTATION

Evolution by natural selection is, in general, slow and gradual. However, with the passing of a few million years, the resultant characteristics may differ drastically from the beginning. These slowly-paced changes are different from changes that happen over shorter time frames, hence, the debate of gradualism and punctuated equilibrium.

Mutation and speed Of Evolution

I am lactose intolerant, like about 60% of the global population. A few questions pop into my mind right after I found out. Is intolerance the norm or the exception? How fast does this characteristic develop? Is it gradual or punctuated? When and how did we start to have this problem? Can this be the result of natural selection?

Human babies get their nourishment from mothers' milk. They digest the lactose in the milk by the lactase enzyme in their digestive tract. When the babies grow up, between the ages of four and five, the production of lactase slows or even stops. After that, drinking milk causes stomach cramps and potentially life-threatening diarrhea. In the absence of lactase, lactose simply rots in the guts. This situation must be the original intent of our biological function since mothers are not supposed to nurse babies beyond four or five years old. Weaning must be the norm.

Around 10,000 years ago, this began to change. We know this timing because we have used the molecular clock technique to determine this. A genetic mutation appeared somewhere near modern-day Turkey that jammed the lactase-production gene permanently in the "on" position. The original mutant was probably a male who passed the gene on to his children.

People carrying this mutation could drink milk their entire lives. Lactose intolerance in adults is due to the gradual decrease of LCT gene expression after infancy. The LCT gene, located on the long arm of chromosome 2 (2q21), encodes an enzyme of lactase. A DNA section controls LCT gene expression, called the regulatory element, which is the MCM6 gene. Those who are lactose tolerant exhibit a slight change to the MCM6 gene in as little as three base-pairs, three single nucleotide polymorphisms, or SNPs. This change is the result of a randomly happening mutation.

Now that we know that lactose tolerance is a genetic mutation happening to one specific gene in a chromosome. It just so happens that humans in extremely cold weather in places where there is not a lot of sunlight benefit from this tolerance. Nature may then favor offspring with this tolerance to get more vitamin D by drinking various kinds of animal milk. Here, the environment does its duty of a filter. This trait may be amplified to a different degree, depending on the severity of the climate.

Evolution on Steroids

Genomic analyses have shown that within a few thousand years, at a rate evolutionary biologists had thought impossibly rapid, this mutation spread throughout Eurasia, Great Britain, Scandinavia, the Mediterranean, India, and in between, stopping only at the Himalayas. In an evolutionary eye-blink, 80% of Europeans became milk-drinkers; in some populations, the proportion is closer to 100%. Everywhere else, lactose intolerance is the norm—around two-thirds of humans cannot drink milk in adulthood.

The speed of this transformation is one of the weirder mysteries in the story of human evolution, more so because it is not clear why anybody would favor the mutation in the beginning. In retrospect, this fast evolution may have benefited people in colder climates, and thus, has a purpose. Irrespectively, this switch from intolerance to tolerance highlighted the effect of the mutation, and this evolution seems to have no pre-programmed master plans in the beginning. As well, if mutations, although random, produce some advantages for adaptation, they could kick start the evolutionary process and give it a boost in high speed. Compared with natural selection evolution, evolution due to mutations could move along the evolution much faster. We could say that mutation might be the enabler of evolution on steroids. Or, perhaps, this is a form of punctuated equilibrium at work.

WHAT ARE MUTATIONS?

The chromosomes in our cells carry out multiple tasks, including functioning normally for the growth, reproduction, or simple existence of an organism. Under ideal chromosomal living conditions, they perform their function with various safeguards and repairing processes, so as few mistakes as possible can happen during replication and reproduction. Life is not perfect, though, and irrespective of the failsafe mechanisms built into every task, mistakes still happen. These failsafe mechanisms cannot take care of all possible disturbances when environments change unpredictably. For example, a disturbance could be the irradiation of organisms by abnormal amounts of radiation, in a situation the organisms would not experience during their whole evolutionary existence. In this case, the organism has had no opportunity to even evolve the build in failsafe mechanisms to deal with this abnormality.

These mistakes could be changes on the base pair level, called single nucleotide polymorphism (SNP). They could also happen to the whole gene. The differences from the original chromosomes are called <u>mutations</u>. More specifically, the mutations start by changing a gene's structure, resulting in a variant form that may or may not pass to subsequent generations.

Mutations: Non-reproductive And Reproductive

There are two kinds of mutations: non-reproductive and reproductive. Non-reproductive mutations, or somatic mutations, happen to the DNAs in the non-productive cells, and are frequently caused by environmental factors, such as exposure to ultraviolet light, certain chemicals, or radioactive components. This change of DNAs will pass on to the mutated cell's daughter cells in the course of cell division. As such, they are present only in specific cells and not in every cell in the body. These changes may or may not pose any harm to us; however, in some cases, they can cause problems for human beings that are detrimental. For example, they play a crucial role in transforming normal cells into cancerous ones; however, these changes do not pass on to the next generation because they do not participate in the reproductive process.

Most of the time, somatic mutations create non-life changing genotype differences. As such, polymorphisms can happen on the molecular and/or genetic levels without us knowing that changes have already happened in the DNA. Most SNPs belong to this type of mutation.

Mutations happening to the DNAs in sex cells are, by definition, inheritable and can pass on to the next generations. These mutations are sometimes called germline mutations because they are present in the parent's egg or sperm cells. When an egg and a sperm cell unite, the resulting fertilized egg cell receives DNA from both parents. If the resultant recombined DNA carries the mutation, the child will carry that mutation in each of his/her cells.

Variants And Alleles

The inherited altered or mutated genes are what we call a new variant. These gene variants can be passed from mutated generations to the next generations and become a part of the species' characteristics. As such, mutation is, ultimately, the only means for new variants or new alleles to enter the species.

All genes have two copies, one from the father and one from the mother, called alleles. For a recessive mutation to give rise to a mutant phenotype in a diploid organism, both alleles must carry the mutation; however, one copy of a dominant mutant allele is needed for a mutant phenotype. Recessive mutations result in a loss of function, whereas dominant mutations often—but not always—result in a gain of function. The mutated gene that turns off the lactase operation is a new variant mutation, so there are two versions of the alleles from the same gene controlling lactose intolerance. There is lactose intolerance in a person when both allele versions are turn on, and when only one is on, there is lactose tolerance. Remember Mendel, the father of genetics? He was able to identify something hidden in peas that carried the message as to whether the unripe pea should be yellow or green. That something is the genes with two alleles: Y and G.

mtDNA

Human genomes consist of all 23 pairs of chromosomes, and each of them consists of hundreds of millions of base pairs in a twisted double helix that extends 10 to 15 cm long with two terminals on each chromosome. Some of these base pairs clump together to form genes, as described before. There is, however, some DNA in the human body that is not twisted into linear pairs. They are circular. The likely reason they are present is that when organisms evolved a higher complexity, they retained some of the older organisms' ingredients and functions. This ancient DNA retained by humans is called mtDNA. The mtDNA is the DNA Cann et al. used to study the mutation determining the lineage of our species' age and where they initially lived.

Among the most interesting details of mtDNA is that it is circular. It is inherited only from the mothers' side and is abundant in human cells, it mutates very fast relative to other DNA, and finally, it is simple and easy to count the number of mutations. All of these characteristics lend themselves as the ideal DNA for molecular clocks. It is easiest to introduce mtDNA through the following list:

1. Mitochondrial DNA (mtDNA or mDNA) is the DNA stored in mitochondria. Mitochondria are the cellular organelles within eukaryotic cells (having a nucleus) that

convert chemical energy from food into adenosine triphosphate (ATP), something the cells can use.

2. Nuclear and mitochondrial DNA have a separate, evolutionary origin, with the mtDNA derived from the circular genomes of bacteria enveloped by early ancestors of eukaryotic cells. In the cells of more evolved organisms, mtDNA is left outside of the eukaryotic nucleus. Incidentally, circular DNA is abundant in nature. Viruses and Bacteria all have circular DNA. Human mtDNA may retain some primal characteristics of this ancient DNA, as well.

3. mtDNA is a much smaller molecule relative to the chromosomes and simple, with only 16,569 pairs of base pairs. It has 37 genes, some coding, some not coding, and some in controlled regions. Some regions are hyper variables that are more susceptible to mutation, either single or multiple nucleotide polymorphisms, ideal for molecular clocks.

4. In mammals—including humans—mtDNA is inherited from the mother. In sexual reproduction, mtDNA is usually inherited exclusively from the mother, and the sperm cell's mtDNA is destroyed by the egg cell after fertilization.

5. The fact that mitochondrial DNA is maternally inherited enables genealogical researchers to trace maternal lineage far back in time. Y-chromosomal DNA—paternally inherited only—is used in an analogous way to determine patrilineal history. Both mtDNA and Y-chromosomal DNA stays in their forms and are not complicated by recombination for sexual reproduction. If anything changes in this DNA, it is pure mutation and not reproductive. Mitochondrial and Y-chromosomal inheritance is, therefore, non-Mendelian (The same Mendel that is the father of modern genes).

6. There are about 500 copies of mtDNA in each cell on

average, as opposed to only one set of chromosomal DNA, but it varies: some cells do not have any while some have a lot. In human eggs, the number of mtDNA is in the order of 200,000. The placenta cells also carry an abundance of mtDNA since the content in mtDNA is found very helpful in the intelligence development during childhood. If one is to use mtDNA for any purpose, the best place to look is the cells in the mammalian placenta. Of course, such practice has not been needed since the advent of PCR.

7. mtDNA has the most polymorphism compared to nuclear DNAs. The control region differs by as much as 1.7%, indicating that it is prone to mutation. The current understanding is that mtDNA is subject to damage from reactive oxygen molecules released, as a byproduct, during its operation to produce adenosine triphosphate (ATP). In most eukaryotes (cells with nuclei), this ATP production takes place inside mitochondria, thus the high rate of mutation.

8. Since mtDNA is primal, it has kept a lot of the original bacteria form. They are similar in humans, fish, horses, apes, and the like. We can borrow the study of animal mtDNA to infer how fast mtDNA has evolved over the last few million years.

This brief introduction to mtDNA is intended to be followed up with a detailed introduction to the pioneering work performed by Cann et al. that set the stage of the molecular anthropology age.

SUMMARY

Through the cause and effect analysis of evolution, a linkage is firmly established between microscopic molecular action and macroscopic expression. This linkage validates the evolutionary principle introduced in chapter 3. Whereas evolution is initiated by DNA executing its microscopic causes, the effect is macroscopic (phenotype) and microscopic (genotype) changes in the organisms.

There are two types of evolutionary processes driven by the primal desire to replicate from the microscopic point of view (i.e., DNA). The first one is the gradual change of traits with successive modifications by continuously mixing up chromosome molecules, creating a diversity from which nature selects (i.e., natural selection). The second type is the more abrupt change initiated by mutation, and nature goes through the filtering process to select organisms that mutate favorably for the environment. Although the underlying causes are different, evolving to best adapt to the ecosystem is the same.

It is worth noting that the term molecular anthropology covers a wide range of modern scientific techniques and tools. We use molecular and physical or chemical steps to purify and isolate DNA samples. We then use differential chemical reaction and staining to identify chromosomes and the constituents of these macromolecules. We use special seeding techniques to grow the DNA into crystals. X-ray crystallography and diffraction patterns finally lead to spatial constructs of DNA. We use extensive computers for fast gene sequencing. We cut the DNA into shorter sections to do detailed studies. We emulate nature by replicating and amplifying sections of DNA for repeatedly verifying assumptions. We analyze genes and identify corresponding traits. We deduce mutations that can be inherited. We even use artificial intelligence to continue the refinement of human genomes and their various phenotypes.

We are now all set to tell our story with better certainty and clarity courtesy of these advances. It is time to look back at how a group of scientists have performed the pioneering work that created the uproar in modern human origins and ages and ushered in molecular anthropology as a scientific field of its own.

BIBLIOGRAPHY

1. "A humanized version of FOXP2 affects cortico-basal ganglia circuits in mice," Wolfgang Enard, Sabine Gehre, Kurt Hammerschmidt, Sabine M. Hölter, Torsten Blass, Mehmet Somel, Martina K. Brückner, Christiane Schreiweis, Christine Winter, Reinhard Sohr, Lore Becker, Victor Wiebe, Birgit Nickel, Thomas Giger, Uwe Müller, Matthias Groszer, Thure Adler, Antonio Aguilar, Ines Bolle, Julia Calzada-Wack, Claudia Dalke, Nicole Ehrhardt, Jack Favor, Helmut Fuchs, Valérie Gailus-Durner, Wolfgang Hans, Gabriele Hölzlwimmer, Anahita Javaheri, Svetoslav Kalaydjiev, Magdalena Kallnik, Eva Kling, Sandra Kunder, Ilona Moßbrugger, Beatrix Naton, Ildikó Racz, Birgit Rathkolb, Jan Rozman, Anja Schrewe, Dirk H. Busch, Jochen Graw, Boris Ivandic, Martin Klingenspor, Thomas Klopstock, Markus Ollert, Leticia Quintanilla-Martinez, Holger Schulz, Eckhard Wolf, Wolfgang Wurst, Andreas Zimmer, Simon E. Fisher, Rudolf Morgenstern, Thomas Arendt, Martin Hrabé de Angelis, Julia Fischer, Johannes Schwarz, Svante Pääbo, *Cell*, 137, 961-971 (2009).
2. "The complete mitochondrial DNA genome of an unknown hominin from southern Siberia," Johannes Krause, Qiaomei Fu, Jeffrey M. Good, Bence Viola, Michael V. Shunkov, Anatoli P. Derevianko & Svante Pääbo, *Nature*, 464, 894–897 (2010).
3. "A High-Coverage Genome Sequence from an Archaic Denisovan Individual," Matthias Meyer, Martin Kircher, Marie-Theres Gansauge, Heng Li, Fernando Racimo, Swapan Mallick, Joshua G. Schraiber, Flora Jay, Kay Prüfer, Cesare de Filippo, Peter H. Sudmant, Can Alkan, Qiaomei Fu, Ron Do, Nadin Rohland, Arti Tandon, Michael Siebauer, Richard E. Green, Katarzyna Bryc,

Adrian W. Briggs, Udo Stenzel, Jesse Dabney, Jay Shendure, Jacob Kitzman, Michael F. Hammer, Michael V. Shunkov, Anatoli P. Derevianko, Nick Patterson, Aida M. Andrés, Evan E. Eichler, Montgomery Slatkin, David Reich, Janet Kelso, Svante Pääbo, *Science*, **338**, 222-226 (2012).

4. *"Who We Are and How We Got Here: Ancient DNA and the New Science of the Human Past"*, David Reich, Vintage Publisher, 2018.

9

MODERN HUMAN ORIGIN

The most consequential study on modern human origin was an academic paper published in the professional journal *Nature* in January 1987. The paper's title is "Mitochondrial DNA and Human Evolution," reported by Rebecca L. Cann, Mark Stoneking, and Allan C. Wilson. Its two most significant contributions are (1) the origin of modern humans and (2) the rigorous, scientific, and molecular biological approach to anthropology and evolution.

This work reached the conclusions as to the birthplace and age of modern humans through a well-thought-through and focused scientific experiment with rigorous data analysis. The conclusions are still valid today, irrespective of scientific and technological advances over the last 40 years. Consider the vision and execution of the experiment before these advances— that this achievement has withstood years of critical scrutiny is nothing short of remarkable. For any discussion or conversation concerning our origins, these conclusions are always a good starting point.

As well, their application of the scientific methodology of molecular biology to anthropology has set the standard of today's research on human genetics and evolution. This study, in my opinion, launched the academic branch of molecular anthropology.

WHO CONTRIBUTED THE MOST TO THE ORIGIN OF MODERN HUMAN

At the time of this paper's publication, there were arguments hinting that this work was built upon existing advancements of knowledge and not original. Similar research would, sooner or later, be performed by someone else if this team did not succeed in their feat. As such, this work is nothing spectacular or pioneering. The truth will be told eventually, although maybe later, but it will be told nonetheless, when the pent-up knowledge base finally breaks through, leading to similar conclusions.

I disagree. As is the case in any field, great discoveries or breakthroughs are always built upon a solid foundation of past successes and achievements, vis-à-vis "standing on the shoulders of giants." Consider a similar situation in physics involving the most influential scientist of the 20th century, Albert Einstein. James Clerk Maxwell's electromagnetic theory is declared the most profound and fruitful work since Isaac Newton by Einstein. Maxwell had the mathematical formulation in his famous Maxwell equations; however, he was not able to recognize one significant implication for the big picture. It was left to Einstein to realize that Maxwell's equations necessitated the electromagnetic field propagating at the speed of light, which can not be exceeded by anything. Einstein developed the theory of special relativity based on this recognition, leading to the famous formulation linking energy and mass through $E = mc^2$. Einstein is justifiably recognized as the one who developed the special theory of relativity and not Maxwell. By the same token, I would not hesitate to recognize the work by Cann et al, contributing the most to the study of our origin.

.   .   .

THIS CHAPTER

This chapter includes two parts pertaining to this study. The first part tells the backdrop of how the work came together. It also serves as a quick recount of the state of affairs regarding the understanding of our origins in the 1970s to 1980s. There are also a few amusing anecdotes accompanying what was at the time considered provocative conclusions that made the team and its members public figures. This should bring some smiles to an otherwise serious and tedious academic undertaking. A little humor would serve to lighten the mood while reading this chapter.

The second part details a physicist's retelling of this study in language with which we have become familiar to bring light to the significance hidden in the academic publication. This part dives into details, hoping this familiarity can help while reading this book and other publications on human evolution. Hopefully, after biting the bullet and spending some time getting to know the basics well enough, we will be able to look past most of the academic gibberish or misconceptions of popular science and appreciate the importance of human evolution.

THE RESEARCH AND THE TEAM

A LONG TIME COMING

In the 1970s, these three scientists were already working at UC Berkeley and moved on to other institutes since mid 1980's. Rebecca Cann, is now a professor of cell and molecular biology at the University of Hawaii, Mark Stoneking is currently a member of the Department of Evolutionary Genetics at Germany's Max Planck Institute for Evolutionary Anthropology. Allan Wilson, who sadly died in 1991 at just 56, was one of the earliest, and at the same time, one of the most controversial scientists who pioneered molecular biology and genetic markers to study human origins.

In the science disciplines, a professional publication's author list usually reveals relative contributions to the work. The first author is likely the major contributor to the study and the one who does the writing. The last author is usually the advisor of the group who provides funding and guidance. The others are contributors to at least part of the effort in various degrees.

There are a few related breakthroughs in the background that enabled this study to build upon. Around 1974, the use of new "DNA scissors," i.e., restriction enzymes, was gaining attention in publications. The other breakthrough was CalTech's (California Institute of Technology) preliminary work on isolating and mapping genetic locations in human mitochondrial DNA. Putting the two together, human mtDNA can be broken up at specific locations by specific enzymes. These enzymes are designated as restriction enzymes and was the base for the first large-scale human DNA sequencing by Fred Sanger's (see DNA history in chapter 8) group at Cambridge in the UK.

Around the same time, Cann started working in molecular anthropology and human evolution with two of the world's most eminent experts at Berkeley, Allan Wilson in biochemistry and Vince Sarich in anthropology. They had collaborated in an attempt to put a molecular time scale on human evolution as early as 1969. This concept of molecular clocks was then used in human evolution and the main research subject that dominated Cann and Wilson's efforts.

Wes Brown, who did the work of isolating human mitochondrial DNA at CalTech, pointed out that one can start with purified mito-chondrial DNA and bust it open with restriction enzymes to study them in small sections. These sections of mitochondrial DNA had a fast mutation rate that could generate statistically significant results (see chapter 8 on the cause of mtDNA's fast mutation rates.) The mtDNA's behavior happened to be what the team had been looking for since the time scale had fallen in the ranges of tens of thousands to a few million years.

This group's study, together with their approaches to molecular anthropology, has since ushered in the mtDNA studies on almost everything evolution for the 50 years following.

· · ·

CONFLUENCE OF PALEOARCHAEOLOGICAL EVENTS

Around the time when the group was purifying and studying human mtDNA from various sources representing different geographical populations, it was also one of the most exciting times in paleoanthropology. UC Berkeley was at the center of a few archaeological advances. Although discovered in the early 1970s, the oldest and most famous proto-human fossil in Africa, Lucy (see chapter 5), was fast gaining public recognition. Donald Johanson, Lucy's discoverer, also had many connections with Berkeley. Also at Berkeley was Tim White who was involved in the Lucy discovery and also co-discovered the bipedal footprint trails at Laetoli, Tanzania, with Mary Leakey. White was also the discoverer of Ardipithecus *ramidus* (chapter 5), of course, that was a few years after Cann et al.'s publication.

As a result, there was a wealth of new information, data, and brain power at hand on the subject of the earliest human evolutionary stages. It seemed as if the latest data and evidence were all linked to Africa from fossils found in Africa, dating back 100,000 to 3,700,000 years ago. Lucy was 3,200,000 years old, and the Laetoli footprints were 3,700,000 years old. There were also a few Neanderthal discoveries in the Middle East area around 100,000 years old that seemed to be the intermediate vintage of humans between the 3,000,000-year-old hominins and modern humans. I imagine there must have been a buzz of lively and intellectually challenging discussions about human evolution permeating the campus and hallways.

Incidentally, I was happy to find that Donald Johanson, in his retirement, was an expedition host for a high-end private jet tour through Africa in September 2020. I am sure the tour would be very enlightening with his experience in paleoanthropology. I would love to be on one of his tours if it is offered again in the near future.

MISSING THE MISSING LINKS?

Something was glaringly missing from the human evolution

picture around 1970's. First, there were these Australopithecus *afarensis* fossils from Africa dated to a few million years old. Then there were Neanderthal fossils in the Middle East around 100,000 years old. Finally, some 40,000-year-old cave paintings and stone tools were discovered in Europe. Most experts thought and wrote that modern humans started as the African Australopithecus, became the Middle East Neanderthals and finally evolved into modern humans in Europe.

This line of modern human evolutionary origins seemed a viable interpretation, but as many as 400 Neanderthal individuals were discovered, and none could be identified as the people between Neanderthals and modern humans, between 40,000- and 100,000-years-old. The inevitable questions are, then "Why didn't we find the missing link?", "Who were the new ancestral populations that later spread across the world?", "Would they be descendants of Neanderthals?", Or "Did they come from somewhere else?" Modern human emergence became a pressing matter in the 1970s since we were missing the missing links.

Incidentally, modern humans did not have a monopoly on cave paintings in Paleolithic times. A cave painting was recently discovered in 2017, dated about 64,000 years ago and about 20,000 years before modern humans had reached Spain. The cave painting was not any less sophisticated than those produced by much later modern humans in similar regions. This discovery has no impact on the evolution of modern humans. It does, however, change our perception of Neanderthals' intelligence capacity.

THE MODERN HUMAN STORY COMING TOGETHER

Realizing that there are parts of mtDNA tend to mutate quickly, the team believed that the original location and time signals of modern humans are buried in it and waiting to be discovered. When all of this archaeological data trickled in with boisterous debates, the team had already collected and analyzed mtDNA from a diverse group of individuals from a few geographical populations.

Initial findings pointed to that if you had a female African ances-tor, you would likely be at the base of the human genetic tree because your mtDNA had mutated the most and had accumulated the most extensive divergence. After the African samples, it appeared the next divergent people from a mutation standpoint was Asian, Australian, New Guinean, and Caucasian, in that order. When digging one layer below the geographic layer by performing a genetic phylogenetic analysis, they found that the genetic tree's very base, considered the root of modern human mtDNA, is from the African mtDNA samples. They indicate the bearers of this root mtDNA were most probably descendants from Africans with very few mothers.

The mtDNA phylogenetic analysis also reveals that the ages of mtDNA are not consistent with the ages of geographic groups. For example, geographic Africans do not necessarily carry the oldest mtDNA. Also, geographic Caucasians do not necessarily have the youngest mtDNA—instead, geographic branches are connected with mtDNA genetic lines in a criss-cross fashion. The interconnecting tangle clearly indicated that the concept of "race" is an artificial creation that does not stand a chance as far as genetics analysis are concerned. This point becomes more evident when we introduce quantitative analysis later in the chapter.

It was, however, clear that all branches, either geographical or genetic, could be traced to the same tree base or root from Africa in the past thousands of years.

THE PUBLICATION

Two apparent conclusions emerged in the mid-1980s from this study group. First, the deepest mtDNA root from modern humans came from the oldest African mtDNA group. Second, this genetic root started to grow around 200,000 years ago. It seemed as if the conclusion regarding that single line of modern human history was solid enough to make public.

Right before its publication, it got another corroborating data point from Tim White. White had discovered and confirmed that modern human fossil samples in the Middle East dated to 110,000 years old, which fit nicely into the team's implicit message, that modern humans did not have to evolve from Neanderthals, so there was no need to invent theories to explain the lack of fossil evidence between Neanderthals and modern humans. Modern humans simply were not in Europe between 100,000 and 50,000 years ago. The missing links did not have to be missing since there is no missing link to search for in the first place. Everything was now in line for publication.

THE AFTERMATH
mtDNA Eve

The few mothers sitting at the root of the mtDNA phylogenetic tree have been considered the most recent common ancestors (MRCA) of all modern humans. We frequently refer to them as mtDNA Eve, a name popularized by Roger Lewin, who coined the moniker in a 1987 article appearing in *Science*, headlined "The Unmasking of Mitochondrial Eve." Professor Wilson himself preferred the term "Lucky Mother," and thought the use of the name Eve "regrettable," but the concept of Eve caught on with the public. That designation also showed up in a *Newsweek* cover story (the January 1988 issue featured a depiction of Adam and Eve on the cover, with the title "The Search for Adam and Eve"), and a cover story in *Time* on 26 January 1987. However, the real inference was that the very few women at the base of the mtDNA tree were the universal lucky mothers of all modern people. These women had an unbroken line of maternally inherited genes (this will become clear later in this chapter) that come to us today.

To clarify further, mtDNA Eve was not the only female alive at the time—she was a member of a population with this specific mtDNA type. The other mtDNA types went extinct because the descendants of these mtDNA bearers either left no offspring or had only male offspring. This random extinction of lineages, coupled with a single origin of mtDNA, is sufficient to guarantee that all variations have to trace back to a single common ancestor at some point in the past. In other words, while all of our genes have ancestors, our mtDNA ancestor was not the ancestor of all of our genes. These other genes traced their ancestry back to different individuals (and even different species), living at different times in different places.

Multi-regionalism Debate

Today, there is little controversy on mitochondrial Eve's residence, which is Africa, but that was not the case in the 1980s. Milford Wolpoff spearheaded the multi-regionalism concept in the mid-1980s, which lasted through to early 2000. However, it was hard to perceive that humans arising from Africa, Asia, or Australia could independently represent a single gene pool with such mutational equilibrium as all modern humans today.

Also, it just didn't fit with the gene pools at a molecular level. If humans from different regions were isolated for 50,000 to 1,000,000 years giving rise to geographical populations, why were any two humans so molecularly similar? Besides, only 7% of human genetic diversity can be accounted for by geography, as we know from blood protein work. So, multi-regionalism in its original form was unlikely to work, although it morphed into something essentially accommodating Cann's single regional origin vision.

Other Debates

Another debate erupted as soon as Cann started talking about the preliminary analysis of data at scientific meetings, as early as 1985. The academicians tended to have one of two reactions: either they thought they had known the answer all along, or they thought the team could not possibly be right. Some were dismissive because more than half of Americans did not believe in biological evolution. For them, evolution might have been operative for animals, but it did not apply to humans.

There were, of course, some religious objections, especially when the mtDNA Eve moniker took off, and it had to make clear to people that she wasn't the same woman as Eve in the Judeo-Christian Bible's story of genesis, who lived about 6,000 years ago.

There were objections from population geneticists, too. Like Alan

Templeton, a number of them still had not resolved that this African origin idea could be correct in their minds in the early days. Some even maintained that the Cann team had the right answer, but they did not know why they had it; they were just lucky. If you read the paper carefully to see the background of how this work came together, you would say that the group had a pretty good idea of what they set out to validate and why they knew they had the right answer!

ANECDOTES

Sample Acquisition

The group needed more than just blood samples to purify human mtDNA. One of the team members, Cann, started going to Lamaze classes to get to know pregnant moms and allow her to take their babies' placentas after giving birth. She must have been very persuasive—there may still be a few 30-something person in the Berkeley and Oakland areas with pictures of their DNA sequences in their baby books, thanks to Cann!

It seems a little odd for them to need placentas from pregnant women. The concentration of mtDNA varies in different cells (Chapter 8), with the highest concentration of mtDNA in human eggs. Placenta cells are the next best thing to obtaining and purifying mtDNA. This just shows Cann's resourcefulness and her determination to get the samples for this study.

Today, we recognize that placentas are private and belong to the families, and giving them away for scientific research is almost unthinkable. Most hospitals hesitate to give them to the mothers without due process, according to regulations. I doubt it would be possible to obtain that many samples for that specific study if it were to happen today.

The Bloody Mary Margarita

If you are a bloody Mary or strawberry margarita lover and if you have done similar lab work, you might think twice the next time you pick one up, as the team members had to witness samples being pulverized and purified using blenders. The story goes that some team members could not enjoy these drinks for a while. I would stay away from them, too, if it were me.

Splitting Hairs for Genetic Study

Cann was also said to have some fun with people when the team switched to collecting hair samples from donors. The donors wanted to give the team pubic hairs instead of head hairs because they had to be better sources for human genealogy. I would have liked to have been a fly on the wall to listen in on those conversations.

Legal Tangle

This scientific paper and the subsequent *Newsweek* ("The Search for Adam and Eve") and *Time* ("Everyone's Genealogical Mother") magazine articles created a huge public hoopla that must have changed Cann's life. I read that she had many hate and crank letters and some with strange, scrawling notes. She even had a visit from the FBI after the Unabomber attacks, for whatever reason. For those readers old enough, you must remember the UC Berkeley math professor who terrorized the country for almost 20 years by sending bombs nationwide to various people involved with modern technology, killing three of them. The Unabomber was eventually apprehended in 1996, and a plea bargain was reached in 1998, under which he pleaded guilty to all charges and was sentenced to life in prison without the possibility of parole. To this date, I still don't understand how Cann's work was related to the Unabomber.

Plain Annoyances

In an interview 25 years after the mtDNA Eve discovery, she mentioned that right after the Newsweek article, she would receive random calls in the middle of the night in Hawaii on flight layovers, where she later worked, wanting to talk. I am one of the people who called her out of the blue to request a conversation in 1988. At least I had the sense not to call in the middle of the night. A friend of mine, who was teaching at U. Hawaii at the time, encouraged my call since he believed that all UH faculty members should entertain friendly and knowledgeable parties. I had no idea how big of a deal in the academic circuit and public domain she was or how much time she had to spend on these nonsensical requests.

Fortunately, the meeting did not happen. I would not have been able to converse at an intelligible level and would have completely wasted her time. Now that I have acquired some level of intelligence regarding human evolution and I am curious enough to continue my search, maybe, when I am in Hawaii again, I would like to have the chance to meet her in person.

REBECCA L. CANN, THE HUMANIST AND VISIONARY

In the same 25th anniversary interview, Cann commented:

"Humans are remarkably alike, once we get past our seven or so genes that influence skin pigmentation and 100 or so genes that help model the shapes of our faces, noses, eyes out of 20,000 plus in total. I tell my students they should all celebrate Black history month since they are all Africans genetically. Fossils are an important way to understand the past and incredible records of evolutionary change. But so is our DNA. And it survives so we can pass it on and learn from our studies. We are each uniquely endowed and challenged. We are a new species, we went through a period where we were like an endangered species, a very small, isolated population, and now we are 7 billion. We came very close to going extinct. We could do it again unless we take better care of the planet."

I believe that if you are immersed in the subject long enough, you develop a sense of awe of as to how we are a small part of Nature's enormous evolutionary experiment. One cannot help but become a humanist with an empathetic and global view of our species.

There has always been a desire to study ancient human DNA for various purposes, but mostly for medicinal, health, and evolutionary causes. Once the mitochondrial thing took off, anyone thinking about ancient material thought of mtDNA since there was such a large quantity in the cells. If anything was going to survive in time, it wasn't going to be single-copy nuclear genes. It was more likely something in the mitochondria. Cann envisioned that archaic human beings' mtDNA and the complete genome might someday be fully sequenced as early as 40 years ago, making her a visionary in the early days. The possibility of knowing everything about our genome happened a mere 15 years later through the Human Genome Project.

MARK STONEKING'S PERSPECTIVE

In the same interview piece, Stoneking noted that despite all the criticism and subsequent studies of human mtDNA variation, the study's central conclusion remained unchanged. We have mtDNA data from hundreds of thousands of individuals, complete genome sequences from thousands of individuals. The current view remained that the human mtDNA ancestor lived in Africa some 150,000-200,000 years ago. Even though it has been 40 years since the original publication, the human story is still remarkably similar to what the team had published.

Moreover, their paper brought genetics into the debate over human origins for the first time. Their study also opened a new line of evidence, which ultimately led to a resolution in favor of a recent African origin for modern humans. These modern humans proceeded to assimilate with non-African hominins (e.g., Neanderthals and Denisovans), and the concept of "leaky replacement" is currently the prevailing model for modern human origins and the demises of Neanderthals and Denisovans.

One of Stoneking's later contributions based on the same molecular clock methodology is nailing down the time when we started to regularly put on hide or pelt. The study involved with studying mtDNA mutations in fleas, concluded that the time was 170,000 years ago.

THE STUDY

THE THREE mtDNA TASKS

We are all set to take a closer look at this study. As we become convinced that molecular action is the foundation of evolution, the phylogenetic tree of modern humans should reflect the microscopic actions that determine our family relationships. In a nutshell, this study is to determine modern human mtDNA's most recent common ancestors (MRCA) and the time of MRCA (TMRCA).

The study has many moving parts but can be grouped into three related tasks, each telling a different aspect of our story. For me, they are the steps I sorted out logically, so it was easiest for me to comprehend. All of these tasks make use of mtDNA samples collected from groups as diverse as possible through geographic regions.

The three tasks are: (1) Analyze how divergent mtDNA has mutated for inter- and intra-geographic groups. The group with the most divergent mtDNA might give a general idea of from where we have originally come; (2) Determine the ages and homelands of geographic groups based on mutation divergence; and (3) Sort mtDNA on the molecular level and build the mtDNA phylogeny. Lastly, further determine the locations and ages of mtDNA's MRCA, that is TMRCA.

TASK 1: mtDNA's DIVERGENCE AND THE LOCATION OF OUR MRCA

The first task is to count the number of genetic differences between the mtDNA of any two participating individuals. The differences collectively represent the divergence for the whole group and the individual geographic subgroups. The smaller the divergence is in a geographic group, the younger the group's age, and vice versa. This simple analysis ranks the ages of geographic groups. As the oldest group is from Africa, we can tentatively decide that Africa is where our MRCA originated.

The mutations experienced by mtDNA usually happen to base pairs (e.g., the A-T pairing could change to a G-C pairing, resulting in a different mtDNA sequence). Each single base-pair mutation is defined as a single nucleotide polymorphism, or SNP. The mutated mtDNA constitutes the polymorphism that does not usually have a direct effect on our phenotypes. The SNPs in mtDNA occur relatively infrequently and can be considered a sequential, random process. Not only does the mutation happen randomly in time, but it does not happen to any specific part of the mtDNA. As an organism species continues to survive, the mutations accumulate as time goes on, and the differences between any two individual organisms increases. The larger the number of differences in a group, either in genes or SNPs, the larger the indication that the group has had a longer time to accumulate mutations. There is a point in time when the differences do not have time to accumulate; this time is TMRCA. The organism bearing unmutated mtDNA is our MRCA.

Quantifying Genetic Divergences

The best measure of divergence is comparing mtDNA base pair differences between each possible pair of individuals. Unfortunately, molecular study resolution was not down to the base pair level at the time. However, they found that site mutations can be treated similarly to SNP mutations. They were counting the "site" divergence, where each site difference represented a mutation. There are 147 mtDNAs under study and (147X146)/2 site difference counts to compare, all 10,732 of them. A histogram of the occurrences for a specific number of site differences is recreated from the scientific publication as Figure 13. The histogram reveals how often site differences happen in the group. For example, a site difference of eight happens most frequently, about 1,250 times. All other site differences happen fewer than 1,250 times.

With a total of 10,732 data points taken and the shape of the histogram being almost a bell-shaped normal distribution, it is evident that they represent statistically significant samples, giving credence to the numerical analysis. A weighted average number of 9.47 is now the

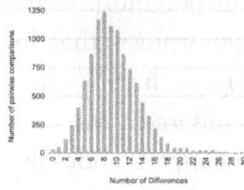

Figure 13. Histogram of pairwise mutation differences recreated from research performed by Cann, et al.

divergence of mtDNA among all people involved.

Data Analysis

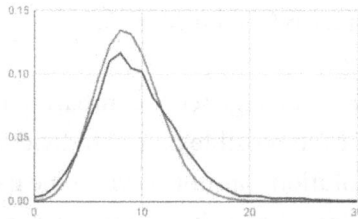

Figure 14. Histogram of Figure 13 scaled as probability (blue) and overlapped with calculated Poisson distribution (red). The scaling is done to ensure that probability of all differences, from 0 to infinity, is 1.0.

When this measured histogram normalized to probability (the blue line) is compared with a calculated Poisson distribution (the red line), Figure 14, as we have discussed in the evolutionary principle in chapter 3, the average divergence and the random nature of the mutation fall out naturally. The closest match between the two curves leads to the "Poisson Average" of 8.8 through a least-square fitting computation. Either the weighted average or the Poisson Average can be considered the divergence of the mtDNA group of 147 individuals.

The mtDNA from 147 individuals came from five geographic regions: 20 Africans, 34 Asians, 46 Caucasians, 21 Aboriginal Australians, and 26 Aboriginal New Guineans. It should be reasonable to expect that if a group of people has been in existence for a longer time, the mtDNA would be allowed more time to accumulate mutations, thus the larger divergence. One should expect a similar histogram for older geographic categories that pushes the peak to higher numbers (i.e., to the right). By the same token, the histogram of younger geographic types should pull to the smaller numbers (i.e., to the left).

The team's work rank orders them in divergence to be Africans, Asians, Australians, Caucasians, and New Guineans. One might conclude that this divergence rank order is indicative of the ages of these geographic populations. This is only partially true, as we will see in the next section.

Discrepancies Between Data And Ideal Random Process

Observant readers might see that there are a few minor differences between the blue and red curves. A few possibilities may have caused these discrepancies.

The rate of mutation could have changed over time. There is a correlation between mtDNA mutation and the reactive oxygen molecules released by ATP operation since they are near each other (chapter 8). The mutation rate may not have held steady if the biology of ATP generation changed over the last 500,000 years. The cosmic ray influx bombarding the earth is known to have changed, evidenced by the need for radiocarbon dating calibration. Anything impacting ATP biology could potentially change the pairwise comparison at both the higher and lower site differences. The mutations could also vary due to population bottlenecks, leading to fewer changes. Smaller or larger mutation divergence may result in giving the impression of younger or older ages.

Overall, there is a higher frequency of larger mutation differences than the average, which means it is likely there are more cases with site differences beyond the "average." This slight bump up of the occurrences may indicate that the age of modern humans is most likely older than inferred from the "average" divergence.

. . .

TASK 2: DETERMINING AGES THROUGH mtDNA DIVERGENCE

The second task is to provide more definitive evidence for the African homeland and our age. Focusing on divergences based on a geographic population is not the whole story since we are more complicated, and this simple grouping may be misleading. A genetic grouping may make more sense. This section uses divergences according to genetic groupings to determine age estimates. The detailed molecular grouping will be the subject of the next section.

It seems logical that we can easily translate "divergence" numbers directly to age. We might equate an average divergence of 8.8 to a certain age if we know how many mutations per thousand years or the equivalent. However, there has to be a calibration on the divergence rate at the starting point.

There has been a fair amount of solid work on mtDNA, not only by this research group but also by many other groups. It was established that the divergence by mutation in mtDNA is almost uniform in primates, rhinoceroses, rodents, the genus Equus (horses and the like), and ungulates (other hooved animals). This number is a two to four percent divergence every million years.

The team scaled the average divergence based on histograms for the geographical grouping (or genetic grouping, as will be discussed later) to this percentage divergence accordingly. They found out that the oldest African mtDNA (the definition of the oldest African mtDNA will be in task 3) have a divergence of 0.57%. The age of the oldest African mtDNA lineage would then be between $0.57/2=0.285$ and $0.57/4=0.1425$ million years (142,500 years). If we are all connected to this oldest African mtDNA, the time when the first mutation occurred would be our age (i.e., the TMRCA and the unmutated mtDNA would be the MRCA). Our common ancestors who carried this mtDNA would then be our MRCA.

What is great about this line of deduction is that the average age of mtDNA—between 142,500 and 285,000 years, or 214,000 years—falls just out of this the data tabulation without any speculation or data manipulation. The uncertainty is inherent in the ability to determine the percentage of divergence among all mammals. We will be using an average number of 200,000 years as our age for the rest of this chapter and book, but we have to keep in mind that this uncertainty always accompanies the 214,000-year number.

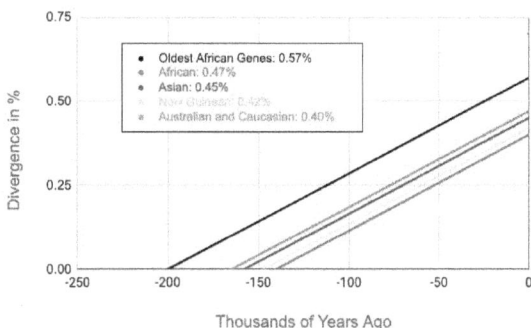

Figure 15. mtDNA divergences through time and the rough ages of the respective geographic groups. The straight lines represent the progression of divergence along time. The intercepts at zero divergence are the age of the geographic groups.

All human geographic populations are younger than the deepest African lineage. Figure 15 captures mtDNA divergence through time and the rough ages of the respective geographic groups. Assuming that mutations happen at a constant clip through the ages, the divergences grow as straight lines through time. The starting points in time of these lines are the beginning of these specific populations. Caucasians are the youngest group at the age of 0.40/0.57 of the old African lineage (i.e., 150,000 years). It would be interesting if we could also pinpoint the locations where the branching off happened. We will do exactly that in the migration story later in chapter 13, although with a little more recent and accurate mtDNA phylogenetic tree.

TASK 3: THE mtDNA PHYLOGENY

Simply grouping mtDNA divergence according to geographic

groups is a reasonable starting point. Indeed, it gives us a rough idea of the relative age of geographic populations. It is not, however, a modern human genealogy tree, per se. This geographic grouping is like the uncertainty genealogists encounter when they only include known living family members when a genealogy tree is compiled—one must dig deeper to discover correct pedigrees.

The third task does precisely this by sorting out the details of mtDNA changes, creating a molecular phylogenetic tree. Before going any further, it would be interesting to note again that this mtDNA phylogenetic tree leads to a complete collapse of the definition of races based on people from different geographical locations.

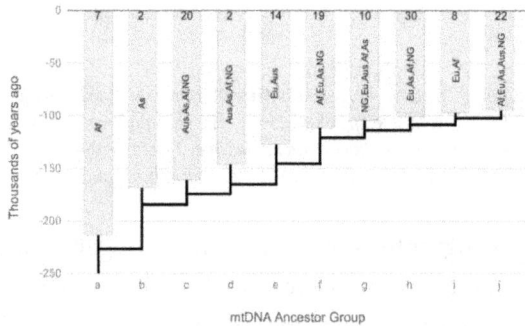

Figure 16. mtDNA genealogy linking the modern human population to common ancestral females designated as the group "a." The ten groups, from "a" to "j," cover all 133 types of mtDNA found in the 147 participants.

By sorting the 400 mutations into groups (some parallel, some sequential), they found 133 types of human mtDNA from the 147 individuals. The next step was to put them into a phylogenetic tree based on an algorithm that searches for the most direct interconnection between common molecular traits. The tree in Figure16 is an mtDNA genealogy linking the modern human population to common ancestral females designated as group "a." The ten groups, from "a" to "j," cover all 133 types.

Right at the root is the deepest African mtDNA group that

branches off to other groups wherein all five geographical groups are dispersed in various mtDNA groups. Written on each of the ten groups are the individuals carrying that specific mtDNA group. For example, only people from Africa geographically have the mtDNA group "a," the oldest African lineage according to the tree. As well, group "g" mtDNA can be found in people from New Guinea, Europe, Australia, Africa, and Asia. If that is not confusing enough, people from Asia can carry the mtDNA from groups b, c, f, g, h, and j.

Applying the same practice to find out the percentage of divergence of geographic populations to the genetic groups, a to j, each group's ages are determined. Group "a," at the root of the tree, has a divergence of 0.57%, translating to 214,000 years old. The bottom of each of the bars indicates the group's respective ages, shown in this mtDNA phylogenetic tree.

It is clear that if you use geographical groupings, you are bound to exclude other people in other groups that may have close genetic relationships. Conversely, if you use genetic phylogenetic tree groupings, you will have trouble fitting phylogenetic groups into a single population. In other words, assigning people to geographic groups or mtDNA groups alone does not tell the whole story.

Although it is not shown in detail in this figure, there is an exclusively New Guinean subgroup in the j group. The age, determined by mtDNA divergence percentage, is around 0.18% or 70,000 years. This works pretty well with the most recent discoveries, indicating that Australian Aboriginals arrived there 65,000 years ago. Since then, both the people from Papua New Guinea and Australia were isolated because of rising water when the ice age waned, starting their mtDNA accumulation, resulting in the groups' ages. This equivalence of 0.18% and 70,000 years is another calibration point corroborating the consistency between geographic dating and molecular clocks.

"Race" Is Meaningless

As far as human beings are concerned, we often quibble and argue over the superiority of one group of people over another. Since the beginning of history, we have arbitrarily assigned race or factions to ethnicities and geographic locations. The situation worsens when we further judge people by their resourcefulness, particularly since the onset of imperialism around the 16th century. It did not get any better when New Imperialism came around in the late 19th century. The Enlightenment movement alleviated some of racism's pain, yet rampant racism has persisted globally.

In light of the mtDNA phylogenetic tree and the complicated and intertwined relationship between mtDNA from various geological groups, the concept of race associated with geography is meaningless.

UPDATED mtDNA PHYLOGENY

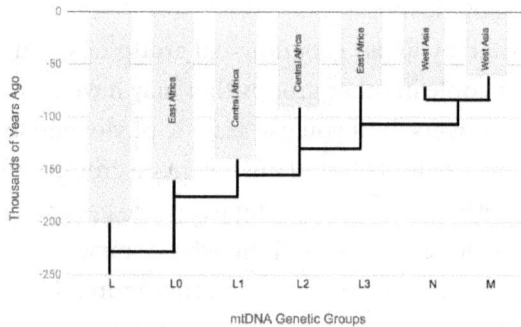

Figure 17. A more up to date mtDNA phylogenetic tree based on SNPs. It is common to use the designation of letters from L to M at the highest levels these days.

A simplified and more up to date mtDNA phylogenetic tree is shown in Figure 17. Whereas Cann et al. designated "a" through "j" for mtDNA groupings, it is more common to use the designation of letters from L to M at the highest levels these days. These points and dates may not be 100% consistent with the above mtDNA phylogeny details, but it starts from the same beginning point at 200,000 years ago.

Each of the branches—ages—are labeled with a location indicating where and when the branch-off happened. There are a lot more details above this mtDNA tree that account for everyone on the planet. In other words, everyone on the planet belongs to one of the seven branches in this chart. I can see how I fit into this chart: I belong to the M group based on my *23andme* profile.

OTHER CONTEMPORARY mtDNA STUDIES

There are a few other contemporary mtDNA studies, but none make the concrete and almost irrefutable connection between the age of modern humans and origin as clearly as this work.

At least one other study—by Johnson et al.—focused on mtDNA. This group also concluded an African origin. The study is more of a methodological slant than results. As such, they had not linked their tree with the time; thus, no conclusion is made on the age of modern humans. Another study also tackled mtDNA, focusing on intra-species variation, but the relationship with human evolution was not the primary goal, and it missed the hidden significance of the variability of mtDNA. There were also studies on genetic distance in modern humans based on nuclear DNA. Two general trends are consistent with each other. First, a few cases indicate that the differences in genes inside racial groups are larger than between racial groups, showing that traditional race does not have a genetic correspondence. Second, most studies agree that Africa is our birthplace, which is consistent with this mtDNA study.

SUMMARY BY ABSTRACT OF THE STUDY

I hope this chapter has done justice in paraphrasing this research in a non-academic language. To sum up this research for its significant importance, I would like to quote the publications' abstract verbatim, as follows:

Mitochondrial DNAs [sic] from 147 people, drawn from five geographic populations have been analyzed by restriction mapping. These mitochondrial DNAs stem from one woman postulated to have lived about 200,000 years ago, probably in Africa. All the populations examined except the African population has multiple origins, implying that each area was colonized repeatedly (by different generations of modern man).

MODERN DAY MOLECULAR ANTHROPOLOGY

This book took shape in the middle of 2019, more than 30 years from when this pioneering work was first published. Their work started a few years earlier with a clear understanding of molecular clocks, mtDNA, genealogy, molecular biology, and anthropology. They used their knowledge intelligently, without modern-day scientific and technological infrastructures, and constructed a clear vision of how modern human came about. Their achievement is highly commendable. Just imagine what they could have accomplished if they had modern-day science and technologies at their disposal.

POLYMERASE CHAIN REACTION (PCR)

The science of molecular genetics has been moving at almost lighting speed, looking back. It took a lot of effort to obtain and purify these samples during the mid- to late-1970s. It is much easier today with the advent of polymerase chain reaction (PCR). We can obtain samples for testing with a single hair or a simple cheek swab, as everyone who watches crime dramas on TV knows.

PCR was invented by Kary Mullis in 1983 and not available when Cann et al. did their work. Part of the PCR process is cycling samples through pre-set temperature ranges to amplify a single strain or part of the DNA to a large quantity identical to the beginning strain for lab use. The innate nature of replication works behind the scenes, and PCR simply leverages that nature to replicate the same strains many times. It has been the cornerstone of any work involving DNA in major genetic laboratories these days. For this PCR invention, Kary Mullis was awarded the Nobel Prize in chemistry in 1993.

PCR makes possible the study of ancient DNA from our archaic Homo *sapiens* relatives, which was recognized by Cann and her group as early as 30 years ago. With this process, getting samples from any person for genetic or ancestral analysis takes only a swab from the inside of your cheek as long as the action is agreeable between involved parties.

FULL GENOME SEQUENCING

The ability to decode our full genome and detect SNP—single nucleotide polymerization—is widely available in laboratories and institutions these days. I recall a discussion I had with some kids doing SNP counting in a biological lab in Saratoga High School in California. Such a feat was unthinkable in the 1980s. The counting of accumulated SNP mutations is down to an art, and we can count SNP distances between humans and any other animals in mtDNA. Based on this counting, one can determine which mammals are genetically closer to us: chimps or gorillas. A group of scientists had actually put together the most plausible processes of how we—hominins— became a separate species from the chimps.

NUCLEAR DNA AS MOLECULAR CLOCKS

Our ability to decode our complete genomes has enabled us to determine the age of mtDNA Eve more precisely these days. We can also use the Y-chromosome to determine the most recent common ancestor of the y-chromosome (Y-MRCA, informally known as Y-chromosomal Adam). The owner of this y-chromosome would be the most recent common ancestor from which all currently living men are descended, patrilineally.

Y-chromosomal Adam

Similar to Mitochondrial Eve, Y-chromosomal Adam is not permanently fixed to a single individual. As of 2015, estimates of the Y-MRCA age ranges from around 200,000 to 300,000 years old, roughly consistent with the emergence of modern humans, deter-mined by mtDNA. Of course, you can also project back to find out our relative's age, if such DNA can similarly survive as mtDNA. For example, Y-chromosomal data taken from a Neanderthal from El Sidrón, Spain, produced a Y-TMRCA of 588,000 years ago for Neanderthals, meaning that Neanderthals are about 600,000 years old. With the advent of using protein leftovers in fossils, a more ancient dating of hominins may be possible.

mtDNA for dating

Chapter 6 introduces a few fossil dating techniques, mostly through analyzing samples with nothing to do with genetics or DNA. Since we have become better acquainted with the mutations of mtDNA, we can now use these mutation counts to date the ages of the samples. When we count the SNP mutation difference between an unknown ancient human sample and that of ours or that of mtDNA Eve's, the sample age could be determined with the same accuracy as the age of modern humans.

SUMMARY

This pioneering study contributes to anthropology in two aspects. First, it concludes that modern humans are 200,000 years old, and they hail from Africa. Second, through its rigorous scientific methodology, this work ushers in molecular anthropology as an independent academic branch of its own. In particular, with today's scientific and technological advancements and infrastructures, we can use the same methodology to peek further back in time and deeper into our evolutionary roots.

This chapter spends a lot of effort detailing the molecular clock. The rephrasing of this scientific work from my non-anthropologist's viewpoint is through my physicist's prism. It may give the reader a deeper appreciation of the logic behind our evolution, and hopefully, by extension, the evolution at large on planet Earth.

The totality of the characteristics of mtDNA, anthropological background, the mechanism of mutation, how they diverge, how they create different types of mtDNA, and people all seems complicated and even challenging. There is, however, an underlying fundamentality in the divergence and evolution based on the evolutionary principle discussed in chapter 3. Once you clear out the cobwebs of complex molecular interactions mechanisms, the mutations are still tractable by identifying and counting them. By comparing the mutation data collected and an ideal calculation for event probability, the nature of the random process of microscopic molecular action in evolution is bubbling up from its foundation.

Pioneering work like this, in general, does not just spring up out of the blue for any given subject. Rather, it builds on the existing knowledge base that was fast improving during the 1980s, but it took the teams' vision, expertise, experience, broad knowledge base, and talent to successfully execute the studies. The significant long-term impact on our history and the academic field cannot be understated. This situation is similar to the realization that an isotropic 3.3-degree Kelvin background radiation is related to the remnant energy left over from the universe's initial big bang. It took visionaries like A. Penzias, my old boss, and R. Wilson to connect their experimental findings to cosmology. They were eventually awarded the Nobel Prize in 1974 for their discovery, confirming the origins of the universe's big bang beginning. Judging by the study's significant contribution to our understanding of evolution in addition to its being pioneering and monumental, the work of Cann and her team is definitely Nobel-worthy in my opinion.

With the molecular anthropology foundation having been solidly laid through this pioneering work, we tend to look at everything about ourselves from the molecular perspective. In addition to searching for our direct origins, we can now apply molecular anthropology principles and make better acquaintance with our species, Homo *sapiens*, including our extinct relatives like the Neanderthals and Denisovans.

BIBLIOGRAPHY

1. "U-Th dating of carbonate crusts reveals Neandertal origin of Iberian cave art", D. L. Hoffmann, C. D. Standish,

M. García-Diez, P. B. Pettitt, J. A. Milton, J. Zilhão, J. J. Alcolea-González, P. Cantalejo-Duarte, H. Collado, R. de Balbín, M. Lorblanchet, J. Ramos-Muñoz, G.-Ch. Weniger, A. W. G. Pike, *Science*, **359**, 912-915 (2018).

2. There are a few studies for the average length of a human generation for contemporary human beings, but our ancient ancestors have not been clarified as far as I know. The 25 years per generation is an oversimplification of our reproduction process; however, it is in the ballpark for numerous studies.

3. "The complete mitochondrial DNA genome of an unknown hominin from southern Siberia," Johannes Krause, Qiaomei Fu, Jeffrey M. Good, Bence Viola, Michael V. Shunkov, Anatoli P. Derevianko & Svante Pääbo, *Nature*, **464**, 894–897 (2010).

4. "Mitochondrial DNA and two perspectives on evolutionary genetics," Allan C. Wilson, Rebecca L. Cann, Steven M. Carr, Matthew George, Ulf B. Gyllensten, Kathleen M. Helm-bychowski, Russell G. Higuchi, Stephen R. Palumbi, Ellen M. Prager, Richard D. Sage, Mark Stoneking, *J. Linn. Soc.* **26**, 375-400 (1985).

5. "Identifying and Interpreting Apparent Neanderthal Ancestry in African Individuals," Lu Chen, Aaron B. Wolf, Wenqing Fu, Liming Li, Joshua M. Akey, *Cell,* **180**, 677-687 (2020).

6. "Mitochondrial DNA and human evolution," Rebecca L. Cann, Mark Stoneking, Allan C.Wilson, *Nature,* **325**, 31-36 (1987).

7. "Maximum Likelihood estimation of the number of nucleotide substitutions from restriction sites data," Nei, M., and Tajima, F., *Genetics,* **105**, 207-217 (1983).

8. "Radiation of human mitochondrial DNA types analyzed by restriction endonuclease cleavage patterns," M. J. Johnson, D. C. Wallace, S. D. Ferris, M. C. Rattazzi & L. L.

Cavalli-Sforza, *Journal of Molecular Evolution,* **19,** 255-271 (1983).

9. "Intraspecific Nucleotide Sequence Variability Surrounding the Origin of Replication in Human Mitochondrial DNA," BD Greenberg, J E Newbold, A Sugino, *Gene,* **21,** 33-49, (1983).

10

NEANDERTHALS, DENISOVANS, AND MODERN HUMANS

The last chapter uses scientific methodology to substantiate the microscopic argument that each of us is a member of the Homo *sapiens sapiens* subspecies, without exception. Realizing that it is possible to construct a continuous genealogy starting with MRCA and TMRCA, if we want, this closeness between ourselves should unite us human beings on a macroscopic level because of our underlying microscopic homogeneity.

THE HOMO SAPIEN FAMILY

This chapter tells the story of our Homo *sapien* family (not the "family" under the Linnaeus's categorization). It consists of at least three members. The first is Homo *sapien sapien*, that is, modern human. Our cousins include Neanderthal and Denisovan, who perished about 40,000 years ago. We call them archaic Homo *sapiens*. There may be a few more that we know existed but cannot find or identify yet.

We can be sure about our bloodline because our genetic codes experience slow and constant genetic recombination and random mutations. Consequently, by examining our DNA and enumerating accumulated changes, we can unravel our ancestral line backward, toward the time and location of our earliest existence. It would make sense that if we sample DNA from our closest species relatives, we can decipher our intertwined relationships. Similarly, we can extend this microscopic to macroscopic analysis further back to the emergence of humans 7,000,000 years ago, if we only had all of the DNA and genomes of our ancient relatives and ancestors.

The breakthroughs enabling us to achieve a part of this feat started about 15 years ago when scientists and paleoanthropologists searched diligently to find precious quantities of Neanderthal and Denisovan remnant DNA. Although there is no Neanderthal and Denisovan DNA population with which to construct a typical and generic genome and mitogenome (the full sequence of mtDNA), the knowledge we gained is quite impressive. With these genetic codes, we can now establish a family tree of our extended Homo *sapien* family.

As far as the most obvious physical features and traits are concerned, with the help of genome and comparative anatomic analysis, we have some idea of the appearance of Neanderthals and Denisovans. We might also ponder whether and how species family members, us, and these archaic Homo *sapiens* communicated with each other.

A family tree is not complete until you include your relatives by blood and marriage. For example, we might—or might not, in some cases—like to find out who our in-laws are and where they came from. Once we found out how those in the Homo *sapiens* family interact with each other, we realized there were some positives and negatives from the mixed marriages. We were able to identify a few microscopic changes leading to macroscopic traits. These positives and negatives may have had an impact on our daily lives without us realizing their origins until now.

We can work backward in time by 200,000 years based on the DNA of modern humans because our evolutionary records are stored in our genomes, evidenced by the work performed by Cann et al. Modern advances in molecular anthropology extend that timeframe to 1,000,000 years, based on our genomes and those of 40,000-year-old people belonging to the Neanderthals and Denisovans. The follow-up question should be, "Wouldn't it make sense for us to fill in the voids in our evolutionary past if we could find the genomes of all hominins?"

THE CHAPTER

We first introduce the discoveries in sequencing the genomes of both Neanderthals and Denisovans. Scientists have used decoded genomes to postulate our relationships with them and between them from a microscopic perspective because a macroscopic approach is not viable at this time. These genomes are useful to corroborate and refine the part of the family tree that is exclusively for the species of Homo *sapiens*. Beyond the genetic family tree, we explore the possibility based on genomes, whether family members communicate effectively, and how alike or different we look.

Next, we explore inter-subspecies relationships within our species. In the last chapter, we have seen molecular evidence that the interaction of all modern human geological populations was frequent, rendering the term "race" meaningless. There is no reason that wouldn't happen between Neanderthals, Denisovans, and modern humans—they overlapped in time and location for at least a few thousand years, after all. Although both Neanderthals and Denisovans left the family 40,000 years ago, these unions led to traits that have both benefited us and gave us problems at the same time. We will use a few examples to illustrate these influences through genetic introgression.

DNA OF HOMO SAPIENS

FULL MODERN HUMAN GENOMES

We have successfully decoded our generic genome through the completion of the Human Genome Project. We have since continued to fill in the details and archived the rapidly cumulated knowledge of our genomes in the public domain, accessible by any interested party. For example, you can get the code for a full genome from the interactive UCSC Genome Browser. UCSC is a participating member of the Human Genome Project.

FULL NEANDERTHAL GENOMES

Modern human genomes, including nuclear and mitochondrial DNA, are relatively easy to get since every one of us has 30 trillion copies. We just need to be aware of the multitudes of legal and ethical ramifications before offering our DNA to any genome research projects. Sequencing ancient and remnant DNA from fossils is, however, a different matter. There are a few obstacles to sequencing Neanderthal genomes. The youngest Neanderthal genomes would be as old as 40,000 years and not in good shape. All DNA is fragile after the organisms hosting them die and are prone to breaking apart into smaller segments without the living organism to maintain their integrity. Ancient DNA is broken into shorter segments if it survives through fossilization.

The first step for an extensive and thorough analysis of remnant DNA is to replicate the DNA millions of times with identical outcomes through the process of PCR. PCR amplification is powerful and does the replication job quite routinely today, but it is also indiscriminate. It will amplify all that is in the samples, whether from the fossils or impurities inadvertently introduced into the samples. One has to exercise extreme caution while isolating the real fragments, either before PCR or during analysis.

Finally, the fragments need to be stitched together into the full genome correctly. Since DNA stitching was never done before, a significant effort was required to develop the methodology and its implementation. The broken segments of archaic human DNA found are typically in the order of hundreds of base pairs. The process of stitching the fragments together and returning the full genome is worth special mention. In particular, we have to accurately reassemble the entire genome of 3.2 billion base pairs without knowing what they should be.

This last part is not exactly correct. It would be reasonable to assume that the human genome and that of the Neanderthals have a lot in common. There are good reasons for filling in most of the missing gaps based on existing human genome libraries. With careful comparison and a wealth of knowledge of human genomes, scientists were able to string together the whole genome from the remnants of Neanderthal fossils. The feat for Neanderthal mtDNA was first reported in 2008, and the full Neanderthal genome, all 3.2 billion base pairs, in 2010. The team achieving this task was led by Svante Pääbo, with whom we should be familiar with by now—he is a Swedish geneticist specializing in evolutionary genetics at the Max-Planck Institute for Evolutionary Anthropology.

We did not undertake the sequencing task merely out of curiosity without purpose. The knowledge of this full sequencing yielded new revelations almost immediately after it was made public in 2010 and enlightened some genetic relationships between Neanderthals and us.

Pääbo disclosed two of the cases in a book he wrote. Immediately after publicizing their draft genome in a 2010 conference, a scientist reported that Neanderthals and modern humans share the same lost molecular piece, partially responsible for something called the penile spine. This part is present in all apes but missing in Neanderthals and modern humans.

The second case is that both modern humans and Neanderthals are missing a genetic part that limits apes' brain sizes in general, and they can continue the evolution toward a larger brain size unimpeded. This may explain why both of us have almost equivalently large brain sizes. On the other hand, there must be some adverse side effects of the larger brain size; otherwise, why does it exist in apes in the first place? One speculation could be that we cannot carry a big braincase throughout our lives, particularly during childbirth. There is no academic follow up on the subtlety of our brain size, as far as I know.

Jumping ahead in the Denisovan genome's story a little, I have not found any specific mention of these two subjects concerning the Denisovan genomes.

FULL DENISOVAN GENOMES

Denisovans were discovered in 2010 when the DNA from an ancient bone fragment found in Denisova Cave in Siberia was sequenced, expecting to find Neanderthal genomes. Researchers were surprised it did not belong to a Neanderthal. They were able to reconstruct the entire high-quality Denisovan genome in 2012 based on the same methodology used to reconstruct Neanderthal genomes. This work was also led by Svante Pääbo at the Max Planck Institute and published in *Science*.

This achievement is essential since the DNA differed enough from that of Neanderthals to prompt the "discovery" of a subspecies of our relatives. Comparative anatomy was of no use to indicate differences between this species and Neanderthals—the DNA in the fossil did. This discovery begs the question: "What do Denisovans look like, anyway?" We will try to answer that a little later.

Two fragments of the pinky, proximal phalanx of a girl was the only Denisovan fossil ever recovered until very recently. This changed when the mandible fossil was re-examined after its initial discovery in 1980. The mandible being from a Denisovan was determined microscopically, after the Denisovan genomes was sequenced. In this case, the identification was not through DNA since it had deteriorated entirely and none could be recovered from the fossil, but an analysis of collagen protein in its teeth confirmed the jawbone had come from a Denisovan because modern humans and Neanderthals have different genes for collagen, and thus, different collagen.

This fossil, being 160,000 years old and having been located in Tibet, China, is intriguing in and of itself. It is interesting to imagine that our close but lost relatives had ventured to Tibet before modern humans began their migration out of Africa. We also got fairly close with one another and shared the particular trait of hardiness required when living in locations of high altitudes, such as Tibet.

With fewer than two Denisovan individuals identified through fossil genetics, it is unlikely to have a good idea of their physical attributes, but knowing that they are genetically close to modern humans and Neanderthals, it is not too far-fetched to conjure up their looks, even just conceptually. For as little physical evidence Denisovans have left of their existence, they have left indelible evidence inside of us.

HOMO SAPIENS FAMILY TREE

FAMILY TREE DETERMINED BY mtDNA

From ample fossil evidence, we know that we are closely related to Neanderthals. We also know this to be true through our DNAs. Denisovans were discovered through their genomes and their close relationship with Neanderthals. By transitivity, modern humans must also be related to Denisovans. In the time before we were alone on this planet, three types of people, all from the species of Homo *sapiens*, were all alive at the same time. Modern humans have used their prerogative to name themselves Homo *sapiens sapiens* and their subspecies relatives of Homo *sapiens neanderthalensis* and Homo *sapiens denisova*. We use Neanderthals and Denisovans for most of the book for convenience.

Exactly how close we are related to each other in our mtDNA? Thanks to advances in science and technology, we can now precisely count the number of SNPs caused by mutations in our family members. Using the molecular clock concept and counting SNPs from broad human samples, scientists have provided clues to the Homo *sapiens* family tree. J. Krause et al. reported their findings in 2010 using mtDNA from one Denisovan—one early, modern human —during the late Pleistocene age (30,000 years), six Neanderthals, one modern chimp, one modern bonobo, and finally, 54 modern human beings.

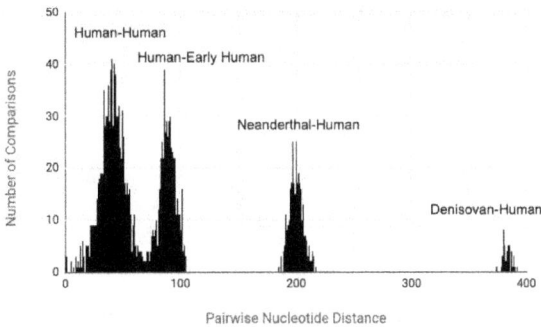

Figure 18. The histogram analysis of the pairwise nucleotide distances caused by mutations amongst the modern humans, early modern humans, Neanderthals, and Denisovans. It tabulates the frequencies of these pairwise differences between any two individuals. The first peak (on the left) is was the human SNP divergence for the 54 humans, with a divergence of 48. The second peak is at an SNP divergence of 88 between modern humans and an early human about 30,000- thousand years- old. The third is the divergence between humans and Neanderthals, with an average of 202. The last one (on the right) is the divergence between humans and the Denisovans, peaking at 385.

The analysis of pairwise nucleotide distance caused by mutations generated the histogram in Figure 18. It tabulates the frequencies of the pairwise differences between any two individuals. Including a chimp and bonobo in the study implicitly recognizes that chimp, bonobo, and human share a common ancestor. Bringing chimp into the comparison with humans marked the first time they were part of a genetic analysis. In essence, chimp's mtDNA can be considered 7,000,000 years old ancient DNA.

This comparison histogram clustered into four groups. The first one (on the left) is the human SNP divergence for the 54 humans, with an average distance of 48. The second peak is at an SNP divergence of 88 between modern humans and an early human about 30,000-years-old. The third is the divergence between humans and Neanderthals, with an average of 202. The last one (on the right) is the divergence between humans and the Denisovan, peaking at 385. Far outside of this figure and to the right is the mutation distance between modern humans and modern chimps, peaking at 1,462 positions.

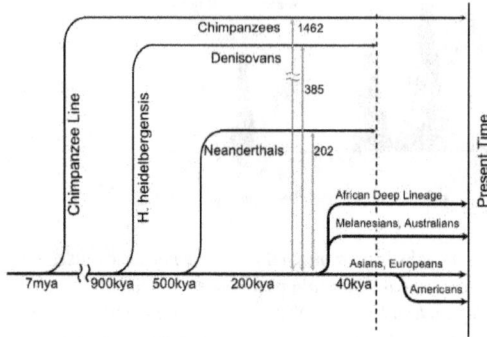

Figure 19. The intra Homo sapien *species family tree. It focuses on the last 1,000,000 years, roughly since the beginning of* Homo sapiens *family. The blue lines represent the number of SNP differences in their mtDNAs.*

Based on this histogram, Denisovan mtDNA carries almost twice as many differences as the mtDNA of modern humans, as does Neanderthal mtDNA. This means that Neanderthals and humans are closer relatives than Denisovans and humans by a factor of two. We can quantify how close we are to each other if we use mtDNA as a simple metric. We can estimate the TMRCA of the Homo *sapiens* family, assuming the divergence between human and chimpanzee mtDNA is 6,000,000 years ago (according to Krause's analysis). The time when the Denisovans, Neanderthals, and modern humans shared the most recent common mtDNA ancestor was about 900,000 years ago. This ancestral line was almost twice as deep as the most recent mtDNA ancestor of modern humans and Neanderthals, about 465,000 years ago. We can now put a more specific timeline to the intra-species family tree, as shown in Figure 19, the abbreviated family tree from chapter 5.

WAIT, NOT SO FAST—FULL GENOMES TELL A DIFFERENT STORY

Based on mtDNA analysis, our relationship with Neanderthals and Denisovans seems pretty conclusive. Their nuclear genomes, however, suggest a much younger common ancestor between European Neanderthals and Denisovans. The nuclear genome study dates their common ancestors to around 400,000 years ago and characterizes Denisovans as a sister group to Neanderthals. This possibility is designated as Milestone 7[1] in our phylogenetic tree in chapter 5.

Later, traces of an even more archaic human were identified in the Denisovan nuclear genome. A mitogenome sequence related to the Denisovan has also been found in a 400,000-year-old specimen from Sima de los Huesos (Spain), whose nuclear genome is closely related to Neanderthals. This discovery pointed to another possible archaic people that was neither Neanderthal nor Denisovan but some other descendant of Homo *erectus* or Homo *heidelbergensis*.

It may stretch the imagination a little too far when one tries to infer the Denisovans' affinity with Neanderthals or modern humans using morphology. One research group concluded that, on the one hand, the anatomy of the Denisovan pinky suggests it belongs to Homo *sapiens* but different than that of the Neanderthals. On the other hand, the Denisovan mandible morphology indicates they descended from the same ancestor of modern humans.

Together, this data suggests that either the Denisovan mitogenome was replaced with that of a more archaic human following an admixture event or it represents the mitogenome of the common ancestor between Neanderthals and Denisovans before they were replaced in the later Neanderthal lineage.

Denisovan 0, 1, and 2

A 2019 study indicated more than one Denisovan variety that we designated as Denisovan 0, 1, and 2. Denisovan 0 is assigned an Altai origin. Denisovan 1 split off from Denisovan 0 around 360,000 years ago, whereas Denisovan 2 split off approximately 280,000 years ago. It is still debatable as to whether they can be considered as subspecies.

. . .

A POSSIBLE THIRD ARCHAIC HUMAN GROUP

The full genome analysis hints at a third ancient people having a genetic influence on Denisovans, Neanderthals, and modern humans. Teeth dating some 80,000 years ago yielded DNA from a Denisovan individual in Denisova Cave in Siberia, confirming that a third group coexisted with Neanderthals and human ancestors.

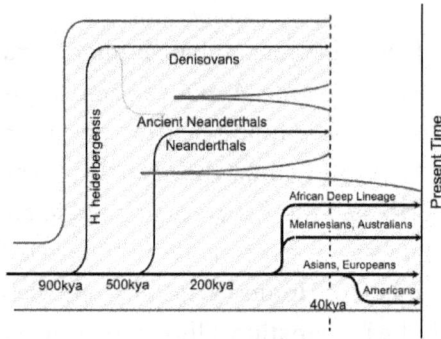

Figure 20. Homo sapiens *family tree represented in bands. The graph's beginning point is the common ancestor of the genus of* Homo erectus *about 1,200,000 years ago.*

THE FAMILY TREE ACCORDING TO FULL GENOMES AND MITOGENOMES

Pulling all the scattered information together, we come up with a family tree based on various Homo *sapien* populations represented as bands in Figure 20. The graph's beginning point is the common ancestor of the genus of Homo *erectus* about 1,200,000 years ago. The human population, represented as a band, moves along, continuously mingling with the population until 1,000,000 years ago when Homo *sapiens* started to take shape.

Before the main population split into two bands, there is evidence of an unknown species, most likely an ancient Neanderthal group, branching off from Homo *heidelbergensis*, that eventually blended with Neanderthals, as indicated by the orange line. Our family tree certainly has a lot of unsolved mysteries.

This main population split 600,000 years ago into the upper and lower bands. The upper band became the common ancestors of Neanderthals and Denisovans. Denisovans and Neanderthals continued to trudge along, mingling with each other, represented by the figure's orange line. Around 400,000 years ago, the genetic distinction became more apparent, and Denisovans and Neanderthals were considered separate yet closely related sister groups.

The other—the lower—Homo *sapiens* band, continued to evolve until 200,000 years ago when we, modern humans, emerged as the subspecies we are today.

This is the current understanding of our Homo *sapiens* family tree as of late 2019. Keep in mind that this third ancient Neanderthal group existed in the background (represented by the orange line) between 400,000 and 1,000,000 years ago. This other group may mess up the family tree a little if we can be more confident as to who they are.

While discussing the emergence of modern humans in chapter 9, we argued that the theory of multi-regionalism for modern humans does not work well from a DNA point of view. On the other hand, if you zoom out far enough to view the evolution process from 1,000,000 years ago, multi-regionalism might make sense for Homo *sapiens* as a species. Combining the fossil record, the migratory paths of Homo *sapiens*, and this molecular evidence, it is clear that modern humans evolved in Africa. In contrast, Neanderthals and Denisovans evolved somewhere in the Middle East or Eurasia. As such, the theory of multi-regionalism for the rise of Homo *sapiens* species as a whole may make some sense.

MINGLING AMONG SUBSPECIES

We have dispelled the concept of "race" within modern humans through ample evidence in our mtDNA in the last chapter. This indicates that we moved around in the intervening years and had frequent relationships outside of our geographic group. Did this happen among modern humans, Neanderthals, and Denisovans if they had the opportunity? Indeed, it did, and there is evidence left of this in our genomes.

NEANDERTHALS AND DENISOVANS

The oldest genetically identified inter-subspecies relationship found is between Neanderthals and Denisovans. The comparison of the Denisovan nuclear genome with that of a roughly 100,0000-year-old Neanderthal in Denisova Cave revealed that Denisovans experienced gene flow from a Neanderthal population.

A bone fragment, also from Denisova Cave, has been analyzed and found to have belonged to a female individual that was the hybrid of a Neanderthal mother and a Denisovan father. Her maternal Neanderthal contribution is more closely related to the genome of the 40,000-year-old European Neanderthal than to that of the 100,000-year-old Neanderthal from Denisova Cave in Asia. Furthermore, the paternal Denisovan genome of the hybrid appears to bear traces of an ancient Neanderthal admixture. This genetic evidence is why the orange arrowed line split off from the Denisovan line in Figure 20. This data indicates that the gene flow between Neanderthals and Denisovans was not a rare occurrence.

It was evident that Denisova Cave was a popular hot spot for our ancestors. The 120,000-year-old remains of an individual Neanderthal were recently discovered in the same Denisova Cave, predating other Neanderthal residents by 80,000 years. Ninety thousand year old remains of a Denisovan-Neanderthal hybrid found in the same cave laid bare the fact that the two groups cohabited at or near the same shelter and interbred. The Denisovan Cave must have been inhabited through generations of hominins. The earliest inhabitants might well have been previous generations of Neanderthals.

MODERN HUMANS AND NEANDERTHALS

From our discussion on dating their fossils, we know that Neanderthals disappeared around 40,000 years ago. Their roaming range extended from Spain in the west to Siberia in the east. There is evidence that fossils of modern humans have been found in the Middle East as early as 100,000 years ago. The time and location overlap between them might have been extensive. It should not surprise anyone that Neanderthals and modern humans have inter-bred even though they are about 400,000 years apart in their evolutionary journeys. Recall that modern-day chimps and bonobos can still crossbreed after being separated for 1,500,000 years despite their apparent morphological differences.

The interbreeding of modern humans and Neanderthals must have been successful because many modern human populations carry Neanderthal genes in their DNA. I, for one, am living proof of this. When *23andme* analyzed my DNA, I found out that I have 226 Neanderthal variants in my gene pool. I am in the minority, though—more than 92% of the population in *23andme* data bank have more Neanderthal variants than I do. The highest number of Neanderthal variants in the *23andme* data bank is 397. There are 6,000 Neanderthal variants; it is not clear how many of the 6,000 variants *23andme* has tested and shared with its clients. The general population of Asians and Europeans carry anywhere from two to three percent of Neanderthals in their genomes.

MODERN HUMANS AND DENISOVANS

We also know that the gene flow between Neanderthals and Denisovans occurred as described in the last section because they had a long time to do just that in either of the scenarios in the abbreviated Homo *sapiens* family tree shown as Figure 21. The co-location of Neanderthals and Denisovans and of Neanderthals and modern humans implies that modern humans and Denisovans overlapped in space, too. Once researchers had reconstructed the entire, high-quality Denisovan genome in 2012, it became clear that, like Neanderthals, Denisovans interbred with modern humans when they cohabited somewhere in Eurasia. Further, the analysis also suggests the some of our introgressed DNA likely came from multiple Denisovan populations within the last 50,000 years.

Denisovan DNA makes up four to six percent of the genomes of people native to Melanesia's islands, a sub-region of Oceania. They left their genetic mark in other Pacific island populations and some modern East Asians to a lesser extent. It is mostly absent from the genetic code of most other people.

FAMILY BY BLOOD AND OTHER ASSOCIATIONS

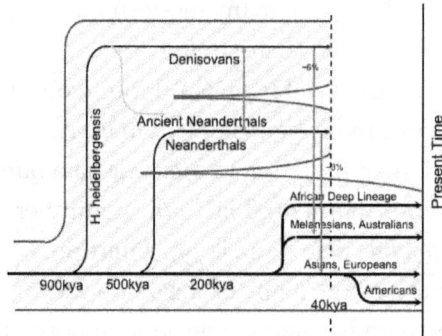

Figure 21. The genetic contribution to modern humans from Denisovans and Neanderthals. The mixing between Denisovans and Neanderthals is not quantified for now.

It might be time to pull together a more comprehensive family tree, including the deep lineage of modern humans, Neanderthals, and Denisovans as shown in Figure 21.

The percentage of Neanderthal DNA in modern humans is zero or close to zero in people from African populations and is about two to three percent in people of European or Asian backgrounds. This two to three percent of genes from Neanderthals has stayed steady and widespread in us, indicating that the interbreeding happened but stopped about 40,000 years ago. The percentage of Denisovan DNA is highest in Melanesian populations (four to six percent), lower in other Southeast Asian and Pacific Islander populations, and very low or undetectable elsewhere in the world.

The following is a scenario of the interaction between the three groups. Modern humans from Africa did not interbreed—or they interbred a little—with either Neanderthals or Denisovans. Instead, they stayed behind and did not have the chance to interact with either. At the same time, modern humans from Europe and Asia interbred with Neanderthals in the past after leaving Africa before they spread beyond the region of interaction in the Middle East.

The Melanesians have the most Denisovan DNA, possibly because they have not intermingled with people from other places after they initially interbred with Denisovans in the Middle East region. Southeast Asian and Pacific Islander populations have less of a Denisovan contribution to their genes than the Melanesians. It could be that the Melanesian, Southeast Asian, and Pacific Islander groups traversed through different regions, interacting with other Denisovan populations to reach their final destinations.

FAMILY PORTRAITS

Can you tell who is who when all of the Homo *sapiens* family members—modern humans, Neanderthals, and Denisovans—stand side by side in a family portrait? What are the key features that tell us apart?

MODERN HUMANS

We know what we look like by looking in a mirror. You may not be the poster child that typifies our subspecies, but each of our traits would have a normal distribution if you characterized everyone living today. For example, we would have a normal distribution of height, and there is an average height. We have an average color of hair, skin, and eyes. The average shapes of our noses are neither too flat nor aquiline. If you compare the two extremes on either side of the normal distributions, you are bound to find that we might be very different in one aspect or another, but in the end, you are not likely to mistake us for Neanderthals if you know what they look like.

NEANDERTHALS

Figure 22. A life-sized Neanderthal by the Dutch Kennis brothers and on displayed in the Natural History Museum at South Kensington, London.

Through the abundant Neanderthal fossils' skeletal and muscular anatomy and creative artwork, we have a pretty good idea of what Neanderthals looked like when they roamed the earth. A life-sized Neanderthal has been reconstructed by the Dutch Kennis brothers and is on display in the Natural History Museum at South Kensington, London (Figure 22). Our Belgian Neanderthal is in his twenties and stands 155 cm tall, to which Adrie Kennis says, "The scientists bring the knowledge, and we make the characters." Would we confuse him as one of us if he stood among us? For one thing, they are not the brutes popularized by Marcellin Boule. They are not huge, but they do look a lot more robust than most of us. On the other hand, he might have just been someone who had hit the gym hard. I probably would not notice him if he wore a T-shirt, a pair of jeans, had a clean groom on his hair and beard and traveled in the New York subway system.

DENISOVAN

Figure 23. A Denisovan face constructed based on the activities of the genes with obvious phenotypes common to modern humans and Neanderthals illustrated by Maayan Harel, National Geographic phenotypes, *Sept 19, 2019.*

We have very few Denisovan fossil fragments, so reconstructing their looks is not as easy as it is for Neanderthals; however, this does not discourage scientists from speculating based on genetic evidence. A skeletal structure may be constructed based on the activities of genes common to modern humans and Neanderthals, related to phenotype appearance. Since any common phenotype is the expression of numerous genotypes, we needed to use readily identifiable, prominent, unique connections between genes and looks. Figure 23 is the result of their attempts in which scientists try to accomplish this feat by comparing phenotype differences with existing skeletal disorders associated with these genes. This approach is fundamentally flawed, but I believe this is the only published work that attempts to imagine Denisovan features.

They speculate that Denisovans look more like Neanderthals than human beings—this similarity should not be a surprise. There are some subtle differences though. One, the Denisovan pelvis is as wide as a Neanderthal's but distinctively different from ours. Two, the Denisovan skull is wider than both the Neanderthals' and ours, pointing to a larger braincase and volume, meaning that Denisovans might have been as smarter as we are. Three, the Denisovan jaws are longer to accommodate larger teeth, maybe due to a diet consisting mainly of vegetation, implying that they did not hunt as much as Neanderthals.

. . .

THE DNA FANTASY IS STILL A FANTASY, AFTER ALL

Chapter 8 has debunked the fantasy of synthesizing a criminal's face based exclusively on human DNA, and this most recent work seems to lend further credence to this possibility. The imagined Denisovan only displays the most noticeable features that might link the genes to related disorders. It infers and assumes, rather presumptuously, that our ancient relatives' carrying these abnormal genes was the norm, based on scarce DNA samples. It is, by no means, an accurate representation, given the broad, general overview of the species of hominin, especially when it went extinct around 40,000 years ago. These renditions are an oversimplification of how genes interact with genes. The fantasy of reconstructing full facial features based solely on DNA is still just that: a fantasy.

DID WE TALK TO OTHER MEMBERS IN THE FAMILY?

Sometimes, science fiction inspires real science. It is not necessarily the fiction that hits home in the imagination of scientists, but the out of the box thinking it provokes, prompting them to ask unlikely questions not normally conceivable by academia. I cannot help but think about the book by John Darnton again: *Neanderthals*. Specifically, the book poses the question of whether they could speak and communicate with modern humans. It claims that Neanderthals were as smart as human beings, but it is possible that they could not talk due to their vocal cord anatomy, which is also uncertain at best for the time being.

If I were confused by the New York City subway and a Neanderthal gentleman in a T-shirt and jeans were standing next to me, I might not hesitate to ask him how to get to Yankee Stadium. I would also expect a response from him. Is this a realistic expectation? Anatomically, Neanderthal vocal cords and throat anatomy was very similar to ours. Their FOXP2 seems to have acquired the same amino acids as humans, believed to have happened at least 300,000 to 400,000 years ago. Whether Neanderthals—or Denisovans, for that matter—could speak will remain unresolved unless we can relate the ability to speak through comparative genome-wide association (GWS) study and anatomy. I would recommend this particular subject as an independent research project if I could work with either the Broad Institute or the Max Planck Institute.

THE IMPACT OF INTER-SUBSPECIES RELATIONSHIPS

HYBRIDIZATION AND CROSSBREEDING

The idea that closely-related species can benefit from cross-breeding—known in evolutionary terms as adaptive introgression—is not new. Some use the term hybridization to describe such activities. I am not sure that cross-subspecies breeding can be considered hybridization, but for the sake of not casting domesticated cattle as being hybridized for meat or milk, or cultivated plants for their yield, we will use the term crossbreeding to describe inter-subspecies relationships.

You might have heard that children of mixed-race parents look prettier, but this is, however, a myth. First of all, prettiness is purely subjective. From a crossbreeding point of view, it does not intrinsically have a direction making offspring either more or less beautiful. The probability of having beautiful children over ugly children is the same if the genetic math works out. Our ideas of beauty have nothing to do with evolution at all. In the end, the final judgment is in the hands of the environment. Or, in the case of breeding leaner cattle for meat, it is in the hands of the breeders who simply chose leaner cattle to parent the next generation. By crossbreeding, you have the probability of generating more diverse organisms or species that can better adapt to the environment and survive collectively.

Without crossbreeding, pure gene lines would take a long time to adapt to the changing environment through natural selection and mutation evolution. In the case of migrating organisms as a subspecies (or species) expands into a new territory, it grapples with a new set of challenges: different climate, food, predators, and pathogens. Species adapt through natural selection in combination with spontaneous mutations that are helpful to spread gradually through a population, but natural selection is slow, and mutations rarely strike, making adaptation a slow process. A more expedient option is to mate with species that have already adapted to the region and co-opt some of their helpful DNA. It is not clear if early humans would have known the benefits to intentionally crossbreed to better adapt to the environment. Again, this act was not intended to go one particular direction; it just happened.

How did human subspecies crossbreeding happen? We migrate and disperse once we become a more mature population. As modern humans began to spread out of Africa for their last mass migration roughly 70,000 years ago, they encountered other species that looked remarkably like them, the Neanderthals and Denisovans, two archaic humans sharing an ancestor with us approximately 500,000 years earlier. This motley mix of humans coexisted with modern humans in Europe, the Middle East, Asia, and other locations for at least a few thousand years. We now know that they interbred, leaving a lasting legacy in our DNA.

As a result, the DNA of non-Africans has roughly two to three percent Neanderthal DNA, and some Asian and Oceanic island populations have as much as six percent Denisovan DNA. The genome of a 40,000-year-old human whose remains were unearthed in Romania harbored as much as six to nine percent Neanderthal DNA. It is interesting to note that modern humans no longer keep that high level of Neanderthal DNA anymore.

ADVANTAGES OR DISADVANTAGES?

With the topic of Neanderthal/modern human AND Denisovan/modern human crossbreeding settled; one wonders what good came from the interactions. Namely, what were the benefits and consequences of these unions? Was it just a curious feature of human history that didn't have any impact, or did it alter the trajectory of human evolution? In retrospect, it seems that modern humans steamrolled through the world—how might this disturbance affect the path of our grandiose plan, if it does at all?

Neanderthals and Denisovans lived in Europe and Asia for hundreds of thousands of years, enough time to adjust to the cold climate, weak sun, and local microbes. These adjustments could be through slow changes due to natural selection or more abrupt mutations; both are under the influence of the environment eventually. It was fortuitous for modern humans to pick up a gene variant from a population that had already been there for 300,000 years rather than adapt slowly. Indeed, Neanderthal and Denisovan genes with the most significant signs of selection in the modern human genome mostly have to do with how humans interacted with the environment.

As far as what modern humans picked up genetically, in some cases, the genetic mixing is so deep that in some spots of our genome, we are more Neanderthal than humans. It seems pretty clear that at least some of the variants we inherited from archaic hominins were adaptive, helping us survive and reproduce.

Such observations are common between species, and it should not be unexpected that it happens to relationships inside a single population of species. The genetic boundary between subspecies seems to be porous. Following this same line of thought, maybe the boundaries of species are not watertight, either. This concept of soft or permeable species boundaries is an important starting point when we get to the subject of human speciation.

What survival advantage did this instill in our ancestors? Scientists are starting to pick up a few hints. Most of these genes are tied to our immune system, skin, hair, and perhaps our metabolism and tolerance for cold weather, all of which might have helped migrating humans survive in new lands. Then again, some might not have any consequences.

INTROGRESSION FROM NEANDERTHALS TO MODERN HUMANS

There are plenty of examples of the impact crossbreeding has on modern humans. Overall, Neanderthal variants are related to a higher risk of neurological and psychiatric disorders and a lower risk of digestive problems.

COVID-19

The effect of the Neanderthals' genetic introgression into modern humans has a very contemporary and immediate impact on them. Since the beginning of 2020, more than 120,000,000 humans globally have confirmed being infected by the new coronavirus that causes severe respiratory difficulties leading to more than 2,500,000 deaths. COVID-19 is the worst epidemic since the 1918 pandemic, and its rampage has shown no sign of abating at the time of this writing. It is of the utmost importance to understand whether there are genetic dispositions for contracting the disease for treatment or prevention. Identifying a genetic vulnerability to the virus is most beneficial to understanding the virus. A recent study attempted to achieve this feat:

A recent (Sept. 2020) genetic association study identified a gene cluster on chromosome 3 as a risk locus for respiratory failure upon SARS-CoV-2 infection. A new study comprising 3,199 hospitalized COVID-19 patients and controls finds that this is the major genetic risk factor for severe SARS-CoV-2 infection and hospitalization (COVID-19 Host Genetics Initiative). Here, we show that the risk is conferred by a genomic segment of ~50 kb that is inherited from Neanderthals and is carried by ~50% of people in South Asia and ~16% of people in Europe today.

The crux of this study indicates that this genetic region is almost identical to that of a 50,000-year-old Neanderthal from southern Europe. Further analysis has shown that, through interbreeding, the variants came over to the ancestors of modern humans about 60,000 years ago. It is still not clear yet, however, whether this Neanderthal variant will render Europeans more susceptible to the COVID-19 infection than people in South Asia.

Freckles

A comparison of human and Neanderthal genomes revealed that the most common adaptive Neanderthal-derived genes are those linked to skin and hair growth. One of the most striking examples is a gene called BNC2 on chromosome 9, connected to skin pigmentation and freckling in Europeans. Nearly 70% of Europeans carry the Neanderthal version of this gene. This is why a lot of Europeans are freckle-faced when young.

Diabetes

The most concrete and well-studied examples are the diabetes genes we inherited from Neanderthals. The discovery of a gene variant associated with type 2 diabetes is the second case. Modern humans have acquired a trait from Neanderthals, notes paleo-geneticist Svante Pääbo, whose team also discovered the Denisovan people. Another team also showed that Mayans, in particular, have inherited a gene variant from Neandertals that increases the risk for diabetes.

Researchers have focused on type 2 diabetes for years, the most common form of the disease, accounting for 90-95% of diabetes cases in humans. In type 2 diabetes, the body either does not generate enough insulin—a hormone the body needs to use sugar for energy —or its cells ignore the molecule.

A risk gene for type 2 diabetes, known as SLC16A11 on chromosome 11, went undetected in previous research. People who carry the higher-risk mutation of the gene, which is active in the liver, are 25% more likely to have diabetes than those who lack it. People who inherit copies of this gene variant from both parents are 50% more likely to have diabetes.

The higher-risk version of this gene is present in up to half of people with recent Native American ancestry, including Latin Americans. This gene mutation is more common in Latin Americans, and it could account for as much as 20% of their increased levels of type 2 diabetes.

We have come to understand the biological function of SLC16A11 and how changing its sequence in Neanderthals and eventually leaking into modern humans increases the risk of type 2 diabetes. We may, in the long run, be able to develop improved prevention or treatment.

These results, however intriguing, do not lead to a simple gene editing to make our type 2 diabetes problem go away. Like most genetically predisposed diseases, type 2 diabetes is a complex disease influenced by multiple genes, environment, and behaviors. This finding is only one piece in a large and complex puzzle that is still in the research phase, and any resulting health benefits will take time.

INTROGRESSION FROM DENISOVAN
Living At The High Altitude

Our knowledge of the Denisovans started from a short section of a pinky in the Denisova cave, and now they have a new address in Tibet. A new fossil of a Denisovan mandible was discovered in Tibet, of all places in the world. The discovery in Tibet makes sense. A study in 2014 indicated that the mutant EPAS1 gene on chromosome 2 could have been inherited from archaic hominins—the Denisovans.

Denisovans have the ability to move easily through higher elevations thanks to this gene. How the DNA made its way to Tibet is anyone's guess, but Denisovans are such a mysterious group that anything we learn about them is not just exciting but useful.

Tibetans—in particular, the Sherpas, known for their Himalayan hardiness—exhibit similar patterns in this mutated EPAS1 gene, which further fortifies that the gene is under selection for adaptation to Tibetans' high-altitude life. EPAS1 is also known to encourage increased athletic performance in some people. As such, this gene has been referred to as the "super athlete" gene.

High Altitude Living Does Not Need EPAS1

I once wondered whether Peruvians living in the Andes above 4,500 meters altitude also have the EPAS1 gene. I visited Rainbow Mountain in Peru in early 2018, a new tourist site located in the Andes of Peru in the Cusco region. Before getting there, I stayed at Cuzco, which is 3,400 meters high, to acclimate to the altitude. It was hard work, getting around and climbing stairs in Cusco. I figured I needed to book a horse to ride instead of hiking up the 5,200-meters-high Rainbow Mountain like all the youngsters with whom I was traveling.

Little did I know that it would be a different kind of horse ride.

The reins were in the hands of a walking—or more appropriately, running—guide. It was snowing up in the mountains, with a couple of inches of snow already on the ground, though it was the middle of summer. The local guide just held onto the reins and pulled the horse forward, running while wearing a worn-out pair of open-toed leather sandals. He was no taller than five feet and ran like nobody's business. He guided me up to the top of the mountain and told me to wait for him to come back to take me down while he went back to the staging area to fetch another person.

I was amazed at his ability to function so well at such high altitudes. One can only wonder if the Andeans also had the mutant EPAS1 gene to utilize the oxygen more effectively than us. I did some research and found out that was not the case. The native Inka people —Quechuan—were descendants from Asia, more specifically, originally near the Altai Mountains. They migrated to the Americas about 15,000 years ago, bringing a narrow gene pool and little to none of the Denisovan variants. They have spent 12,000 years in the mountains. Irrespective of their time spent at a high altitude, they do not carry a mutation similar to EAPS1 genes. Andean highlanders have adapted to such thin air by adding more oxygen-carrying hemoglobin to their blood. These adaptations are not, however, permanent and are part of acclimatization. If they go back to the low land, their hemoglobin levels will drop to that of the lowlanders within a few weeks. Their tolerance for the high altitude is not a phenotype caused by mutated genes. However, they do possess a variant of EGLN1 that does help their ability to carry oxygen in their hemoglobin.

Since either the genetic change for adaption by the Denisovans or an increasing hemoglobin level achieves the same goal for high-altitude living, you might ask what is the difference between these two adaptations? Is there an advantage to either one? As it turns out, the density of Sherpa hemoglobin is even lower than other people in the world. The edge to the Denisovan genes' adjustment to their physiology is that they can live with lower oxygen levels because they simply do not need that much oxygen. The Andeans are just like any of us who still need proper amounts of oxygen to survive. This lower

density of hemoglobin for Denisovans may be advantageous to
reduce blood clotting, thus reducing heart disease in the cold
weather.

It probably took Denisovans around 500,000 years to acquire the
genes to feel comfortable in high altitudes. Sherpas got the benefit of
living at high altitudes from interbreeding with Denisovans over a
few generations. However, the irony is that we never had the opportunity to return the favor once we had this beneficial gene. Denisovans
went extinct for some unknown reasons, one of them might be
caused by the much larger population of modern humans.

Immunity To Microbes

Findings by a team from the Garvan Institute of Medical
Research showed that some modern humans acquired a gene variant
from Denisovans that heightened their immune reactions, indicating
an adaptation of the immune system to a changing environment.

There are harmful variations of a gene called TNFAIP3 that
causes autoimmune issues like inflammatory bowel disease, arthritis,
multiple sclerosis, psoriasis, type 1 diabetes, and lupus. The study
reveals that some modern humans, including those with Indigenous
Australian, Melanesian, Maori, and Polynesian ancestry, acquired a
variant TNFAIP3 on chromosome 6 from Denisovans that increases a
range of immune reactions and inflammatory responses, including
responses that protect us from disease-causing microbes.

The study, published in *Nature Immunology*, is the first to demonstrate how a single DNA sequence variant from an extinct human
species can change the activity of the modern human immune
system.

Discovering An Immune Switch

The TNFAIP3 gene encodes for a protein called A20 that helps
"cool" the immune system by reducing hyper-immune reactions to
foreign molecules and microbes. Variant TNFAIP3 correctly codes
the A20 protein that can optimally dial-in levels of immune
responses. This lowered reaction to some microbes is another advantage of mixing with our Denisovan relatives.

The team also found the variant gene in genome data extracted from the Denisovan girl dating to 50,000 years ago, recovered from a cave in Siberia. This variant was, however, notably absent from Neanderthal remains recovered from the same cave. It is then reasonable to conclude that this gene variant emerged after the Denisovan and Neanderthal lineages split 400,000 years ago.

SUMMARY

Through fully sequenced Neanderthal and Denisovan genomes, we gain quite a few crucial microscopic insights into our species. We now can connect the microscopic and macroscopic parts of our past and consolidate our Homo *sapiens* family tree, including modern humans, Neanderthals, and Denisovans. There is also molecular evidence of the existence of a yet to be identified member in this family tree.

There has been ample microscopic evidence that all three members of our family tree were relatively friendly and crossbred in more than a few incidents. We have confirmed this inter-subspecies relationship in the form of variant genes in modern humans. This relationship has given modern humans some advantage when it comes to our ability to deal with everyday challenges. We also inherited some disadvantages with which we must deal, using modern medicine, such as diabetes.

Finally, while we follow the progression of using molecular anthropology to move back in time to the early stages of our evolution, it is tempting to continue to go even further back. The most intriguing mystery to me was our speciation, 7,000,000 years ago. The question is, then, whether we have enough DNA from our intermediate ancestors, like that of the genus Australopithecus, to make sense out of our speciation. As it turns out, we may already have some 7,000,000-year-old DNA within our reach: the high-quality DNA of modern-day apes. We may gain some insight into how we parted ways with the live fossils that are chimps.

BIBLIOGRAPHY

1. The research referenced in this chapter usually involves large scientific teams. They are necessarily large since modern-day molecular anthropology requires multidisciplinary talents that can only be found in diverse backgrounds and organizations. They also require resources of advanced equipment and sophisticated software in international collaborations. I decided to cite full author lists out of respect for the dedication and contribution of everyone. These large author lists remind me of a similar situation in particle physics. The experimental discovery of the Higgs Boson, sometimes coined as the God particle for the standard model, published by teams in the Large Hadron Collider (LHC) in Physics Letter B, is 29 pages long. The author list occupies eight of the printed pages, consisting of 3,000 co-authors.

2. "The complete genome sequence of a Neanderthal from the Altai Mountains," Kay Prüfer, Fernando Racimo, Nick Patterson, Flora Jay, Sriram Sankararaman, Susanna Sawyer, Anja Heinze, Gabriel Renaud, Peter H. Sudmant, Cesare de Filippo, Heng Li, Swapan Mallick, Michael Dannemann, Qiaomei Fu, Martin Kircher, Martin Kuhlwilm, Michael Lachmann, Matthias Meyer, Matthias Ongyerth, Michael Siebauer, Christoph Theunert, Arti Tandon, Priya Moorjani, Joseph Pickrell, James C. Mullikin, Samuel H. Vohr, Richard E. Green, Ines Hellmann, Philip L. F. Johnson, Hélène Blanche, Howard Cann, Jacob O. Kitzman, Jay Shendure, Evan E. Eichler, Ed S. Lein, Trygve E. Bakken, Liubov V. Golovanova, Vladimir B. Doronichev, Michael V. Shunkov, Anatoli P. Derevianko, Bence Viola, Montgomery Slatkin, David Reich, Janet Kelso & Svante Pääbo, *Nature*, 505, 43-49 (2014).

3. "The complete mitochondrial DNA genome of an

unknown hominin from southern Siberia," Johannes Krause, Qiaomei Fu, Jeffrey M. Good, Bence Viola, Michael V. Shunkov, Anatoli P. Derevianko & Svante Pääbo, *Nature*, **464**, 894-897 (2010).

4. "A High-Coverage Genome Sequence from an Archaic Denisovan Individual," Matthias Meyer, Martin Kircher, Marie-Theres Gansauge, Heng Li, Fernando Racimo, Swapan Mallick, Joshua G. Schraiber, Flora Jay, Kay Prüfer, Cesare de Filippo, Peter H. Sudmant, Can Alkan, Qiaomei Fu, Ron Do, Nadin Rohland, Arti Tandon, Michael Siebauer, Richard E. Green, Katarzyna Bryc, Adrian W. Briggs, Udo Stenzel, Jesse Dabney, Jay Shendure, Jacob Kitzman, Michael F. Hammer, Michael V. Shunkov, Anatoli P. Derevianko, Nick Patterson, Aida M. Andrés, Evan E. Eichler, Montgomery Slatkin, David Reich, Janet Kelso, Svante Pääbo, *Science*, **338**, pp. 222-226 (2012).

5. "A high-coverage Neandertal genome from Vindija Cave in Croatia," Prüfer K, de Filippo C, Grote S, Mafessoni F, Korlević P, Hajdinjak M, Vernot B, Skov L, Hsieh P, Peyrégne S, Reher D, Hopfe C, Nagel S, Maricic T, Fu Q, Theunert C, Rogers R, Skoglund P, Chintalapati M, Dannemann M, Nelson BJ, Key FM, Rudan P, Kućan Ž, Gušić I, Golovanova LV, Doronichev VB, Patterson N, Reich D, Eichler EE, Slatkin M, Schierup MH, Andrés AM, Kelso J, Meyer M, Pääbo S, *Science,* **358**, 655-658 (2017).

6. "A Complete Neandertal Mitochondrial Genome Sequence Determined by High-Throughput Sequencing," Richard E. Green, Anna-Sapfo Malaspinas, Johannes Krause, Adrian W. Briggs, Philip L.F. Johnson, Caroline Uhler, Matthias Meyer, Jeffrey M. Good, Tomislav Maricic, Udo Stenzel, Kay Prüfer, Michael Siebauer, Hernán A. Burbano, Michael Ronan, Jonathan M. Rothberg, Michael Egholm, Pavao Rudan, Dejana Brajković, Željko Kućan, Ivan Gušić, Mårten Wikström, Liisa Laakkonen, Janet

Kelso, Montgomery Slatkin, Svante Pääbo, *Cell,* 134, 416-426 (2008).

7. "Analysis of Human Sequence Data Reveals Two Pulses of Archaic Denisovan Admixture," Sharon R Browning, Brian L Browning, Ying Zhou, Serena Tucci, Joshua M Akey, *Cell*, 173, 53-61 (2018).

8. "No Evidence for Recent Selection at FOXP2 among Diverse Human Populations," Elizabeth Grace Atkinson, Amanda Jane Audesse, Julia Adela Palacios, Dean Michael Bobo, Ashley Elizabeth Webb, Sohini Ramachandran, Brenna Mariah Henn, *Cell,* 17, 1424-1435 (2018).

9. "Reconstructing Denisovan Anatomy Using DNA Methylation Maps," David Gokhman, Nadav Mishol, Marc de Manuel, David de Juan, Jonathan Shuqrun, Eran Meshorer, Tomas Marques-Bonet, Yoel Rak, Liran Carmel, *Cell,* 179, 180-192 (2019).

10. "Neanderthal Man, In Search of Lost Genomes," Svante Pääbo, 2015, Basic Books publisher.

11. "Multiple Deeply Divergent Denisovan Ancestries in Papuans," Guy S. Jacobs, Georgi Hudjashov, Lauri Saag, Pradiptajati Kusuma, Chelzie C. Darusallam, Daniel J. Lawson, Mayukh Mondal, Luca Pagani, François-Xavier Ricaut, Mark Stoneking, Mait Metspalu, Herawati Sudoyo, J. Stephen Lansing, and Murray P. Cox, *Cell,*177, 1010-1021 (2019).

12. "A late Middle Pleistocene Denisovan mandible from the Tibetan Plateau," Fahu Chen, Frido Welker, Chuan-Chou Shen, Shara E. Bailey, Inga Bergmann, Simon Davis, Huan Xia, Hui Wang, Roman Fischer, Sarah E. Freidline, Tsai-Luen Yu, Matthew M. Skinner, Stefanie Stelzer, Guangrong Dong, Qiaomei Fu, Guanghui Dong, Jian Wang, Dongju Zhang & Jean-Jacques Hublin, *Nature,* 569, 409–412, (2019).

13. "Morphology of the Denisovan phalanx closer to modern humans than to Neanderthals," E. Andrew Bennett,

Isabelle Crevecoeur, Bence Viola, Anatoly P. Derevianko, Michael V. Shunkov, Thierry Grange, Bruno Maureille, and Eva-Maria Geigl, *Science Advances*, **5**, 2019.

14. "The genome of the offspring of a Neanderthal mother and a Denisovan father," Viviane Slon, Fabrizio Mafessoni, Benjamin Vernot, Cesare de Filippo, Steffi Grote, Bence Viola, Mateja Hajdinjak, Stéphane Peyrégne, Sarah Nagel, Samantha Brown, Katerina Douka, Tom Higham, Maxim B. Kozlikin, Michael V. Shunkov, Anatoly P. Derevianko, Janet Kelso, Matthias Meyer, Kay Prüfer & Svante Pääbo, *Nature* **561**, 113-116 (2018).

15. "Denisovan, modern human and mouse TNFAIP3 alleles tune A20 phosphorylation and immunity," Nathan W. Zammit, Owen M. Siggs, Paul E. Gray, Keisuke Horikawa, David B. Langley, Stacey N. Walters, Stephen R. Daley, Claudia Loetsch, Joanna Warren, Jin Yan Yap, Daniele Cultrone, Amanda Russell, Elisabeth K. Malle, Jeanette E. Villanueva, Mark J. Cowley, Velimir Gayevskiy, Marcel E. Dinger, Robert Brink, David Zahra, Geeta Chaudhri, Gunasegaran Karupiah, Belinda Whittle, Carla Roots, Edward Bertram, Michiko Yamada, Yogesh Jeelall, Anselm Enders, Benjamin E. Clifton, Peter D. Mabbitt, Colin J. Jackson, Susan R. Watson, Craig N. Jenne, Lewis L. Lanier, Tim Wiltshire, Matthew H. Spitzer, Garry P. Nolan, Frank Schmitz, Alan Aderem, Benjamin T. Porebski, Ashley M. Buckle, Derek W. Abbott, John B. Ziegler, Maria E. Craig, Paul Benitez-Aguirre, Juliana Teo, Stuart G. Tangye, Cecile King, Melanie Wong, Murray P. Cox, Wilson Phung, Jia Tang, Wendy Sandoval, Ingrid E. Wertz, Daniel Christ, Christopher C. Goodnow & Shane T. Grey, *Nature Immunology,* **20**, 1299–1310 (2019).

16. "The major genetic risk factor for severe COVID-19 is inherited from Neanderthals", Hugo Zeberg and Svante Pääbo, *Nature,* (2020). https://doi.org/10.1038/s41586-020-2818-3

17. *"On the Origin of Species By Means of Natural Selection, or, the Preservation of Favoured Races in the Struggle for Life,"* Darwin, Charles, Public Domain Books Publisher, 1859.
18. "Observation of a new particle in the search for the Standard Model Higgs boson with the ATLAS detector at the LHC," G. Aad, and 3,000 other contributors, *Physics Letters B,* **716,** 1-29 (2012).

11

HUMAN SPECIATION

The strongest motivation that drove me to take the biological anthropology course was for humans' origin. I found out very soon that there was much emphasis on the slow and natural selection evolution adapting to environments, consistent with Darwin's gradualism concept. However, one of the most crucial questions of how we became human was glossed over in both course work and textbook. Out of 600 pages of a college-level biological anthropology textbook, only ten are devoted to macroscopic human speciation. As well, the concept or definition of species was given only a half-page of elaboration, emphasizing that it was complicated and ambiguous. Considering the enormity of the subject of human origin, the textbook and course work seemed to be light on or even avoiding the subject.

While genetic recombination in sexual reproduction and its interplay with the environment can account for natural selection evolution, using the same argument to explain the separation between humans and chimpanzees contradicts the premise of natural selection itself. Humans and chimpanzees do not have the same number of chromosomes. As a result, the fact that speciation happens would seem to challenge the traditional concept of a species. There must be some mechanisms beyond simple genetic recombination within species, causing the split or emergence of a new species.

Realizing that the answers are not in the classroom or the textbook, I had a few after class discussions with the professor to find alternatives. As knowledgeable as she was—and she was—I could not get a sensible, definitive direction. When I had an assignment to make a special topic presentation on modern human ancestry, I decided to explore the human speciation mechanism and include that if I was able to put my arms around the subject.

After an extended research, I found a plausible yet provocative answer in a research report in the literature. This report analyzed the molecular and genetic differences in our genomes and those of our relatives and inferred the activities leading to speciation. This study was thorough, logical, reasonable, and able to account for various contradictions. It took advantage of every scientific and technological infrastructure tool available, leading to a likely macroscopic scenario based on microscopic evolutionary actions. Although this is just a small part of our story and would take a considerable amount of details to finalize, I felt that it pointed in the right direction. I included that mechanism in the special topic presentation to the college sophomore class, and it ended up being a part of their midterm exam.

This speciation ushered in our existence and moved us away from the chimps to continue our march to modern humans. That such an essential step in our past could be deciphered (of course, only partially at this time) in the laboratories is a testament to the power of genomic study explored in the last three chapters. By diving into the speciation theory, this chapter completes the connection between microscopic and macroscopic activities from the beginning of our earliest existence.

Chapter 9 takes us back 200,000 years, based on modern human genomes. Chapter 10 extends this further back to 1,000,000 years to include the full genomes of Neanderthals and Denisovans. The extension into the past is possible due to available, relevant genomes of the organisms we want to connect. As such, the older the genome, the better we can understand our past, to a degree. Even though we are missing the intermediate genera's genomes between us and our family's MRCA, we have the highest quality genomes from our living relatives, from living apes, albeit not the genomes from a 7,000,000-year-old vintage.

There is one more key concept to anchor the theorization of our speciation. We have to re-define the classical sense of species, or more accurately, we need a generalized version of it. More specifically, it is not the artificial definition that distinguishes one species from another. It is defined by the degree of accumulated genetic differences that stops one species from interbreeding with another.

This chapter's presentation starts with the macroscopic concepts of how speciation happens, leading to a revisit of the genetic definition of species based on molecular biological advances in the last 50 years. The second half details a plausible human speciation theory.

MACROSCOPIC SPECIATION SCENARIOS

A more classical definition of species is briefly described in chapter 4 to place ourselves in a conventional taxonomy for all animals. Mammals are the same species if they can successfully interbreed and produce offspring. We have used this as the basis for continuing to refine and confirm the taxonomy. It has also served as a more basic guideline than superficial trait similarities, which are not enough to guarantee the ability to interbreed—organisms may look very different yet still can interbreed. Of course, when genes and chromosomes are better understood, the concepts of species are then further modified to be organisms with the same number of chromosomes. The ability to interbreed needing the same number of chromosomes is as good a starting point for a discussion on speciation as any.

In terms of the classical species formation process, an existing species could evolve into another species if given a new environment and time. The environmental condition can simply change, or the species happens to move into a new territory. Either way, natural selection evolution and positive feedback are in operation for the adaptation that continuously changes the organisms. When the continuous changes become too different from the older species, a new species emerges.

There are a few scenarios in which speciation can happen on the macroscopic level. They are scenarios because they are, at best, theories that may not be provable since the time scale involved is beyond our experimentation. These scenarios are postulated to distinguish one mechanism from another. They are based on how single, uniform populations eventually become more than one, each with distinct traits, rendering interbreeding impossible. The beginning population could be allopatric (separately located), parapatric (side-by-side located), or sympatric (co-located). Since our interest is in human speciation, we will briefly describe each in general while focusing on its applicability to humans. At the end of each of the scenarios, we briefly discuss how well it works with human beings. We will also consider whether it is consistent with the microscopic genetic speciation processes, which we will introduce in the second half of the chapter.

ALLOPATRIC SPECIATION

By definition, the allo- prefix and -patric suffix already tells a story. Allo refers to different and patric location. Allopatric speciation arises from a population forced to divide and reside in separate areas due to geographic changes. In this scenario, the trigger for a new species' emergence could be a geographic separation, creating multiple populations of the same species. For example, a river that cuts into its banks can grow wider over time. Eventually, the river's course becomes a canyon separating the populations and interrupting any contact between them.

Over thousands of generations, random mutations and genetic differences by natural selection accumulate in each separate population until they are different enough to be considered distinct species, and they cannot crossbreed. Their reproductive isolation comes from genetic differences, differences in the mating process, or morphological differences. Such circumstances of isolation and divergence frequently happen in nature.

The chimps and bonobos' separation is a classic example of allopatric speciation through a widening Congo River, 1,500,000 years ago. Since then, they accumulated genotypic and phenotypic differences and may become two altogether different species a few million years from now. They are very different in appearance: whereas bonobos have a slender build, bright pink lips, and a black face, chimpanzees have a robust build, they have dark lips, and their face color changes with age. Appearance-wise, it is not clear they can crossbreed. If human beings had not intervened to put them together and encourage them to mate and produce offspring, they would still be reproductively isolated.

The debate of whether they are the same species continues as of today. Biologically speaking, they have the same 24 pairs of chromosomes; they can crossbreed, albeit not voluntarily, so they should be considered the same species. On the other hand, it may be interesting to contemplate whether they are, in fact, the same species if they continue to be separated geographically for another 10,000,000 years.

Could this mechanism be in operation when chimps and hominins started to diverge from each other? We do not know precisely where the population of our common ancestors lived 7,000,000 years ago and whether any natural barriers separated the population into two or more groups. There is no evidence anywhere coming close to the situation like that between chimps and bonobos. I am not convinced that this allopatric speciation scenario by itself is the operative speciation mechanism for humans and chimps.

PARAPATRIC SPECIATION

Parapatric speciation is a process initiated by populations located nearby but which occupy a broad geographic terrain. When two groups of the same species occur adjacent to one another, and there is continuous gene flow between them, speciation of one from the other might arise if one or both populations exist over an extensive geographic area. This situation can entail at least one part of the population being located remotely enough from another so that new traits and varieties can develop and adapt to local challenges.

Subsequently, a zone of overlap develops where new populations, now almost two species, continue to interbreed, even their phenotypes and genotypes are diverging. This scenario assumes that the same species' interbreeding changes slowly into hybridization between the two species; the overlapping regions would become hybrid zones. This assumption has an implicit recognition that species barriers are not insurmountable. Eventually, accumulated natural selection modifications and random mutations from either population grow to the point where it disrupts hybridization and gene flow. Afterward, one or both new species emerge and become geographically isolated or choose to stay away from the other species, further accentuating their morphological, genetic difference, and reproductive isolation.

Although we do not know where the population of human and chimp ancestors resided, it might have been a large enough area to allow for independent evolution in some corners. It seems reasonable that this could have happened to the common ancestors of humans and chimps.

There is still something not right if this is the mechanism behind humans and chimps parting ways eons ago. How did our common ancestors give rise to two species with different numbers of chromosomes, though they were most likely initially identical? A careful look into the respective chromosomes shows they might not be that different, after all. Human chromosome 2 might only be two chimp chromosomes fused end to end.

A split between humans and chimps is then possible if we blend this macroscopic scenario with a microscopic situation that an infrequent mutation caused the last chromosomal number change. There could be multiple individuals bearing the same mutation if the population is large enough. The hybrid zone gives the mutating species the chance to reproduce the new organisms with a unique number of chromosomes. This may be the final straw that eventually permanently separated humans and chimps. There may have been enough individuals with the same, new chromosomes who could successfully generate offspring generations after generations.

This speciation scenario seems the likely mechanism for humans and chimps.

SYMPATRIC SPECIATION

Sympatric speciation is the speciation process that happens inside an existing population. It occurs when ecological factors create more than one phenotype in a single population. No spatial separation of the parent species is involved. Each subpopulation moves genetically away from the other, perhaps due to limited resources, until two species have formed in place of the original one.

By itself, sympatric might not easily explain our split from chimps since the two groups with mildly different phenotypes lived in the same location. The crossbreeding must have happened often enough, leading to fast amorphization of the population's phenotypes. Probably the most apparent phenotypical differences were minor, like hair color or skin hues. For sympatric to work, it would necessitate that one group was distinct enough from the other, could not tolerate the sight of each other (different mating protocols, maybe), and physically moved away from the other group. Long time isolation from the original group afterward would result in speciation.

Such a scenario is not likely for complex organisms like humans and chimps if we subscribe to Darwin's gradualism. Each phenotypical change would have been minor inside a population with a constant gene flow, which may not have been enough to cause isolation in reproduction to break up a species to form a new one.

MACROSCOPIC SPECIES CONCEPT

Any of these empirical speciation scenarios assume a well-defined species in the beginning. Speciation also ends up with one or more different, new species, equally well defined. How does the new species differ from the parent species once they have disappeared? Can they still crossbreed, hypothetically? If they can, the speciation process is incomplete, according to the macroscopic species defini- tion. If they cannot, how does one characterize the organisms in tran- sitioning to a new species? Are they not a species themselves? At what point in the evolutionary process can we consider it a completed speciation process? Amid this confusion, what is becoming clear is that irrespective of any scenario, speciation does happen. It just does not conform to the traditional macroscopic view of species.

If the evolutionary principle in chapter 3 is true, evolution and speciation continue to happen in a continuum, and there is no break or pause for completed speciation and species. In that sense, one cannot define any organism strictly in the traditional species' frame- work since organisms are always in flux or transitioning from one species to another. A species might be a good starting point for speci- ation, and it might also be a suitable endpoint of the speciation process if such a thing exists, but more importantly, any organism thought to be in the speciation process has to be an equally well- defined species.

Irrespective of the confusion, the concept of macroscopic species has served us well and will continue to serve as a guideline to study animals close to one another. Following this, we revisit the concept of species from a few microscopic perspectives. Once it is clear that the definition of species is necessarily complex due to permeable bound- aries, it would be logical to introduce this study and the theory of speciation theory to which I alluded to earlier.

MICROSCOPIC SPECIES CONCEPT

THE BCS DEFINITION: REPRODUCTIVE ISOLATION

The empirical definition of species based on morphology, inter- breeding ability, and genetic compatibility (i.e., the same number of chromosomes) is similar to the concept of reproductive isolation proposed by Mayr and Dobzhansky in 1942. More specifically, Mayr defined that "species are groups of actually or potentially inter-breeding natural populations that are reproductively isolated from other such groups." This biological species concept (BSC) empha-sizes discontinuity and complete reproductive isolation and has driven the direction of genetic research through the late 1990s. At the core of this isolation concept, BSC necessarily requires that reproduc-tive isolation applies to the whole genome where the gene flow is not permitted. Microscopically, there are strict dividing lines between the genomes of different species, and no gene exchange can happen. Although the modern-day BSC concept is different from when Mayr invented the definition in the early days, it has a few problems that lead to the breakdown of BSC.

THE BREAKDOWN OF BSC

Darwin's Vision

The concept of BSC has served the academic world well, but it contradicts Darwin's idea of continuity between varieties and species. Darwin recognized that whatever the species, it has to allow for multiple species to originate from a single ancestral species. One of his most straightforward statements on species is in the summary at the end of *The Origin of Species*: "Hereafter we shall be compelled to acknowledge that the only distinction between species and well-marked varieties is, that the latter are known, or believed, to be connected at the present day by intermediate gradations, whereas species were formerly thus connected.' To paraphrase, Darwin believed that variety and species are just a matter of degree of repro-ductive isolation. As such, the isolation is not strict but a little slushy and sloppy in nature. In that sense, BSC does not acknowledge that divergence between lineages can persist in the face of gene flow. Even the modern version of BSC stands on shaky ground from the onset, vis-à-vis Darwin's vision.

Hybridization Facts

Throughout our thousands of years of farming, humans have intentionally crossbred and hybridized plants and animals to tailor crops and livestock for our benefit. We have scientifically studied the long-held practices of artificial hybridization and introgression over the last 50 years—hybridization is a fact of life in stark contrast to BCS's reproductive isolation rules.

Speciation Facts

BSC's isolation prohibits gene flow between species. The fact that it does not permit hybridization poses a glaring logical problem. In the face of 8,700,000 animal species on earth at the last count, all of which have come from the same common ancestor about one billion years ago, how did new species come about if no gene flow was permitted? If we accept the fact that speciation does happen, BSC must not be universally true. As far as we know, speciation is the norm, and BSC is, at best, a vision of the species in a tiny sliver of time.

SOFTENED SPECIES ISOLATION

If reproductive isolation is intrinsically incomplete, it is logically acceptable that genetic isolation varies along the genome. There have to be regions along the genome that show introgression from or to other human species. Indeed, this is the case based on studies in advanced molecular biology and anthropology. A case in point is the evident introgression of Neanderthal genetic variants in modern human genomes. In the sense of softened isolation, the gene flow is no longer strictly prohibited.

Species definition or concepts based on the old BCS is then, at best, a guideline to distinguish different species that are morphologically different and unable to interbreed. However, for closely related species, what matters is how they interact on microscopic genome levels. As a result, various degrees of isolation along the genome start to form the basis of a permeable species boundary concept.

SPECIES BOUNDARIES

Species are supposed to be the most fundamental biological unit, distinct from one another. Carolus Linnaeus devised categories for biological organisms specifically for this purpose. The discussion in this chapter so far has kept reminding us that interspecies gene flow and hybridization are possible. Is there a middle ground on this? Let us take a look at how strict the dividing lines between species are, or in more established terms, species boundaries.

Now that the boundaries of species are not strict, we can compare the genomes of different species region by region, gene by gene, or even atom by atom. In particular, there has been evidence that there are regions of the human genome that are potentially more amenable to hybridization and introgression. These regions have been prone to introgression for Neanderthal or Denisovan variants in the human genome. In essence, genomic boundaries are porous; they are not sacred lines that no genome can cross. Genomic boundaries are soft, leaky, and permeable.

DETERMINING HUMAN SPECIATION

The rest of this chapter will zoom in on the first split milestone of our phylogenetic tree in chapter 5 and how the published study resolved the speciation process based on genomes of ours and many of our other relatives, close and not so close. By looking at different parts of the gene flow, we see that some parts cross boundaries earlier than other parts; thus, they are older than other parts. Such a difference in the age of gene flow is the basis for determining when these introgression events—and subsequently, the speciation—happened.

We know the boundaries are permeable to allow hybridization and introgression. We also see that they do not stay permeable for eternity since the species continue to diverge further as time goes on until separate species emerge. In the end, hybridization becomes rarer as time rolls on, and eventually, it just stops, even though the genetic permeability has not dropped to zero. Our interest is, then, to determine the timing of this eventuality between humans and chimps.

It is important to note that there is no predetermined rate as to how fast this speciation happened. However, it does depend on the organisms' abundance, as discussed in chapter 3. The speciation pace will experience an additional push in the positive feedback evolution processes if the environment changes along with the humans. In the end, larger populations accelerate the eventuality of speciation. For the case of human and chimp speciation, it happened to take 4,000,000 to 5,000,000 years.

It is likely that the dividing lines—the genomic boundaries—and species boundaries between closely related species are fuzzy. Some of the genes in genomes might represent characteristics from other species and vice versa. Some genes in genomes might indicate an older ancestral line, whereas some may represent younger vintages. These differences enable scientists to track down the age of parts specifically coming from other species.

It has been a few million years since human speciation happened, and the details of what happened are necessarily complicated, unknown, and require a lot of statistically significant data and logical analyses. Under these premises, we should not be averse to any ideas of our speciation. The ideas may be simple, complicated, or even provocative, as long as they come from rigorous scientific discipline and it is consistent with the groundwork we have disseminated in this chapter.

Most physicists, including myself, would go for a simple, unified physical model for the universe. It would be nice if this speciation were as simple as possible, but it seems we are not getting our wish. Many factors are involved in the speciation process, so I do not expect it to be as simple as the gravity being describable by a simple equation. An out of the box, human speciation process is what I am going after. As far as this study is concerned, I am not aware of any research addressing the colossal subject of our speciation reaching, as I believe, a more plausible mechanism than the one I introduce here. Introducing this study would be a good wrap on the subject describing the most straightforward path to modern humans from a proto-human.

It is worth a quick introduction to the institute and team that performed this research. The research team consists mostly of scientists from the Broad Institute, a biomedical and genomic research center located in Cambridge, Massachusetts, United States. The Institute partners with the Massachusetts Institute of Technology, Harvard University, and the five Harvard teaching hospitals. In addition to this work, it has done important and innovative research on ancient human DNAs and pioneering that as an independent research area. Before getting started with this book, I contemplated doing some hardcore research at reputable institutes, of which Broad was one of my options.

For the original work and details, one can refer to the work published in June 2006 in *Nature* magazine entitled "Genetic evidence for complex speciation of humans and chimpanzees," led by David Reich and his team. The following is my interpretation of that work in a language that is as intuitive as possible without any biological prerequisite.

GENERAL PREMISE: VARYING DIVERGENCE ALONG GENOMES

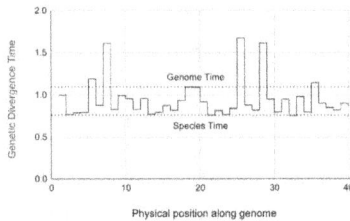

Figure 24. The genetic divergence along the human genome is recreated from the work by David Reich, et al. indicating the difference between species (youngest) time and genome (average) time.

The basic assumption of this work is the recognition that if you follow the genetic divergence of two closely related species—like humans and chimps—the genetic divergence in terms of mutation-induced SNPs between two species varies substantially across the genome. After converting the degree of divergence to time from standard molecular clock rates of genetic mutations, one can infer there are regions/genes that have diverged more than others along the genome. In other words, the larger the divergence, the older that part of the introgression. This divergence then conveys essential information about the timing and process of when that specific part of the genetic exchange happened.

Figure 24 is of the converted divergence times counting from the beginning of various parts along the genomes of humans and chimps. The Genome Time dashed line is the average divergence time between the two species if one ignores the variations. However, the species time—denoted as the dashed line of Species Time—indicates the most recent time when the two were together and had gene flow before parting ways. In other words, the speciation time is the age of the youngest part of genetic divergence between them.

As can be seen from the figure, genetic divergence time varies by as much as a factor of two, building in the complete speciation calendar's uncertainties by the same factor. Because of the variability of genomic divergence, there must have been phenotypes consistent with our morphological record. There could also be a genotype that corroborates the fossils' ages if we have the species' full genome. In essence, we may even be able to "see" physical, or phenotypic, evolution in action if we follow the specific genomic changes along our evolutionary journey.

This specific speciation study used genomes from humans, chimps, gorillas, orangutans, and macaques. They are almost the most diverse genomes available to us as Hominidae family members. In principle, this is an extension of studying modern human MRCA and TMRCA using as diverse a modern human genome as possible.

MASSIVE DATA AND COMPUTATION

The analysis includes comparisons of these genomes for 20,000,000 base pairs of aligned sequences from every species. This number of base pairs provides statistical significance to the proposed mechanisms. I can imagine why massive data collection and computation are needed. I recall my data analysis practice when I studied the fundamental atomic and molecular dynamics of a krypton and fluorine gas mixture. The gas mixture is the primary ingredient for lasers widely used in today's lithography in the semiconductor industry. I tried to fit the experimental data to a presumed physical process, describable using the fewest possible parameters and the most straightforward mathematical model, and I ran into a few technological limitations. The computational power and memory at the time were too limited to handle the massive data I collected. The limitations led to less robust statistical significance and needed more parameters to describe the physical process. I recall an interesting phrase that goes, "One can make a dog wag its tail if you give the modeling enough parameters," when the data is statistically insignificant or calculating power is insufficient. Luckily, we have overcome these limitations these days, with our computational power able to handle the calculations and massive data. With the full genome from our Hominidae family and modern supercomputers aided by artificial intelligence, it is possible to unravel the process of our speciation, giving it a plausible scenario.

Previous molecular genetic studies have focused on the average genetic difference between humans and chimpanzees. By contrast, this study exploits complete genome sequences to reveal the variation in evolutionary history across our genomes and those of our relatives in the Hominidae "family." In theory, by finding genomic regions "older" than others among family members, the time of a common ancestor between humans and chimp can be traced. This new study is the first to measure the changes of DNAs over time ranges of millions of years.

OBSERVATIONS

The time it takes from the beginning of speciation between humans and chimps to the completion of divergence ranges more than 4,000,000 years across different parts of the genome. This range is much more extensive than expected; however, if you consider the variability of genomic divergence around a nominal 7,000,000 years, this 4,000,000-year spread is not surprising.

The youngest divergent regions are unexpectedly recent, being no more than 6,300,000 years-old and probably as recent as 5,400,000 years-old. This finding implies that human-chimp speciation itself is far more recent than previously thought. We might want to revisit the 7,000,000-year speciation time from this study.

However, if one looks only at the X chromosome, it almost entirely falls at the lower end of the time frame. The average of the X chromosome's age is 1,200,000 years "younger" than the average across the 22 autosomal (non-sex) chromosomes.

A quick summary: this new estimate that humans and chimpanzees split less than 5,400,000 years-ago is more recent by 1,000,000 to 2,000,000 years than the previous estimate of 6,500,000 to 7,400,000 years. The older estimates are based on the Sahelanthropus hominin fossil, which has features distinctively different from the chimp lineage.

The speciation process was by no means straightforward, possibly involving an initial split followed by later hybridization before final separation. The speciation model looked complicated, but it has some logical reasoning supported by the original data. For example, one of the high levels of change regions may indicate population divergence at an earlier time. Still another part may show a slower pace with identified introgression from another species. Besides, it might be that there are a few independently evolved mutations—say, for hominins—followed by a merge of mutations from other species —say, chimps—that tells the possibility that they parted ways but got back together again.

GRAPHICAL SUMMARY

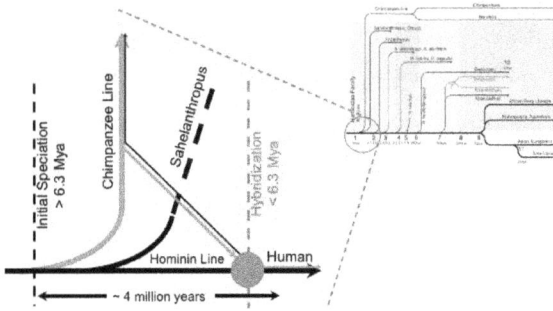

Figure 25. This figure, consistent with the conclusions from
David Reich, et al., summarizes the proposed speciation process
for humans and chimps.

Figure 25 summarizes the proposed speciation process for
humans based on this elaborate study, and for chimps for that matter.

Our common ancestors may consist of a reasonably large population, occupying a wide-open savanna somewhere in Africa. This
population may take up a large geographic region that necessitates
grouping at locations that may have different environments, initiating
the divergence in phenotypes and genotypes. This happened as early
as 8,000,000 to 9,000,000 years ago but earlier than 6,300,000 years,
indicated by the black vertical dashed line.

The hominin line also saw a spur that led to Sahelanthropus, of
which we found a piece of rare fossil evidence without any subsequent beings, indicating a short-lived lineage. The fact that there are
uncertainties about whether Sahelanthropus is along the hominin
line or the chimp line is immaterial (chapter 5) and not factored in
this human speciation model. Around 6,000,000 years ago, the
chimp line came back to interbreed with hominins, and some chimp
genes were absorbed in the hominin line. Similarly, some hominin
genes crossed over to chimps.

The whole speciation process, starting from the initial split to the
emergence of the true hominin line, took a total of 4,000,000 years. It
began 8,000,000 to 9,000,000 years ago and lasted till approximately
5,400,000 years ago.

This microscopic mechanism may lend some support to the parapatric speciation scenario. Our common ancestors must have a large population occupying a large area somewhere sub-Saharan. As the climate and geography changes, a part of the population may have adapted to the now more barren part of the territory, facilitating a more upright posture and bipedal motion to roam. Around 8,000,000 to 9,000,000 years ago, the more upright group began to separate from the other population, which still lived in the lush areas and dwelled in trees. The two groups shared a common area serving as a hybrid zone, allowing interbreeding and gene flow to occur, yet the genomes continue to drift apart. Around 6,000,000 years ago, some tree-dwellers got closer to the upright creatures in the hybrid zone despite their widening differences, but this introgression did not significantly alter the direction of the evolution of the upright creatures. Neither does hybridization significantly change the chimp line from tree-dwelling. Around 5,400,000 years ago, the two groups finally developed a difference rendering it difficult to interbreed, either due to the widening genetic and/or morphological gaps. One final mutation changed the number of chromosomes in one of the two species, making further hybridization even less likely, and the separation between chimps and humans was finally complete.

This graphic representation of the process of human speciation is the result of a bottom-up microscopic genetic analysis. Since there are no physical or macroscopic means to corroborate the mechanism, I believe this is as good and plausible a scenario as it gets for now.

Hybridization Is The Key

The possibility of "hybridization" between separating species— initial separation followed by hybridization and then final separation —could also explain the strange phenomenon seen on chromosome X at a young age. Interbreeding is known to place strong selective pressures on sex chromosomes, translating to a very young age for chromosome X. Thus, the young age of the chromosome serves as more evidence for hybridization.

"Hybridization" has been observed to play a role in the speciation of plants. Still, evolutionary biologists do not generally view it as viable for producing a new species in animals. In light of genetic evidence, hybridization is plausible, even the necessary step involving human/chimp speciation. It is the hybridization process allowed by the softened genomic boundaries that continues gene flow in the face of infrequent mutations. The combination of hybridization and mutation was the last straw to permanently separate humans and chimps.

Continued Refinement Of The Human Speciation Model

"A hybridization event between human and chimpanzee ancestors could help explain both the wide range of divergence times seen across our genomes, as well as the relatively similar X chromosomes," says David Reich, lead investigator. "That such evolutionary events have not been seen more often in animal species may simply be because we have not been looking hard for them."

As the researchers note, it should be possible to refine the timeline of speciation and test possible explanations based on further complete genome sequencing of gorillas and other primates, which is already underway at several centers, including the Broad Institute.

Debates

There are a few debates, as expected in these revolutionary approaches and conclusions, that have questioned the validity of this conclusion. For example, the research group did not consider other explanations for a short time for divergence on the X chromosome. These include natural selection on the X chromosome in the common ancestor of humans and chimpanzees, changes in the ratio of male-to-female mutation rates over time, and less extreme divergence with gene flow. The rebuttal from the Broad Institute group is solid enough that, at this time, I believe this version will stand until stronger evidence and arguments refute the current theory.

AMICABLE SEPARATION?

"It has been nice to be in a family. Now it is time to move on. Let's party"

Figure 26. The cartoon indicates one of the speciation scenarios and the relation between humans and chimps.

The complicated and twisted interaction between species necessitates massive mathematical analyses to untangle the details. It is fair to say that the speciation between humans and chimps is messy. It was not clear whether the separation was acrimonious or amicable, and we will never find out.

Maybe the image in Figure 26 can help summarize the speciation story as a wishful thinking. Of course, this is just the outcome we had hoped would have happened.

Figure 26. In case there is doubt that human and chimp hybridization actually happened, here is a picture proving how intimate human and chimp became.

HYBRIDIZATION EVIDENCE

In case there is still doubt that human and chimp hybridization actually happened at some point in our history, there is a photograph proving how intimate humans and chimps became (Figure 27), a prelude that could easily lead to hybridization. This incident happened in 1968 in movie theaters when Zira and Taylor got pretty close, but Zira might have hesitated because she considered Taylor "so damn ugly." Writing for movie scripts must be fun.

SUMMARY

Speciation is one of the last major lingering questions that has been gnawing at me for a long time. Although not as simple as I would like, I now feel comfortable that the current version of speciation stands on sound arguments. There should be more detailed studies, verification, and refinement in the future of this "big" subject.

The physical distinction between early hominins and chimps must not have been very apparent, or frequent hybridization episodes would not have happened. As time rolled on, the divergence became distinct to the point that we can now talk about features that are definitely human and not belonging to any other animals. We have also pushed our difference—or varieties—without getting close to species boundaries. This is the focus of the next chapter.

BIBLIOGRAPHY

1. "Genetic evidence for complex speciation of humans and chimpanzees," Nick Patterson, Daniel J. Richter, Sante Gnerre, Eric S. Lander, and David Reich, *Nature*, 441, 1103–1108(2006).
2. "*On the Origin of Species by Means of Natural Selection, or, the Preservation of Favoured Races in the Struggle for Life*", Darwin, Charles, Oct. 1, 1859.

12

COMMONALITIES AND VARIETIES

We finally became a species of our own 5,400,000 years ago, our evolution continued change us from our original form. We took on various newer features resulting from the random permutation of genetic codes, absorbing mutations, and enduring the environmental filtering imposed on us. Some of us were better suited than others and continued, whereas some were worse off and went extinct. We are not just different from chimps; we are very different from our early self too. We finally emerged with a new shape and form, having our species wide commonalities and varieties.

BECOMING A SPECIES OF OUR OWN

Numerous common characteristics set us apart from the chimps. These qualities exhibit themselves in both macroscopic morphologies and microscopic genotypes. Morphology-wise, it is evident that we and the chimps are incompatible in so many ways that interbreeding is unthinkable today. Genetically, we are also becoming more distinct because it has been a few million years since the last time there was gene flow between humans and chimps. These commonalities are the most prominent features that tell us apart from chimps, our closest biological relative.

While the commonalities tend to define us, we also vary widely among clusters within our population. These clusters share specific features that identify us as to where we are from, geographically, which tribes we belong to, and into which family we were born. These clusters may collectively handle some infectious diseases better than others. Some may have a skin color that manages body heat better, simply because the group has been adapting to the particular climate longer. All of these are consequences of our continued evolution after speciation.

As a widely varied subspecies, our genomes have not wandered off to the brink of a new species as of yet. In short, we have not seen reproductive isolation anywhere among the 7.8 billion individuals. This ability to interbreed is now both necessary and sufficient to characterize us as a species. We have continued to evolve and change according to the process of natural selection, punctuated by the rare occasions when mutations created variants seeping into our genomes. In effect, we have been evolving along together, solidifying us a species like none other. Our species boundaries are watertight without any danger of being contaminated or diluted by any other animals. Within our species, the current varieties continue to diminish because of our supercharged mobility. The varieties may even be disappearing, whereas collectively, we may evolve into something we cannot even imagine.

This chapter highlights commonalities and varieties from the perspectives of our past, ongoing, and projected future evolution. For species-wide commonalities, we try to include three aspects: (1) traits common to every one of us, (2) the evolution or history of how these traits came about, and (3) the consequences and impact of these traits on us. As for varieties borne out of local adaptations, we would like to make it evident that these are differentiated by very few mutations that happened in the recent past relative to our subspecies. The following list is definitely not exhaustive, but it does highlight the concept of commonalities we share and the varieties we generated in our recent past.

OUR COMMONALITIES

Our common traits include the physical and non-physical, and together they have brought us to the here and now. As for the non-physical attributes, we are the only species that can think. Thinking is the root of many queries: who we are, our mortality, our social positioning, interaction with fellow human beings, where we came from, where we will go from this point, our surroundings, our existence, speech and language expression and abstraction of our experience and feelings, as well as numerous other activities. We are also the only species that does not fear fire, but we respect its power and have harnessed it for our use.

On the physical side, we are the only species of mammals that has shed its fur and exposed its skin to nature but cover it with pelts, hides, and clothing for protection against harsh natural or human-made activities. These traits are a mix of physical and non-physical features. We are the only exclusive and obligate bipedal animals with dexterous hands to perform complicated tasks in coordination with our brains. We have also evolved an extraordinary organ of skin that sweats to prevent overheating and changes color hue to block out the harmful radiation from the sun. While these features are familiar to us, none of these exist in any other animals, including chimps, our blood relatives.

COGNITION AND INTELLIGENCE

Cognition and intelligence are the most deeply rooted traits, not only for how long we have had it at our disposal but also for its influence on humans. What are cognition and intelligence? In modern psychological terms, they are closely related but not the same.

Although they both are physical traits, they are not observable through morphology. Cognition is the basic level of mental activity or

the process of acquiring information and knowledge through observation, experience, sensing, and thinking. It is a mechanism used to
cope with our surroundings, be it the environment or other humans.
Intelligence, on the other hand, is the ability to acquire and apply
knowledge. In other words, it is the capacity of cognition for various
purposes for our collective survivability.

Emotion is an outgrowth of cognition that handles our innate
desires. In addition to managing the knowledge surrounding us, the
capacity to handle emotion is also a part of intelligence, albeit with
the pop cultural, catchy name of emotional intelligence (EI). This
generally refers to the usage, understanding, and regulation of one's
emotions and those of the social group.

There is a subtle interdependence between cognition and intelligence. Without cognitive ability, there is no intelligence since it is
built on cognitive ability. Without intelligence, one cannot perform
well cognitively. This close but subtle relationship was not distin-
guishable before modern psychology. For example, Rene Descartes
did not use different words for thinking and intelligence. He lumped
all of them into one word: "*cogito*." We treat these two as synonymous
for practical and convenient purposes and use them interchangeably
except when particular emphasis is warranted.

Trait Specifics

Cognitive traits include three levels in ascending complexity. At
its lowest level is knowledge acquisition and application, derived
from instinctual survival needs. This eventually gives rise to science,
technology, invention, and materialistic advancements. By the way, all
of these achievements have taken a few million years to get us to the
current state.

The second level deals with self-awareness and abstract thinking,
spawning the question of our existence as well as other, less tangible
activities although not with any less impact, like cave paintings,
poetry, drama, theater, music, and any other form of modern-day art.

The third level expands on the emotional aspect of cognition and
gives rise to empathy, sympathy, morality, ethics, rules, and organization. The pinnacle of this level results in large social structures with

complex hierarchies, for example, countries. There is no judgment made about the pros and cons of large structures at this point; it is merely a statement.

Evolution And History

Our understanding of cognition starts with the task of finding out when it began to take shape and have an impact on our lives. The beginning of human cognition may not be knowable, but it must have happened before we evolved into humans since we can observe a deep level of cognition in apes today. For example, some things relevant to human cognition—such as empathy, mourning, ritual, and the use of symbols and tools—are apparent in great apes, albeit in a much less sophisticated form than found in humans. Their cognition stays at the most primitive level as that of humans.

The second task lies in identifying cognition-related human behaviors along the evolutionary path. We have been able to infer much about ourselves through morphology, artifacts, culture, and genetics. The evolution of cognition can also be inferred from evidence left behind by our ancestors.

When did modern cognition take shape?

After we split from the chimps, human cognition took an evolutionary path along with physical divergence. It is assumed that cognition continues to improve in concert with the increase in brain size. Referring back to the discussion on brain size growth in chapter 7, we can infer that our cognitive abilities evolved synchronically with brain morphology. The evolution of brain size, thus the evolution of cognition, has taken a few leaps in the last 1,000,000 years, whereas the evolution of hands, feet, and body progressed in a plateauing trend. Had this accelerated improvement in intelligence or cognitive advancement outpaced our physical evolution? Do we continue to move further ahead of our slow morphological changes? This is a point worth pondering.

There has been speculation that our cognition and intelligence experienced a recent boost after hightailing it out of Africa some 60,000 to 80,000 years ago. These speculations are commonly known as the great leap forward in human intelligence or the intelligence explosion. The anthropological record yields rich evidence that humans have gone way beyond their ancestors in terms of technological sophistication. We have graduated from stone tools to bone tools, and these tools were specialized for a wide range of activities, from tanning skins (for clothing) to hammering. They were fishing, transporting colorful shells over great distances (probably due to their value as jewelry) for trade, and heating pigments to create different colored paints. They were also involved in burning areas near their homes to help desirable plants to flourish, burying their dead with personal items, and painting elaborate motifs on cave walls.

Emotional intelligence must have enabled us to pull large groups together. There is evidence that these new human behaviors included larger groups of humans living together in social groups. They acted within the confines of groups that were far more hierarchically organized than previous bands of hunter-gatherers. These more structured groups headed out of Africa into Eurasia, bringing their culture with them. Eventually, these revolutionaries absorbed or replaced other human populations like Neanderthals, Denisovans, and possibly others in Eurasia.

Are there any specific genes—more specifically, IQ genes—that we can identify as uniquely related to our cognitive abilities absent from our "lesser" ancestors and when? As we mentioned before, FOXP2 on chromosome 7 has a strong influence on our verbal ability, a significant part of cognition and intelligence. Humans have a modified FOXP2 gene associated with speech and language development. Previous genetic analyses suggested that Homo *sapiens'* FOXP2 gene became fixed in the population around 125,000 years ago. Some researchers believe certain Neanderthal discoveries indicate that this changed gene swept through the population over 260,000 years ago instead. Other researchers also offer alternative explanations for how the Homo *sapiens'* version of FOXP2 could have appeared in Neanderthals living 43,000 years ago.

Though these timeframes are wildly different from the great leap forward, they do not contradict it. Follow-up research cannot pin down the real intelligence explosion in terms of time or magnitude of genetic evidence. At this time, the great leap forward may be just speculation, at best.

Are there IQ genes?

There have been few but significant advances in search of the elusive IQ gene. Though the study's methodology may still be in its primitive stage, using literary survey results as data, a linkage has been discovered between human intelligence and 52 of our genes. They do not directly determine how smart we are per se; instead, they are related to the regulation of the growth of neurons. If we can compare these 52 deciding genes to those of our ancestors (i.e., Neanderthals or great apes), we may start to understand the history of cognitive evolution a little better.

The identified effect of the 52 genes on our intelligence is still small; thousands of genes are likely involved in determining human intelligence eventually. This complex association is certainly not a surprise since almost every facet of us has something to do with our intelligence. When the quality and quantity of intelligence are ill-defined and the potential number of genes involved uncertain, it is expected that the study would have to make use, at a minimum, genome-wide association study (GWAS), and something a lot more powerful, in the future.

Consequences And Impact

What has cognition and intelligence done for us, anyway? With our extraordinary cognitive abilities, we have transformed every aspect of our lives. We have become animals that specialize in learning, thinking, knowing, and analyzing. Our extraordinary power of intelligence has enabled us to do remarkable things.

We have transformed our eating habits with agriculture and cooking and our habitats with buildings, bridges, and roads. Compared to our chimp cousins, we travel over vast distances, moving our bodies in cars, planes, and space crafts. We move our minds to remote places with radio telescopes and tiny places with electron microscopes.

We are political and economic animals, negotiating agreements that affect millions of people and trade instantly in rarefied currencies with strangers in different time zones. We know about time; we understand it to some degree, and we can measure it precisely. We communicate with symbols spoken and written. Using language, we have developed extensive knowledge of our history and diversity and all aspects of the natural and physical world.

Our lives are enriched by a fabulous range of beautiful, intricate, and provocative objects through art, architecture, music, and dance. We engage in sports, elaborate rituals that channel and redirect impulses of aggression with the power wielded by large organizations.

Of course, one of the most interesting attributes of our cognition is that we continue to ask about ourselves, how we came to be, and where we are relative to other beings and times. Meanwhile, we contemplate where we are going in the future and may even control our evolution.

With our superior capacities of cognition and intelligence, I hope we take long and measured thought when utilizing our cognitive abilities to benefit our fellow Homo *sapiens* and our habitats.

FIRE USE

Trait Specifics

Fire use is a derived trait that owes its origin to human cognition, and just like cognition, it is not a physical feature. It is specifically human and not something that other animals use, not even chimps.

It is well-known that most animals are afraid of fire. Some of you may have had direct encounters with wolves while camping in the wild during your Boy Scout or Girl Scout years, but you must have been taught—or seen in the movies—that you can fend them off and keep them at bay using torches and fire. Fearing fire is an instinct seared into the wolves' genes after millions of years of painful experience with fire. Wildfires may have been ignited by lightning or inadvertent sparks in the bushes. Of course, the ignition owes its origins to electrostatic phenomena—either powerful lightning or sparks from hot and dry foliage—which is just a part of nature, as we now know, but wolves, and all mammals, for that matter, didn't know that, and the pain and fear was real to them.

As for human beings? Sure, fire can and will cause burned skin, pain, and dangerous situations that we sometimes cannot outrun. However, we have the cognitive ability to recognize that not all fires are bad for us. We are smart enough to discern situations in which fire may benefit us, but we respect it and realize its potential to cause a great deal of pain and damage. More importantly, we learn its properties and use its power to our advantage in a controlled manner. We acquired the skills to start a fire whenever we needed to use it, protect kindling, and start it by rubbing combustible materials furious enough.

We use fires to protect ourselves from predators. We cook food for consumption and build fire pits to maintain warmth. With fire, we can extend our activities way into the night. We groom our companions and delouse them by the fire pits, chat about successes or failures in the day's hunts or outings, exchange ideas about how our next day might be more successful, and where we should go next. We contemplate how we can best organize the members of our group for future activities by the fireside. Social activities and culture breed and grow.

Evolution and History

The earliest evidence of definitive fire control was by a member of the genus Homo in the range of 1,700,000 to 2,00,0000 years ago. Evidence for "microscopic traces of wood ash" for the controlled use of fire by Homo *erectus* beginning some 1,000,000 years ago has broad scholarly support. Flint blades burned in fires roughly 300,000 years ago were found near fossils of early modern humans in Morocco.

Fire was used regularly and systematically by early modern humans to heat-treat silcrete stone to increase its flake-ability for toolmaking approximately 164,000 years ago at the South African site of Pinnacle Point. Evidence of the widespread control of fire by anatomically modern humans dates to about 125,000 years back.

Consequences and Impact

Harnessing fire drastically benefited early hominins. It facilitated protection against potential external harm coming to them. Combined with better-equipped hunting practices and altered food sources, it indirectly changed our anatomy. Later on, food consumption, huddling around the campfire, social interaction, and organization eventually created human culture. We might go as far as recognizing us as "Creatures of Flame."

WE ARE FURLESS

Trait Specifics

Among primates, humans are unique in having nearly naked skin. Every other member of our extended family has a dense covering of fur, from the short, black pelage of the howler monkey to the flowing copper coat of the orangutan, as do most other mammals. Yes, we humans have hair on our heads and elsewhere, but compared to our closest living cousins, the chimps, we are as naked as having just been shaved in a barbershop.

Evolution and History

Why Did We Lose Our Fur?

Fur is a type of body covering unique to mammals. Indeed, it is a defining characteristic of the class: all mammals possess some fur or hair, and most of them have it in abundance. It provides insulation and protection against abrasion, moisture, damaging rays of sunlight, and potentially harmful parasites and microbes. It also works as camouflage to confuse predators, and its distinctive pattern allows members of the same species to recognize one another. Furthermore, most mammals can use their fur in a social display to indicate aggression or agitation. When a cat "raises its hackles" by involuntarily elevating the hairs on its neck and back, it is sending a clear signal to challengers to stay away.

Keeping Cool and Whiskey

When we descended from trees and started our lives on the open savanna with bipedalism, we lost the cozy, cool habitats of deep, fertile forestry in which other great apes continued to dwell. We started to wander long distances for food, resources, and other purposes. With our size and activity, we had to rid our bodies of excess heat generated by exertion. Having fur over our bodies did not help the cause.

How do we know this is the case? We are not the only naked mammals. A few of the largest terrestrial mammals—namely, elephants, rhinoceroses, and hippopotamuses—have also evolved naked skin. Keeping cool is a big problem, especially when these animals live in hot places and generate plenty of heat from prolonged walking or running. These animals must carefully regulate their core body temperatures—or thermoregulation—because their tissues and organs, specifically the brain, can be damaged by overheating. Fur-covered mammals forced to exercise energetically or for prolonged periods in the heat of the day may collapse from heat exhaustion. The larger an animal is, the harder it takes to rid its body of excess heat through body surfaces. How fast fur-shedding can happen as a result of this necessity is not clear. However, woolly mammoths, a close relative to Asian elephants, grew their fur for protection against cold climates, which was known to have happened since their separation from elephants about 7,600,000 years ago. This fur evolution could be measured on the same time scale.

We can understand this basic concept through simple math. One of my favorite drinks is whiskey, especially smaller cask whiskeys, which have deeper flavors than regular ones with similar aging. As the cask dimension is changed to half of the standard barrel, whiskey barrel volume is reduced to one-eighth, whereas the surface area of the barrel is only reduced to one-fourth. The barrel surface to whiskey ratio, a measure of how much the barrel flavor dissolves into the whiskey, increases relatively by a factor of two. The liquid whiskey interacts twice as much with the barrel surface, rendering a flavor twice as rich in the same period of aging. Of course, whiskey flavor is determined by a lot more other factors than just by this ratio.

The same logic applies to heat dissipation for animals. The larger the animal, the larger the heat generation in proportion to body volume, except their body surface areas cannot keep up. Something has to change to keep their bodies—or more importantly, their brains —cool, and shedding their fur seemed like a good idea.

In addition to the lack of fur, we have sweat glands to help manage our body heat. Since we also use sweating to remove heat from our bodies, it makes no sense to keep the fur to keep the water from evaporating. We will talk about the evolution of the sweat gland under the skin subject later.

When Did We Become Naked?

There is evidence that humans have been furless for at least 1,200,000 years and possibly as long as 3,000,000 to 4,000,000 years. By 1,200,000 years ago, all humans had acquired a version of the MC1R gene on chromosome 6, which influences the expression of color pigment in our skin. Like our ancestors, chimps and bonobos have dark fur, but colorless skin. With the loss of our fur, humans needed a new way to protect themselves from the harsh African sun, so the time we lost our hair must have preceded the change in skin color by some time.

To understand the evidence for the 3,000,000 to 4,000,000 year date, we have to look at lice. Humans are unique among primates for being exceptionally lousy: we have hair, body, and pubic lice, while other primates only have one louse species. Presumably, apes are covered with fur and hair, making their whole bodies habitats for lice, while humans are not, so pubic lice occupy a different niche than head and body lice.

Fur and body lice are closely related, and our lice are, in turn, related to the chimpanzee louse. The point at which our lice speciated from the common ancestor with the chimp louse corresponds to the time when we speciated from our common ancestors with the chimps. However, the human pubic louse's nearest relative is the gorilla louse. They diverged 3,000,000 to 4,000,000 years ago, long after the human/gorilla split. Humans likely picked up the gorilla louse from the environment, something that could only happen after losing most of our body hair, leaving only the pubic area as an oasis of hairiness ripe for colonization by foreign lice. They, in turn, evolved into a specific louse species exclusively living on humans. The 1,200,000 years ago and 3,000,000 to 4,000,000 year ago dates set the lower and upper bounds for when we lost our hair and fur. The genetics of human lice also tell us when we began to wear any kinds of clothes we took in the early days. We will dive into the details a little more when we cover the pioneering work by Stoneking et al., using lice to determine the age of another human feature.

We Are Not Entirely Naked After All

However we became naked, evolution left a few body parts covered. Any explanation of why humans lost their fur must also account for why we retain it in some places.

Hair in the armpits and groin probably serves to propagate pheromones and help keep these areas lubricated during locomotion.

Hair on the top of our heads was likely retained to help shield against excessive heat. This notion may sound contradictory but having dense hair on the crown creates a barrier layer of air between the sweating scalp and the hot surface of the hair on top. Thus, on a hot, sunny day, the hair absorbs the heat while the barrier layer of air remains cooler, allowing sweat on the scalp to evaporate into that layer of air. Tightly curled hair provides an optimum head covering in this regard because it increases the thickness of the space between the surface of the hair and scalp, allowing air to blow through.

Much remains to be discovered about the evolution of hair on the human head. Still, it is possible that tightly curled hair was the original condition in humans and that other hair types evolved as humans dispersed out of tropical Africa.

Consequences and Impact

Going furless was not merely a means to an end; it had profound consequences for subsequent phases of human evolution. The loss of most of our body hair and the gain of the ability to dissipate excess body heat through eccrine sweating helped to make possible the dramatic enlargement of our most temperature-sensitive organ: the brain. Whereas the australopithecines had a brain that was, on average, 600 ccs, not much larger than the size of a chimp brain, Homo *ergaster* had a brain much larger. Within a million years, the human brain swelled another 400 ccs to reach its current size. No doubt, other factors influenced the expansion of our gray matter, but the shedding of body hair was a critical step to becoming brainy, indeed. This naked creature was all set to grow its brain and increase cognition, initiate a positive feedback cycle for the evolution of our intelligence.

SWEATY AND COLORED SKIN ORGAN
Trait Specifics
Human beings are sweaty and colorful. Shedding human fur made sure the excess heat generated from within could escape without the insulation of our fur as a part of the process called thermoregulation. This radiation of body heat and convection of air around our bodies are heat management mechanisms. Another means of removing heat may have been sweating, which is equally efficient for two reasons. One, sweating carries away liquid at the same temperature as our bodies. Sweating is so efficient that we can remove more than ten liters of sweat every day. If the surrounding temperature is moderately lower than your body temperature, 100 calories of heat can be removed from your body in an hour. Second, once the sweat is out of your body, it evaporates in a little breeze. As such, the more sweat glands, the better the heat management. We have as many as ten times more sweat glands than our closest relative, the chimps.

Early hominins are believed to have had colorless skin covered with black fur, like the chimps. You can make a quick observation of your pet dog or cat by examining its skin color under the fur. You should not be surprised if their skin is pinkish in color. After we shed our fur, we were left with colorless, translucent, pink skin.

With the fur or hair gone, the skin became the last defense against the harsh tropical African sun beating on our bodies. Somehow, our skin developed a thin layer of pigmentation that helped block UV light. Skin color strikes a delicate balance by allowing enough sunlight to seep through and manufacturing enough of the vitamin D required by our bodies.

History and Evolution

When did this metamorphosis to sweaty and colorful skin happen? There is no fossil record of skin, but researchers do have some idea of when our ancestors started to engage in everyday activities. Studies have shown that an early member of the Homo genus, Homo *ergaster*, evolved to nearly the same body proportion as us by about 1,600,000 years ago. These body biomechanics are amenable for prolonged walking and running. Thus, the transition to naked skin and a sweating system must have accompanied this new way of life.

Another clue as to when hominins evolved naked skin has come from investigations into skin color genetics. It was shown by examining sequences of the human MC1R gene on chromosome 16, which is, among other genes, responsible for producing skin pigmentation, a specific gene variant always found in Africans with dark pigmentation, which originated as long as 1,200,000 years ago. The evolution of permanently darker skin was a requisite evolutionary follow-up to losing our sun-shielding body hair. This estimate provides a minimum age for the dawn of nakedness and colored skin.

It is reasonable to conclude that we went through this fur-shedding, sweat gland, and skin-coloring development from 1,600,000 to 1,200,000 years ago, based on both traditional anatomical analysis typical of anthropology methodology and more modern molecular anthropology.

CLOTHING OUR BODIES

Traits Specifics

Humans gradually lost their body hair starting around 1,600,000 years ago because it helped them survive in Africa's hot climates. Later on, with their advanced intelligence, they found that coverings over sensitive areas, such as reproductive organs, protected them from being injured due to exposure to the elements, scrapes, bruises, or the occasional melee with other animals or fellow human beings. This meager protection must not have been enough to satisfy their needs because we know they started putting on something heavier, covering more than just vital areas, based on more recent molecular anthropology studies. It is possible, yet not provable, that these extra coverings served other needs, most likely against colder climates. When we make full use of the knowledge of human migration and molecular anthropology, we might be able to tell a more complete "story of clothing."

Evolution and History

It would be ideal to find remnants of clothing to use in our dating techniques to determine their vintage. Unfortunately, we don't have that luxury because one, clothes would have decayed away like our flesh, and two, we have not been able to find any ancient clothing remains except for on Ötzi, a man dating to about 5,000 years ago.

Ötzi is the well-preserved natural mummy of a man who lived between 5,100 to 5,400 years ago. The mummy was found in 1991 in the Ötztal Alps—hence the nickname "Ötzi"—near the Austrian and Italian border. He is Europe's oldest known natural human mummy, and he has offered an unprecedented view of Chalcolithic (Copper Age) Europeans. That is interesting, but it does not answer the question of the beginning of clothing history. He was already fully-clothed with sophisticated cloth items from various locations, indicating extensive trading and craft smiths as early as 5,000 to 6,000 years ago all over Europe. The evolution of clothing was well established by that time.

With no hard, physical evidence of when we began clothing ourselves, we turn to genetics once more. We have to look for human lice again, which are symbiotic with humans. Thanks to Mark Stoneking, a geneticist at the Max Planck Institute in Leipzig, Germany, who came up with an ingenious way to determine the starting point for covering our bare skin. Recall that Stoneking is involved with the study by Cann et al., who got molecular anthropology rolling. Using a similar molecular clock concept on mtDNA, Stoneking was able to resolve our clothing history.

Human lice have three variations: head lice, body lice, and pubic lice. We have used the pubic lice to infer the beginning of us baring our skin based on the same principle. Both the head lice and body lice are parasites that lived on the hosts over a long evolution. They cannot survive more than 24 hours if they leave their hosts, which are humans. They are morphologically similar to each other, and as we found out, they are genetically close as well. Body and head lice likely split from each other when we started to cover ourselves with cloth. This relationship allows scientists to learn about evolutionary changes in the host based on changes in the parasite. The principle is simple—this study used mtDNA sequencing to calculate the time body lice began to diverge genetically from human head lice. The 2003 study estimated that humans began wearing clothes consistently about 107,000 years ago when hair and body lice became two distinct species. A later and more refined analysis using newer data and calculation methods better suited for the question has pointed to an earlier date for clothing: it is as old as 170,000 years.

This result shows that humans started wearing clothes well after they lost body hair. Based on genetic skin-coloration research, that time was about 1,600,000 years ago, meaning humans spent a considerable amount of time without body hair and clothing, except maybe for skimpy loincloths for rudimentary protection.

The last Ice Age occurred about 120,000 years ago, but the study's data suggests humans started wearing clothes in an earlier ice age, 170,000 years ago in Africa.

The Impact Of Clothing Ourselves

It is interesting to think that humans could survive in Africa for hundreds of thousands of years without clothing or body hair. It was not until they had clothing that modern humans moved out of Africa into other parts of the world.

These results soundly debunk a more recent clothing date, originating from frigid locations like Europe or Eurasia at high latitudes.

BIPEDALISM

We devoted much of our effort to bipedalism in terms of the why and what in chapter 7. Suffice it to say that the feature is an evolutionary outcome borne out of adapting to environmental changes through millions of years. In chapter 7, we attributed a part of bipedalism to receding forest lines, laying bare the open savanna grassland for which bipeds were better suited. The evolution of bipedalism is relatively gradual, and it started somewhere around 5,000,000 years ago and did not complete the transformation until Homo *erectus* began dominating the landscape. The gradual "big hole" movement implies slow bipedalism evolution.

Simply said, bipedalism is what moved us from the trees down to the wide-open terrain, allowing us to roam expansive ranges and migrate to significant portions of the earth as early as 2,000,000 years ago (see next chapter). Like any other trait that differentiates us from other animals, bipedalism works together with other human characteristics. It makes us who we are today, even though it took as long as 7,000,000 years to achieve this evolutionary task to now.

OPPOSABLE THUMBS
Trait Specifics
It is likely that the emergence of opposable thumbs and the shortening of fingers happened simultaneously. As was discussed in chapter 7, it took a long time—at least 2,000,000 years or 80,000 generations—from Ardipithecus to Homo *habilis*, who had thumbs similar to ours. It took another 2,500,000 years of evolution to get to our hands in the current form and shape. Our hands are dexterous, with the capability of using existing stones as tools, manufacturing new stone tools, expressing thoughts in art or even music, to the point at which we created writing, painting, and games, and doing each task with relative ease. Just imagine achieving all of that without opposable thumbs!
Evolution
Many animals have opposable thumbs, but ours are more opposable than any others. These characteristics seem to have co-evolved

with our tool use (starting with Homo *habilis*) and brain development (Homo *habilis* had about half our brain size, which is still more than any living apes besides us). The evolution of opposable thumbs is not a stand-alone feat. Other parts of the hand, like the shortened fingers, also evolved in coordination with thumbs into a form that lets us exercise our agility and gives us the ability to perform complicated and intricate tasks.

Scientists may have found the genetic root of opposable thumbs. A patch of DNA once regarded as "junk" may hold the key to upright walking and opposable thumbs. When this part of human DNA was spliced into the mice genome, it activated genes in their thumbs and big toes. Known as HACNS1 on chromosome 2, the sequence is positioned in a genomic stretch that had not been noticeable before. Many of these seemingly non-functional sequences have since been found to regulate gene activity and are a lot more functional.

After comparing human and chimp genomes, researchers noticed that HACNS1 had accumulated 16 variations since we split 7,000,000 years ago, an impressive number, given our nearly identical genomes. When these human genes are incorporated into mice genomes, their paws become a little more human-like. So, perhaps, HACNS1 is what allowed human beings to develop tools and civilization.

Let us hope the scientists didn't let any mutant mice escape! One of my car's electric wiring was chewed out by rats when I was on a month-long that cost more than $1,000 to fix. The genetically-altered mice might be able to jump-start the car and drive it away, given their opposable thumbs—who would want that?

CHIN
Trait Specifics
We all have chins. Whether strong, weak, angular, or square, we have them. Just to be clear, modern humans have prominent chins and Neanderthals, not so much. Those before archaic Homo *sapiens* had almost none. The question is why and what purpose they serve. There are a few hypotheses.

Sexual selection seems like an obvious answer since an attractive chin increases your chances at mating, but a feature needs a function before it can appear in the first place. Only then can it be assigned some aesthetic value. Chin aesthetics are another example of beauty in the eyes of the beholder and not determined by genes.

Evolution

The other, the better answer is that it is all about chewing. The jaw exerts enormous forces when it bites and chews—up to 70 pounds per square inch for the molars. Conscious clenching increases this figure, and people who grind their teeth in their sleep may exceed the average force tenfold. What's more, the jaw moves along more than just one axis, chewing both up and down and grinding from side to side. So, the thinking goes, chewing might increase bone mass in the same way physical exercise builds muscle mass. Bone mass, in turn, may produce the chin. However, the theory's problem is that it does not account for Neanderthals and other primates—including the great apes—which lack prominent chins. Still, they have far more powerful bites than we do, the massive brow ridge muscle notwithstanding. The theory that chins are better for chewing is out.

Consequences

So, why did we grow chins at all? The answer is that maybe we did not. Some suspect the face shrank away from behind the chin as primitive and pre-humans became modern humans, making the chins appear larger relative to everything else. It was not until we had our chins that we set about assigning value to strong, weak, angular, round, cleft, or dimpled ones, depending on your tastes. Those tastes and the mating choices that arise from them ensure that the chin is here to stay. It might be biomechanically useless, but you would look awfully silly without one.

OUR VARIETIES

After our split with the chimps, the evolutionary process continued to render our uniqueness even more unique with our common repertoire. Evolution has honed our commonalities to survive better, and at the same time, weeded out more than 30 other hominin species.

When Homo *sapiens sapiens* came along, our shape and form took on a semi-steady status (in the short time we have existed, about 200,000 years), setting the stage for our further evolution. Our population has grown considerably more massive and spread out to every corner of our diverse planet, where every new habitat may require a unique adaptation. As a result, evolution has spawned various local adaptations and created a variety of clusters that have better survivability for local environments. We have people better adapted to hotter or colder climates. We have people better adapted to higher altitude living, agricultural living, and nomad lifestyles.

Each of these adaptations may take a long time—at least a few hundred generations—and are initiated by a few mutations happening randomly irrespective of the environment. Diverse alleles may or may not express themselves in phenotypes until there are demonstrable advantages to prolong that particular lineage of people in the ever-changing environment. These advantageous mutations are inherited through generations to create a family, tribe, or geographic group sharing the same adaptation and features. The various groups sharing intragroup similarities are the varieties on which we will focus for the rest of this chapter.

Since these varieties represent minor tweaks to our genes and apparent features, they do not create any barriers to intermingling. They may cause seemingly drastic differences today, but they may not last very long due to our mobility and propensity for migrating from place to place. Because these varieties are relatively mild, there is no point in overemphasizing them except for a few of the more prominent ones.

SKIN COLOR

One of our most apparent varieties is our skin color. The shades of skin color, although natural, have created an artificial division within our species. This division has perpetuated the concept of race, which has incited animosity among us for thousands of years. As will become apparent again when this section is through, the concept of race is just a trifle difference caused by a few gene mutations. Artificially created boundaries between people with different shades of skin does not make scientific sense.

Researchers agree that our early australopithecine ancestors in Africa probably had colorless skin beneath hairy pelts. "If you shave a chimpanzee, its skin is light," or colorless, says evolutionary geneticist Sarah Tishkoff of the University of Pennsylvania, the lead author of a new study. "If you have body hair, you don't need dark skin to protect you from UV radiation."

Common Concepts Of Skin Color

Until recently, researchers assumed that after human ancestors had shed most of their body hair sometime around 1,600,000 years ago (see the previous section for the vintage of our naked body), they quickly evolved darker skin. The darker skin, then, functions as a protective shield against the effects of UV radiation. When humans migrated out of Africa and headed to the far north, they evolved lighter skin as an adaptation to limited sunlight.

Genetics And The Evolution Of Skin Color

There is no point in characterizing our skin color into different color groups. Our skin color is actually a continuum, from light to dark, from yellowish to reddish, practically running the whole gamut of color. From a genetic perspective, we can break them into three major groups—pale, light, and dark—identifiable with separate genes.

Pale Skin Gene: SLC24A5

According to recent research about skin color using genetic and molecular clock analyses, the notion of skin color, in general, is only partially true. A "depigmentation gene," called SLC24A5 on chromosome 15 linked to pale skin, swept through European populations over the past 6,000 years. Depigmentation represents skin that is void of most pigmentation rather than one color or another. The story of the evolution of skin color isn't so black and white after all, pun intended.

Interestingly, this gene is also frequently found in many people from Ethiopia, dating to 30,000 years ago. The two alleles of this gene (SNP ID: rs1426654) are ancestral, or the non-variant (G) allele predominates in African and East Asian populations (93–100%), whereas the derived (A) allele is almost a constant fixture in Europe in modern days. However, the fact that the ancestral (G) allele is virtually fixed not only in Africans but also in East Asians suggests that light skin at high latitudes evolved independently in East and West Eurasia. As such, the gene variant responsible for pale skin had a source a lot earlier and in locations other than Europe.

On the other hand, though many East Africans have this gene, they do not have white skin, probably because it is only one of several genes that decide skin color.

Light Skin Genes: HERC2 And OCA2

There are two variants on the second and third genes neighboring SLC24A5: HERC2 and OCA2 on chromosome 15, associated with light skin, eyes, and hair in Europeans that arose in Africa too; these variants are ancient and shared in the light-skinned San people. These two variants arose in Africa as early as 1,000,000 years ago and spread to later Europeans and Asians. It is likely the light skin gene variants in modern Europe have origins in Africa.

Dark Skin Gene: MFSD12

The fourth gene related to skin color is MFSD12. Two mutations that decrease the expression of this gene are present in high frequencies in people with the darkest skin. These variants appeared about 500,000 years ago, suggesting that human ancestors before that time may have had moderately dark skin rather than the deep black hue created by these mutations today.

These same two variants are common in Melanesians, Australian Aborigines, and some Indians. They may have inherited variants from ancient migrants from Africa who followed a "southern route" out of East Africa, along the southern coast of India to Melanesia and Australia. (We will detail our ancestors' migration story in the next chapter.) However, this idea counters other genetic studies last year that concluded that Australians, Melanesians, and Eurasians all descend from a single migration out of Africa. Alternatively, this great migration may have included people carrying variants for both light and dark skin, but the dark variants were later lost in Eurasians.

Summary Of Skin Color Genes

In sum, four genes control the skin color predominantly: MFSD12 on chromosome 19 and SLC24A5 and HERC2 and OCA2 on chromosome 15. Both light and dark pigmentation came from Africa from various periods in the past. Depigmentation variants are found in Africa/Asia and Europe.

These results add to established research undercutting old notions of race. You cannot use skin color to classify humans any more than you can use other complex traits like height, nose shape, or body construct. Tishkoff says, "There is so much diversity in Africans that there is no such thing as an African race." How true!

LACTOSE TOLERANCE

By now, we know that lactose tolerance is because of a mutated variant of the LCT gene located on the long arm of chromosome 2. We have already elaborated on the genetic reason for lactose in chapter 7. Briefly, this mutation is dated to about 10,000 years ago. People who can digest lactose are often from northwest Europe and some parts of Africa. On the one hand, we keep saying that evolution is slow; on the other hand, here is an example that evolution can be incredibly swift. In an evolutionary eye-blink of 10,000 years, 80% of Europeans became milk-drinkers; in some populations, the proportion is close to 100%. Everywhere else, lactose intolerance is the norm; around two-thirds of humans cannot drink milk in adulthood.

E

AR WAX AND BODY ODOR
Trait Specifics
About ten years ago, a friend of mine and his wife went to Kazakhstan to adopt two girls, six and seven. Being first-time parents, while helping the kids get ready for their baths, they grabbed a few Q-tips and prepared to clean their ears. They were surprised to see

that their daughters' ear wax was white/grey in color, dry, and crusty, drastically different from their own, which was yellowish and gooey. The Q-tips were useless. They had to use an earwax scraper to clean their daughters' ears instead. Obviously, there are at least two earwax types that we know of, one is dry, white, and crusty, and the other is wet, yellow, and gooey.

Evolution and History

As it turns out, the gene that controls earwax type is at the rs17822931 location on the ABCC11 gene on Chromosome 16. There are two alleles of the ABCC11, different only by one SNP, the wet type allele, A, and the dry type allele, G, where the dry type is a recessive order, and the wet type is a dominant order. This mutation happened about 40,000 years ago.

The wet and yellow earwax is found in Caucasians, whereas the dry and white ear wax is found in Asians. It is not surprising that my friends' daughters, being Asians, have different earwax than their parents.

The allele for dry earwax appears to have originated from a mutation in northeastern Asia about 2,000 generations or 50,000 years ago and spread outward because it was favored by natural selection for some reason. It is widespread in eastern Asia, becomes much less common in Europe, and is very rare in Africa.

Body odor is said to serve the function of spreading pheromones for various purposes, just like other animals. The ABCC11 gene is also partly responsible for this variety. However, phenotype-wise, there is not a direct correlation between wet earwax and body odor.

HAIR, BREAST, AND TEETH

In contemporary Western culture, the concept of beauty focuses on a few superficial physical features. First is the hair: thick or thin? Blond, black, raven, or brunette? Curly or straight? Then comes body measurements: facial structure, cheekbone prominence, height, and breast, waist, and hip sizes. Finally, the teeth: are they aligned in smooth curves or crooked?

At the root of these characteristics is a mutation identified as a single SNP on the EDAR (short for Ectodysplasin receptor EDARV370A) gene on our chromosome 2. This mutation is widespread in Eastern Asians found at location rs3827760, which occurred about 35,000 years ago.

The phenotype of this mutation includes all three of these traits: hair, breast, and teeth. This mutation favors smaller breasts, sharper incisor teeth, and thicker hair. It must have some advantages for its carriers because it is found in the majority of Asian people today. There is no obvious evolutionary advantage accompanying this mutation for any of these characteristics.

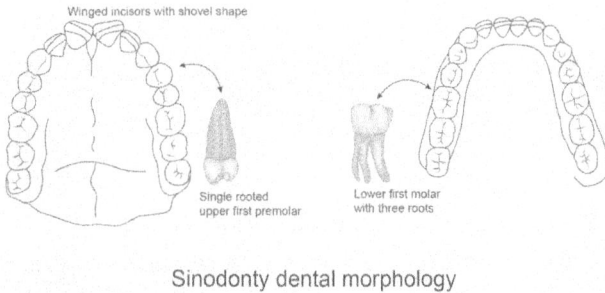

Figure 28. Shovel shaped incisors, crooked teeth alignment and different root structures in sinodonty discovered in East Asians and Native Americans.

As for teeth, these variant-carriers have a trait called sinodonty (Figure 28), characterized by shovel-shaped upper first and second incisors (a total of four). The backs of these teeth are shaped like shovels or spoons, as opposed to being flat like chisels. They are also "not aligned with the other teeth," thus the impression of having crooked or ugly teeth. This feature is a significant income source for orthodontists who make a good living from "correcting this problem" for youngsters about 13- to 15-years-old worldwide.

There is another not-so-obvious difference for these carriers when you drill down to the root of the upper first premolar and lower first molar (pun intended half-heartedly). The upper first premolars have one root for carriers as opposed to two roots in non-carriers.

The lower first molar has three roots for carriers as opposed to two in non-carriers. These traits are not visually apparent, meaning their parents do not have to deal with expensive orthodontics.

Incidentally, shovel-shaped dental characteristics and firmer roots are also present in Homo *erectus* specimens like Peking Man and Neanderthals. However, the morphology of these shoveled incisors is distinct from the modern human form of shovels. Neanderthal's anterior tooth morphology may be an adaptation to the heavy use of their canines and incisors in processing and chewing food and using their teeth for activities other than feeding.

The coincidence of these shovel teeth in modern humans and that of 40,000-year-old Neanderthals may have resulted from convergent evolution at work if it has evolutionary advantages. We have not yet identified any benefits, though.

EYE COLOR

There is evidence that as many as 16 different genes could be responsible for eye color in humans; however, the two primary genes associated with eye color variation are OCA2 and HERC2, both on Chromosome 15. We mentioned this genetic variation in the last section, and the eye color seems to correlate with skin color.

SUPER-ATHLETES

Some modern humans function well at high altitudes because of the difference of a single, mutated variant of EPAS1 on chromosome 2 that we inherited from our Denisovan relatives. Even though this variant did not originate in modern humans, people that can function in the mountains and those that cannot are the two varieties. Some modern humans picked up this variant from the Denisovans about 50,000 years ago, as discussed in the last chapter.

SUMMARY OF VARIETIES

There are other varieties among us. We may be in a group that is not allergic to poison oak through a mutation of CD1A, B, or C gene on chromosome 1, like Native Americans. Our tribe may have inherited some Denisovan variants and are relatively resistant to specific pathogens. The list goes on.

Common to all varieties generated within our subspecies are the surprisingly few genes responsible for physical features. Each of the varieties listed above takes less than ten genes to make the apparent difference; that is, ten out of 25,000 genes defining all of us, which is a small percentage of less than 0.04%. Our skin color difference is no more significant than our tolerance to lactose and a lot less significant than whether our earlobes are attached to our jawlines, where 50 genes are involved. Whatever the varieties of modern humans, we cannot escape the fact that we are the same subspecies with minimal genetic differences.

SUMMARY

NON-STOP EVOLUTION

Humans have had more than 5,000,000 years to evolve important body structures and mental capabilities. These features made us collectively more adaptable to our living environment and spawned a few differently equipped ancestor branches from the day we became our own species. Through the vast span of a few million years, many of our hominin ancestors went extinct along with many of our less adapted features. What remains are the commonalities we share, as listed in the first half of the chapter. These common features seem settled down for modern humans, coming onto the scene around 200,000 years ago.

The modern human subspecies continues its non-stop evolution, and we have generated a few varieties among us resulting from local adaptation. The pace of this variety of evolution seems to be so fast that we can almost witness the changes happening right before our eyes. Two reasons for the faster evolutionary pace are our unprecedented mobility and fecundity, or large population.

. . .

EVOLUTION NEVER TAKES A BREAK

Evolution is relentless. It does not discriminate whether evolving organisms are humans or not. We, a subspecies of Homo *sapiens sapiens*, will continue to evolve as long as we continue to survive and maintain our existence, whether we like it or not.

One of the evolutionary outcomes is relentless genotypical and phenotypical divergence. New species emerge when varieties push through species boundaries. However, human beings, or more specifically, our subspecies, do not fit that mold. If anything, our genes are becoming more uniform or narrow within our modern human subspecies.

First of all, we evolve fast, as we alluded to earlier, because we have mobility to which no other animals come even close. We rely on our feet, bipedalism, and other utilities; we also rely on what we have invented that nature, at least on earth, has not seen before. Our population is so big, and we get so close to one another through our mobility, which practically shortens the evolutionary positive feedback loop and quickly sharpens our uniqueness as a species.

We can almost watch our evolution happen in front of our eyes, albeit not in one or two lifetimes. We may have witnessed our evolution happening "almost" in real-time as a species. Most notable examples include our wisdom teeth, which have been disappearing; our body temperatures, which have been dropping steadily; and our bone density, which has become lighter, mostly since the rise of agriculture about 12,000 years ago. We have also accumulated genetic changes that made us more resistant to some infectious diseases.

As for the possibility of bumping against species boundaries, we may not see that happen at all. Today, it is unlikely that any macroscopic speciation scenarios—either allopatric, parapatric, or sympatric—would break us into a few new species. Quite the opposite, our fast feedback loop would diminish the varieties, making whole the species even more uniform from this point on. For example, our skin color has become so much more diverse that it runs the gamut, indeed. You would have to put 20 shades into one specific color, and we are not finished with that color diversification yet.

As a result, we are becoming an even more unique species as humans, drifting further and faster away from chimps. We continue to homogenize ourselves. The inevitability is that we will evolve together as a single species, or more appropriately, a single entity. We would all evolve as one in all aspects. Simultaneously, our accelerating evolution may change us into something we might not recognize or cannot imagine in, say, another 10,000 years, if we survive that long.

The first 12 chapters have attempted to connect macroscopic human traits with microscopic perspective through the microscopic evolutionary principle introduced in chapter 3. Under the same evolutionary umbrella, these chapters follow a logical analysis leading to how we became us, based on evidence, whether it is fossil or genetic. In essence, we have laid the broad foundation of molecular anthropology. We are well-equipped to drill down to more detail in any subject of biological human evolution if we so desire.

It is time to turn to another aspect of our being that is more macroscopic yet: the almost simultaneous, species-wide migration and evolution, resulting in our inhabiting the planet. That story, although macroscopic in nature, will be told with both macroscopic and microscopic analyses. The fact is that along with our million-year-long evolution, we managed to fill in all the space available to us on this planet. The question is, then, how did this massive humanity of 7.8 billion populate every corner of the land?

BIBLIOGRAPHY

1. I became aware of the origin of covering ourselves through a CARTA symposium in late 2015 when Stoneking made his lice mtDNA analysis presentation. That symposium is as close to professional conferences in molecular anthropology as I got. CARTA is a privately funded

organization privately and stands for Center for Academic Research and Training in Anthropogeny with a stated goal to "explore and explain the origin of the human phenomenon." It organizes free public symposia addressing particular aspects of human origins and uniqueness for professionals and amateurs alike. The panels usually feature recent relevant studies by scientists, eminent in their respective fields. Any person interested in the subject can attend personally or live and online for free. Considering the organization and symposia quality, I have donated time and funds to ensure its continuing effort and success.

2. "Microstratigraphic evidence of in situ fire in the Acheulean strata of Wonderwerk Cave, Northern Cape province, South Africa," Francesco Berna, Paul Goldberg, Liora Kolska Horwitz, James Brink, Sharon Holt, Marion Bamford, and Michael Chazan, *Proceedings of the National Academy of Sciences*, April 2, 2012

3. "Genetic Variation at the MC1R locus and the Time since Loss of Human Body Hair," AlanR. Rogers, David Iltis, and Stephen Wooding, *Current Anthropology*, **45**, 105-108 (2004).

4. "The evolution of human skin coloration," N. G. Jablonski and G. Chaplin, *Journal of Human Evolution*, **39**, 57–106 (2000).

5. "Origin of Clothing Lice Indicates Early Clothing Use by Anatomically Modern Humans in Africa," Melissa A. Toups, Andrew Kitchen, Jessica E. Light, and David L. Reed, *Molecular Biological Evolution*, **28**, 29–32 (2011).

6. "A common variation in EDAR is a genetic determinant of shovel-shaped incisors," Kimura R, Yamaguchi T, Takeda M, Kondo O, Toma T, Haneji K, Hanihara T, Matsukusa H, Kawamura S, Maki K, Osawa M, Ishida H, and Oota H, *American Journal of Human Genetics*, **85**, 528–35 (2009).

7. "Genome-wide association meta-analysis of 78,308 individuals identifies new loci and genes influencing

human intelligence," Suzanne Sniekers, Sven Stringer, Kyoko Watanabe, Philip R Jansen, Jonathan R I Coleman, Eva Krapohl, Erdogan Taskesen, Anke R Hammerschlag, Aysu Okbay, Delilah Zabaneh, Najaf Amin, Gerome Breen, David Cesarini, Christopher F Chabris, William G Iacono, M Arfan Ikram, Magnus Johannesson, Philipp Koellinger, James J Lee, Patrik K E Magnusson, Matt McGue, Mike B Miller, William E R Ollier, Antony Payton, Neil Pendleton, Robert Plomin, Cornelius A Rietveld, Henning Tiemeier, Cornelia M van Duijn & Danielle, *Posthuma Nature Genetics*, **49**, 1107-1112 (2017).

8. "Loci associated with skin pigmentation identified in African populations," Nicholas G. Crawford, Derek E. Kelly, Matthew E. B. Hansen, Marcia H. Beltrame, Shaohua Fan, Shanna L. Bowman, Ethan Jewett, Alessia Ranciaro, Simon Thompson, Yancy Lo, Susanne P. Pfeifer, Jeffrey D. Jensen, Michael C. Campbell, William Beggs, Farhad Hormozdiari, Sununguko Wata Mpoloka, Gaonyadiwe George Mokone, Thomas Nyambo, Dawit Wolde Meskel, Gurja Belay, Jake Haut, Harriet Rothschild, Leonard Zon, Yi Zhou, Michael A. Kovacs, Mai Xu, Tongwu Zhang, Kevin Bishop, Jason Sinclair, Cecilia Rivas, Eugene Elliot, Jiyeon Choi, Shengchao A. Li, Belynda Hicks, Shawn Burgess, Christian Abnet, Dawn E. Watkins-Chow, Elena Oceana, Yun S. Song, Eleazar Eskin, Kevin M. Brown, Michael S. Marks, Stacie K. Loftus, William J. Pavan, Meredith Yeager, Stephen Chanock, Sarah A. Tishkoff, *Science,* **358**, 867 (2017).

13

HUMAN MIGRATION AND DISPERSAL

I love natural landscapes and I frequently travel to places that are scarcely populated and rarely visited. I have been to the high mountains of the Andes, the deserts in the southwest United States, the oxygen-deprived Tibet, the Patagonian mountain ranges, the wide-open meadowland of Mongolia, and the ice-cold Canadian Rockies. There were stories about the artifacts and folklores at every spot, and ancient people had been there thousands of years before us. I marveled at that all of these locations had been home for many of our ancestors. They had taken residences in almost every possible habitable—and some even barely habitable—area in every corner of the planet. No other mammals have these wide-roaming ranges. One cannot help but wonder what it took for our ancestors to reach these locations from our homeland of Africa.

MIGRATION AND DISPERSAL

MIGRATION, DISPERSAL, AND PEOPLING

Both migration and dispersal refer to general biological processes. Migration is the process of biological organisms moving from location to location without establishing permanent residence for them and their offspring. The migrators may have definite destinations in mind, and the path of getting there is simply a means to an end for survival. Dispersal is when an organism's migration continues to new locations while leaving sites behind for themselves and their offspring. The former might happen when they look for better habitats, whereas in contrast, the latter describes the process for inhabitants to extend and expand their livelihoods and lineages using some locations as home bases. These activities were dictated by what the environment allows them, and it is hard to imagine that they were pre-planned and intentional, at least in the early days.

It is likely that humans migrated and dispersed by following games, climates, geological conditions, and other resources. The distinction between migration and dispersal may not be significant for humans since we do not have enough of a fossil record to tell the difference. It is also impossible to know the intentions of the hominin groups, whether it is to pass through or settle down. Whenever we locate or discover fossils and their artifacts, we assume our ancestors have migrated and lived there for a while and roamed within a certain range surrounding fossil sites. Since this movement is the primary focus of this chapter, any reference to migration includes dispersal from this point on and vice versa.

As far as I can remember, the word "people" was a noun from my grammar study in grade school. However, you may encounter the term "people" in public materials, referring to locations inhabited by a specific group of people (noun). In the context of human migration, early or recent, this word serves as a verb meaning that hominins have populated that location. It also includes its tenses when used as a verb. For example, you might read something like this: "The peopling of North America happened in the thirteenth millennium BCE." This gerund refers to the actions of migrating into North America, establishing it as home, and dispersing from there in the thirteenth millennium BCE.

THE WHERE, WHEN, HOW, AND WHO OF MIGRATION

We have been somewhat successful in finding our hominin ancestors' whereabouts and points in time through the fossils and artifacts they left behind—the "where" and "when" seem obvious. We have not been very successful at plotting out the paths they took to get where they were. This chapter attempts to connect this evidence in time and space to the routes they traversed, including the answer to "how" without digging too deep into the details.

In addition to following their breadcrumbs and litter, we would also like to know "who" they were at the various sites at which they were. More specifically, we would like to know what hominin types they were, thus linking to how they got there. In the end, it should help amend our phylogenetic tree described in chapter 5 with time and location attached to each of the milestones, if possible.

As for modern humans, molecular anthropology can provide a lot more details about "who" were migrating from one location to the next or how long they dwelled at the spot before moving on, through genetic identification.

A TALE OF TWO PEOPLE

Depending on the nature of migration evidence, it is convenient to break the story of migration into two parts based on ages of the hominins. The migration of hominins other than modern humans is predominantly based on fossils and artifacts, which constitutes the first stage of the massive human migration story. In this respect, we lump Homo *habilis*, Homo *erectus*, and archaic Homo *sapiens* together as early humans. The second stage is the migration stories of modern humans based on fossils, artifacts, and genetic evidence.

With our ability to obtain full genomes and mtDNA from modern humans, we can trace our migration paths with a high degree of granularity from father's side, mother's side, and the ancestral line in general. Molecular geneticists and traditional paleoanthropologists work together to map out the routes of various groups upon their departure from Africa. Modern man's migration story is now very lively and can almost relate to us on individual level.

HOW FAR HAVE WE MIGRATED?

EARLY HUMANS

Early hominin fossils and proximal evidence were discovered on major continents as early as 2,000,000 years ago. They were scattered all over Africa and the great Eurasia, in other words, the old world. Considering that our migrating ancestors, most likely Homo *erectus*, followed the game and other natural resources without the benefit of Google Maps, it must have taken a long time to migrate from Africa to as far as China around 2,000,000 years ago. It is difficult to fathom the expanse of time needed to achieve this feat from our vantage point, given our super-fast traveling capabilities with sailboats, steamboats, and airplanes.

How far away from home were early humans? We have evidence that they were in Java, Indonesia, which is 9,000 km away from home. They were Homo *erectus*—Java Man—and they were there around 850,000 years ago. An even earlier hominin fossil discovery pointed to 1,630,000 years ago living in Lantian, China. The distance they traversed is around 9,000 km, too.

The exact routes they took to get to their destinations are unclear. They might have gone through the horn of Africa, hugging the southern shore of Asia, taking advantage of the flat, fertile land before they turned north and east from South Asia. It is also equally possible that they traveled through a northern route through the Middle East and vast central Asia, eastbound. We know this because we pick up the breadcrumbs they left behind on both routes.

One of the most intriguing thoughts to contemplate was the mental status of these hominins as they uprooted an established dwelling, moved on, and established another. What were they thinking as they moved along a path, never before stomped on by any other humans? Just imagine we wandered into a new and expansive landscape while following the game. We may often be threatened by the predators and whatever nature and climate throws at us. Imagine, also, that they did not know whether they would survive the next day and what would come, yet they still decided to venture into the unknown for survival. Our ancestors were indeed very courageous and resourceful.

There is no viable estimate of how long it took them to migrate to their destinations from home. Still, it is safe to assume they migrated at a much slower pace than the generally accepted pace of ten kilometers per year from North America to South America by the Native Indians. Regardless, they were 9,000 km away from home where they settled; they must have started at least a few thousand years earlier.

MODERN HUMANS

As for modern humans, we migrated far and fast very early. The distance they covered is in the order of 40,000 km, an estimate from the middle of Africa to the southern tip of South America, at Tierra del Fuego Province, Argentina. That, by the way, is roughly the earth's full circumference. We also traveled as far as Australia, a distance of 25,000 km from home. We achieved that without the help of any vehicles, except for maybe some vessels across a limited span of water, and we would have soon run out of space to migrate, even if modern culture had not come along. Imagine if we started our trek about 75,000 years ago from Africa and completed that feat in less than 60,000 years!

The speed and range of modern-day migration and dispersal are even more astounding. We have run out of new space to migrate. We might have to explore beyond our world to continue migration and the search for more resources. In a speech given by Michel Mayor, Nobel Laureate in physics for 2019, he emphatically stated that there is no chance for human beings to migrate out to exoplanets after exhausting all the resources on this planet. He should know—he was awarded the Nobel Prize because of his work in discovering exoplanets, which numbers in the range of 4,000 and is increasing, with the closest being a few light-years from earth.

THE COMPLETE HUMAN MIGRATION STORY IN TWO MINUTES

Here is a two-minute summary of our global migration to set the stage for the more detailed stories to follow.

Early human migrations began approximately 2,000,000 years ago in the earliest wave of Homo *erectus'* "out of Africa" movement. There were humans reached as far as modern-day Indonesia and China. Archaic Home *sapiens*, including Homo *heidelbergensis* in Eurasia, who lived around 900,000 years ago, and the likely ancestor of both Neanderthals and Denisovans, picked up the out of Africa trail and reached middle Asia to the east and Spain to the west. These early Homo species were said to have crossed land bridges that were eventually immersed underwater. In the end, these archaic Homo *sapiens* did not survive, as far as we can tell.

Within Africa, Homo *sapiens sapiens*, the anatomically modern human (AMH), evolved into existence roughly 200,000 years ago. They started to migrate and disperse in and out of Africa almost as soon as they were born. Early modern human fossils were discovered in Israel and Greece, dated to 194,000-177,000 and 210,000 years old, respectively. These fossils seem to represent failed migration attempts by early modern humans, who were likely replaced by local Neanderthal populations.

The most significant modern human migration out of Africa happened around 70,000 years ago, although it may not have been a single massive migration. Some of these people migrated toward Oceania, hugging the south shores, the Southern Route, along the Indian Ocean, and finally reached Australia around 60,000 years ago. Some other modern humans turned northbound and spread across Eurasia about 45,000 years ago.

These migrating modern human populations interbred with local varieties of archaic Homo *sapiens*. As a result, some modern humans still have six percent of genetic contributions from regional varieties of these ancient humans.

Modern human migrations are dictated or limited by climate,

among other factors. The last glacial maximum (LGM) was the most recent time during the previous glacial period in which ice sheets were at their greatest extent, started about 26,000 years ago. Vast ice sheets covered much of North America, Northern Europe, and Asia and profoundly affected the earth's climate by causing drought, desertification, and a large drop in sea levels, which were believed to have been 145 meters below today's sea level.

After the LGM, northeastern Eurasian populations started to migrate to the Americas about 20,000 years ago. Modern humans populated northern Eurasia after 14,000 years ago. The Paleo-Eskimo expansion reached Arctic Canada and Greenland around 4,000 years ago. Finally, Polynesia was settled 2,000 years ago by the Austronesian expansion.

This summary, although brief, should give us a good starting point for more details.

EARLY HUMAN FOOTPRINTS

There is indisputable evidence that early humans, most likely Homo *erectus*, traveled far from Africa, reaching Northern China as early as 2,120,000 years ago. As far as we know, none of these people survive today. The latest survivors that are not modern humans might be Neanderthals in the farthest west of Europe. There is also evidence that these early humans migrated as far as Indonesia and survived as late as 50,000 years ago. With such vast periods, scarce fossils, and large territory over which they spread; a chronological account of the migrations might be the best we can do.

EARLIEST EMIGRANTS: HOMO ERECTUS AND HOMO HABILIS

We have not found any fossil evidence of any genus of Australopithecus outside of Africa. We can be reasonably sure that they did not venture out of Africa. There may not have been a long-range migration to speak of for them, except for their early dispersal inside Africa.

Between 2,000,000 and 2,500,000 years ago, our ancestors' home turf spread throughout East Africa to Southern Africa, but not yet to West Africa. Around 2,100,000 and 1,900,000 years ago, Homo *erectus*, and possibly Homo *habilis*, migrated out of Africa via the Levantine corridor to Eurasia. This migration may have been related to the Sahara Pump operation around 1,900,000 years ago when these areas were lush with abundant rainfall and food resources. The rainfall stopped around 1,800,000 years ago, making traversing the Levantine corridor and Horn of Africa more difficult. The migration to great Eurasia slowed significantly, giving a plausible proposal for the out of Africa fossils thinning between 1,700,000 until 500,000 years ago.

HOMO ERECTUS IN THE OLD WORLD

Homo *erectus* dispersed throughout most of the Old World, reaching as far as Southeast Asia. Their migration is tracked by following the Oldowan (of Olduvai Gorge) lithic industry, a primitive stone tool industry. By 1,300,000 years ago, their range extended as far north as the 40-degree latitude. This reference of location shows that, although born in Africa, these people had already adapted to colder weather.

The following lists the most notable sites according to their dated ages.

2,500,000 years ago at Longupo and 2,200,000 years ago at Renzidong, both in China. The evidence of human occupation at these two sites is relatively weak, and we will not dwell on them too much.

2,120,000 years ago at Shangchen in Northern China. The evidence of human presence consists mainly of stone tools. This dating is earlier than Dmanisi in Georgia by 300,000 years and the Yuanmou Man at Yunan, China by 420,000 years. It also predates the emergence of H. *erectus* in Africa, thought to have emerged around 1,900,000 years ago. As we know from our phylogenetic tree in chapter 5, the genus of Homo came into existence 2,000,000 years ago; it is also possible that they could be Homo *habilis* due to their age. There is no direct fossil evidence to determine this either way.

1,900,000 years ago : Riwat in Pakistan. This site of human artifacts was discovered in 1983. The artifacts consisted of flakes and cores made of quartzite. The pebble tools claimed to be 1,900,000 years old and were disputed because they were not found in their original context. The claims of the dating of the site are being continuously researched.

1,810,000 years ago: Dmanisi, Georgia, in the Caucasus. Dmanisi is a town and archaeological site in the Kvemo Kartli region of Georgia, approximately 93 km southwest of the nation's capital, Tbilisi, in the river valley of Mashavera. It was the earliest known evidence of hominins outside of Africa before 2018, when archaeologists discovered the site in Shangchen, China, dated to 2,100,000 years old (see above). A series of skulls that had diverse physical traits found at Dmanisi in the early 2010s led to the hypothesis that many separate species in the genus Homo were a single lineage.

1,700,000 years ago: Yuanmou, Yunnan Province, China. Archaeologists found human fossils and blackened mammal bones, dated to 1,700,000 years ago, indicating evidence of fire use by Homo *erectus*. However, it is not clear how much control they had over fire. The evidence refers to a member of the genus Homo whose remnants, two incisors, were discovered near Danawu Village in Yuanmou County in Yunnan, China. Later, stone artifacts, pieces of animal bones showing signs of human work, and ash from campfires also surfaced from the same site. These fossils are on display at the National Museum of China, Beijing.

1,630,000 years ago in Yunan, China: This 1,630,000 year-old skull was considered the oldest fossil of a Homo *erectus* ever found in northern Asia before the ages of the fossils from Yuanmou were confirmed.

1,500,000 years ago: Ubeidiya (in the general area of Levant countries which were frequented by our hominin ancestors), three kilometers south of Lake Tiberias in the Jordan Rift Valley, Israel, is an archaeological site of around 1,500,000 years ago, preserving traces of

one of the earliest migrations of Homo *erectus* out of Africa. The site
yielded hand axes of the Acheulean type, a hippopotamus femur
bone, and an immensely large pair of horns belonging to a species of
extinct bovid. Bovid is in the cattle family, Bovidae, and is a widespread group of mammals, including goats, sheep, gazelles,
antelopes, and goat-antelopes. The site was discovered in 1959 and
excavated between 1960 and 1974.

1,360,000 years ago: Nihewan Basin, Northern China. The site was
populated by H. *erectus* as early as 1,360,000 years ago based on stone
artifacts found in the region. This discovery site is about a few
hundred kilometers north of Zhoukoudian, where Davidson Black
and his team discovered Peking Man in the 1920s. The occupation of
the Nihewan site predated Peking Man by as much as 600,000 years.

1,270,000 years ago: The archaeological site of Xihoudu in Shanxi
Province is the earliest recorded use of fire by Homo *erectus*.

This widespread dispersal of Homo *erectus* prompted some speculation that they might have built rafts and sailed the ocean. This
speculation is also disputed and did not gain steam.

NATIVE ERECTUS CONTINUED TO DIVERSIFY AND DISPERSE

One million years after its dispersal, H. *erectus* diverged into a few
new species. They evolved continuously from their previous
morphology into forms with minor differences but did not go extinct
until a lot later. Late forms of Homo *erectus* are thought to have
survived until after about 500,000 to 143,000 years ago at the latest
with derived forms classified as H. *antecessor* in Europe around
800,000 years ago and Homo *heidelbergensis* in Africa around 900,000
years ago. In turn, Homo *heidelbergensis* spread across East Africa and
Eurasia 600,000 years ago when they gave rise to Neanderthals and
Denisovans, most likely in west Eurasia.

The original thinking of modern human multi-regionalism
evolved in each of these early populated regions and have been
thought possible due to independent evolution after Homo *erectus*

made Eurasia its permanent home. A genetic study has conclusively disproved the validity of multi-regionalism for modern humans, as discussed in chapter 9. However, by zooming out to include a few other Homo species, multi-regionalism is not that unthinkable.

ARCHAIC HOMO SAPIENS
Neanderthals
In 1856, a group of quarrymen discovered the remnants of a skeleton in the Neander Valley near Dusseldorf, Germany (hence the name), thus starting the quest for human evolution. Since that day in the Neander Valley, fossils of more than 400 Neanderthal individuals have been unearthed from a large swath of land in Eurasia.

We have theorized their emergence as most likely the descendants of Homo *heidelbergensis*, a type of Homo *erectus* in chapter 5. Exactly how they got to where they were, mostly in Europe, is unclear. Suffice it to say that they might have evolved locally sometime between 1,000,000 to 500,000 years ago. Based on their fossils and remnant discoveries, we know they covered a wide range, as shown in Figure 29 where we have shaded the possible range they roamed in light gray color.

Their territory covered a substantial part of modern-day Eurasia. They lived mostly in caves, where they are frequently found as far west as Spain and south of England. They lived as far south as Italy. They also roamed as far east as the Altai Mountain area in South Siberia. Other evidence suggests they even expanded as far north as the 50-degree latitude in Eurasia, a location close to the Arctic boundary. Genetic evidence also suggests the possibility they migrated back to northern Africa.

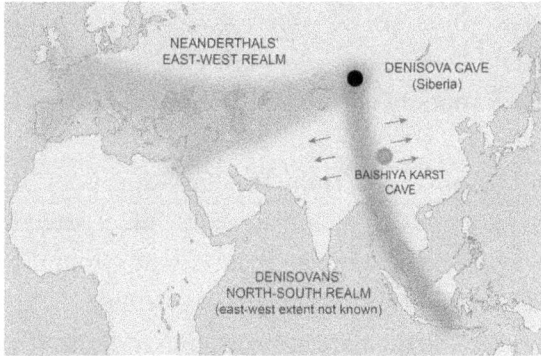

Figure 29. he roaming ranges of Neanderthals and Denisovans.
The black dot indicates the location of Denisova Cave and the
red dot the location of Baishiya Karst Cave.

There have been different estimates of their population through time. By using mtDNA analysis, studies yield varying effective populations, such as about 1,000 to 5,000, 5,000 to 9,000, or 3,000 to 25,000. It was postulated that they steadily increased until 52,000 years ago before declined into the eventual extinction. Reasonable assumptions for the total accumulated population should include a complete population turnover every 29 years, the accepted average life expectancy, their entire existence of 400,000 years, and an average population of 5,000. The number of individual Neanderthals would be 13,000 generations of 5,000 individuals totaling 65,000,000 of them ever born into the world. It is, therefore, not a surprise that we have found as many as 400 fossils attributable to Neanderthal individuals.

Denisovan And Others

Figure 29 also shows a band of light brown, indicating the possible Denisovan roaming range. Since there are few actual fossil records for Denisovans, we had to use genetic and other physical evidence to draw up the fuzzy shades, as shown.

One of the two most notable discovery sites is the area where the Denisovans were first identified in South Siberia. That part overlaps with the farthest eastern range of the Neanderthal habitat because both Denisovans and Neanderthals were discovered in the same cave, either at different times or at the same time. Further, a 50/50 hybrid of Neanderthals and Denisovans was confirmed in research published in 2019. The dark spot in Figure 29 indicates the location of the Denisova Cave.

The other Denisovan site is the Baishiya Karst Cave, shown as red spot in Figure 29, on the Tibetan Plateau in China, dated to about 160,000 years ago. The light brown band extends from the Denisova Cave, across Tibet, and continues to Southeast Asia.

The light-brown shaded area that extends as far south as modern-day Indonesia is based on genetic evidence that Australian Aborigines carry four to five percent Denisovan genes. Until we have further physical evidence, we will not know how they migrated from Middle East, or from where they evolved, all the way to Indonesia. There has even been speculation that Denisovans crossed the Wallace Line, but this is, at best, a suggestion at this time. There has also been some genetic evidence that Denisovan genes have been found in South Americans. The Denisovan mystery seems to continue.

Other archaic human species are assumed to have dispersed throughout Africa, although the fossil record is sparse. Their presence is only postulated based on traces of genetic admixture with early modern humans found in the genome of African populations.

Homo *naledi*, discovered in South Africa in 2013 and dated to about 250,000 to 350,000 years ago, may represent fossil evidence of such an archaic human species. However, the skeleton resembled fossil specimens roughly 2,000,000-years-old. Homo *helmeis* is another possible archaic Homo *sapiens*, as will be mentioned later in its proper context. They were contemporary with Neanderthals or Denisovans but are not considered descendants of the direct lineage line on our phylogenetic chart or archaic Homo *sapiens*. At least for now, the exclusion of H. naledi and H. helmeis from archaic Homo groups is because there has not been enough of a genetic connection between them and other archaic Homo *sapiens*.

Neanderthals spread across the middle part of Eurasia, while Denisovans appear to have spread across Central, East Asia, Southeast Asia, and Oceania. There is clear and compelling evidence that

Denisovans interbred with Neanderthals in Central Asia, where their habitats overlapped, as we discussed thoroughly in chapter 10.

MODERN HUMAN MIGRATION

A LITTLE BIT ACADEMY, A LITTLE BIT POPULAR SCIENCE

For ease of following the storyline about modern human migration ahead, a rudimentary familiarity of haplogroups may come in handy. These terms, originating with academics, of course, are now becoming a part of our everyday, popular science language. Consumer genetic companies like *23andme* and *Ancestry* inform their clients, based on DNA analysis, of their maternal and paternal ancestry in the form of haplogroups. They are used for easier tracing of origins (i.e., "where did we come from"), not only in terms of the original location but also the likely routes taken to get to where we are now. Further, haplogroup information enables the determination of ancestry from our fathers and mothers and how and when they came together.

Haplogroups are becoming a subject of popular science and had seeped effortlessly into fiction. According to the original writer's official website (https://stieglarssonofficial.tumblr.com), The *Girl with the Dragon Tattoo* series is on the *New York Times*' bestseller list for a few years, boasting 90,000,000 copies sold worldwide. Some of you might be familiar with this series, which was the source for a few blockbuster movies, both in Swedish and in English. The sixth installment of the ongoing saga of Lisbeth Salander, the girl, deals with a murder victim who is identified through his mtDNA haplogroup of C4a3b1. The victim's homeland is narrowed down to South Asia by the C4 mtDNA haplogroup designation. The victim's nuclear DNA also carries the EPAS1 variant, known to have come from the Denisovans. The EPAS1 variant in the victim further narrows the victim down to a small village of Sherpa people from Nepal, who are known to share that variant from the Denisovans (See chapter 10 for details). Finally, the murder victim is identified by immediate family members. So, the mtDNA haplogroup is the first step in identifying the region, nuclear

DNA the second for the ethnic group, and finally, a family tree for the specific victim. The academic term of haplogroups, together with the EPAS1 gene, has become a part of everyday language and popular science, so they deserve a little more of an in-depth treatment than how Lisbeth Salander used them to find the murder victim.

HAPLOGROUPS

A haplogroup is a genetic population group of people who share a common genetic ancestor on either the father's side or the mother's side. Haplogroups are designated by letters with refinements consisting of additional numbers and letter-number combinations. *Haplo*, by definition, refers to the singular, and in the genetic sense, a single side of your genetic source. mtDNA is haplo since it carries genetic information from the mothers. The Y-DNA, or more precisely Y chromosome, has genetic information from the father's side, and thus, it is haplo, too. The non-haplogroups are diplo groups, meaning coming from both of your parents. For non-haplogroups, the lineage and genetic family tree are a lot more complicated, and the information derived from them is jumbled together and hard to decipher. However, with modern-day calculation power, algorithms, and artificial intelligence, there have been efforts moving in that general direction.

In general, when a group of organisms stays in one location for some time, it develops local specialties to adapt to the local environment through natural selection and mutation, as was discussed in chapter 9. Mutations to haplogroups happen at a rate that is known. Deviations caused by mutation from the original genes can be used as a basis for family trees with calibrated time at branching points. The locations where this branching happens are inferred from the fossil evidence for older ages and genetic evidence from participating geographic groups. As a result, we are now able to draw actual migration maps with associated haplogroup IDs and dates. Sounds simple, right?

mtDNA Haplogroups And Haplogroup Migration Map

In human genetics, a human mitochondrial DNA haplogroup is a haplogroup defined by its particular characteristics. Haplogroup IDs can be used to determine major branching points on the mitochondrial phylogenetic tree. The letter names of haplogroups (not just mitochondrial DNA haplogroups) run from A to Z. As haplogroups are designated in the order of their discoveries, the alphabetical ordering does not have any meaning in terms of actual genetic relationships.

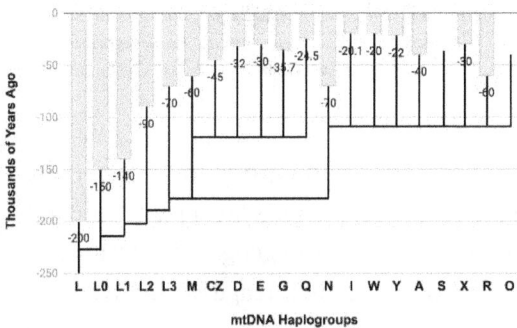

Figure 30. mtDNA haplogroups with more details added to Figure 17.

In essence, the mtDNA phylogeny tree, Figure 30, is the same as the mtDNA phylogeny tree in chapter 9 except we carry the subgroups in more details and to more recent past. Since I like pictorial illustration, this figure collects various published data and summarizes in one graph for convenience and clarity. In fact, the corresponding phylogenetic tree for Y-DNA (figure 32) is put together in the same fashion. The hypothetical woman, mtDNA Eve, at the root of all these groups (meaning the mitochondrial DNA haplogroups), is the matrilineal, most recent, common ancestor (MRCA) for all currently living humans. She is the original L haplogroup carrier sitting at the root of the mtDNA haplogroup phylogenetic tree. The victim in the Lisbeth Salander saga carries the mtDNA haplogroup of C, which is a descendant of M splitting off about 45,000 years ago, as shown in Figure 31.

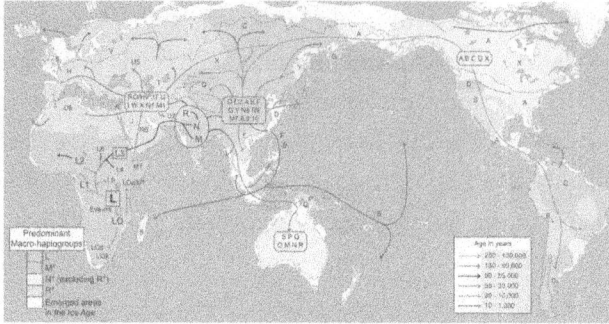

*Figure 31. mtDNA haplogroup migration map. Image from
Wikipedia by Maulucioni, CC BY 3.0: Background color by
ChrisKelly, https://creativecommons.org/licenses/by-
sa/3.0/legalcode*

Figure 31 is the mtDNA haplogroup migration map. The mtDNA
haplogroup ages and branch points are a result of combining
multiple studies on mtDNA from geographic groups. The timelines
are established by counting the lineage of single nucleotide polymorphism (SNP) mutations. A recent study has obtained a reasonably
precise number of one mutation per 8,000 years in the mtDNA of a
serial line.

The branching timelines are established by back counting the
number of SNP mutations at this serial mutation rate. If you are
informed of your mtDNA haplogroup from *23andme*, you should be
able to trace out your matrilinear ancestors' migration path from this
figure. This mtDNA haplogroup migration map also indicates that
the victim in the Lisbeth Salander stories comes from South Asia,
somewhere in India's northwest regions.

Y-DNA Haplogroups and Haplogroup Migration Map

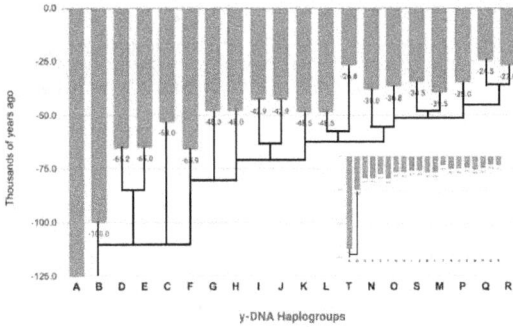

Figure 32. Y-DNA haplogroups using various sources.

In human genetics, a human Y-DNA haplogroup is defined by mutations in the non-recombining portions of DNA from the Y chromosome (called Y-DNA). Figure 32 is the paternal haplogroup, Y-DNA, phylogenetic tree constructed similarly to that of the mtDNA haplogroup. It is more complicated than mtDNA unless you focus only on the part of the chromosome with the most meaningful mutation. This phylogenetic tree is established by YCC, The Y Chromosome Consortium, a scholarship group involved in a collaborative effort to study genetic variation of the human non-recombinant region on the human Y-chromosome.

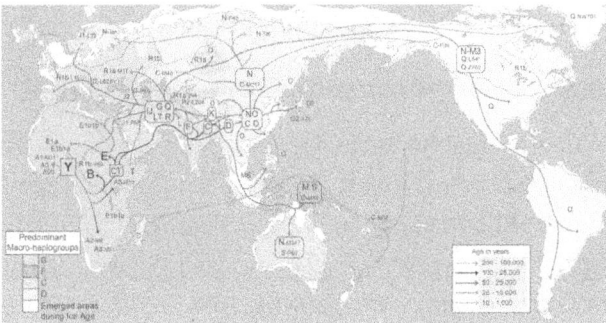

Figure 33. The Yy-DNA haplogroup migration map, Figure 33, shown here is also similarly constructed to , like the mtDNA haplogroup migration map. Image from Wikipedia by Maulucioni, CC BY 3.0
https://creativecommons.org/licenses/by/3.0

The Y-DNA haplogroup migration map, Figure 33, shown here is similarly constructed to the mtDNA haplogroup migration map. There are rough estimates of where various branching happened at specific times and locations from the mtDNA and Y-DNA maps. In principle, I could include more precise locations and times for each of the bars on the mtDNA and Y-chromosome phylogenetic trees; they are widely scattered in popular science and academic literature. I will leave that to the readers who know to which respective haplogroups they belong and who are interested enough to trace their ancestral lines.

Personal Haplogroups And Ancestry

If you happen to work with either *23andme* or *Ancestry*, you may already know where you are with haplogroup identification and your ancestors' migration paths. For example, my maternal haplogroup is M7b1 (this sub-haplogroup is two levels below M and not shown in Figure 31), which started 13,500 years ago descended from M7, which, in turn, began 45,000 years ago, descended from M. Haplogroup M, in turn, descended from L3 50,000 years ago, which started 65,000 years ago, descended from L, 200,000 years ago. Of course, L is the original mtDNA haplogroup of mtDNA Eve. So, Eve is my great-, great-, ...great-grandmother. As for my maternal ancestors' migration, all we have to do is to follow the haplogroup migration map, and voila! you know exactly how your mother's ancestors traveled over the past 200,000 years.

My paternal haplogroup is O-P164 descended from O-M122, descended from O-M-1359, started about 36,000 years ago. The ancestor of O descended from K-M9 about 48,000 years ago. K is descended from FM-89 66,000 years ago. Finally, F is directly from A haplogroup, which started 275,000 years ago. My great-, great-, ...-great-grandfather, Adam, is 275,000 years old. Similarly, if I wanted to trace my paternal ancestor's migration path, the haplogroup map can tell me what I need to know.

How could my Adam and Eve grandfather and grandmother have lived about 100,000 years apart? This is a problem that is not lost on academic experts. A recent work in 2013 dated the age of Adam with proper sampling to be around 180,000 to 200,000 years ago. Now, we are in the ballpark. However, there is no fundamental reason that Adam and Eve have to be the same age. It is just common sense that they would be about the same age.

By putting all available information together and drilling down to the youngest haplogroups, I have traced both my paternal and maternal lineages to about 13,000 years ago. I know, for a fact, that the paternal side of family genealogy extends back to 3,000 years ago. There is a 10,000-year gap that I cannot account for in the whole "where did we come from" story. It seems unlikely that this gap is bridgeable without intermediate genetic and historical evidence, but this is a lot more information than I expected even a few years ago.

In theory, if you are equipped with these two haplogroup migration maps and the two haplogroup phylogenetic trees, you can find out where you and your parents came from and the routes they took while moving to their current locations. You may just be one of the very few of us who know the answer to the question of "where did we come from?"!

This brief introduction to haplogroups serves as a reference for the descriptive narration of modern human migration to follow. You can refer back to these two haplogroup phylogenetic trees and migration maps to confirm your understanding.

THE THREE MODERN HUMAN MIGRATION ENDEAVORS

For this part of the modern human migration story, I leverage the accumulated knowledge about human migration from *Wikipedia* as a reference. I will also make connections between that and what we know of the haplogroup's phylogeny trees and the migration maps introduced above whenever possible.

Our migration narrative is organized into three endeavors out of Africa for easy tracking and completeness. The first endeavor features the modern human population radiating from a central location and spreading to most of Africa. The second endeavor is a continuation of the first, when they found a causeway and moved out of Africa in what we consider the first wave of migration. This wave may have been through the Middle East, but it seemed to fizzle out.

The third endeavor is the second major migration wave out of Africa. These modern humans successfully populated South Asia, and subsequently, Australia. Part of the convoy turned north for other parts of Asia and northwest for Europe. Eventually, they dispersed all over Eurasia, followed by settlements into the Americas. The first two endeavors are relatively straightforward. The third results in us finally populating the globe and requires a more detailed discussion. Our migration story follows the following outline:

Intra-Africa, from 200,000 years ago

1. North Africa: Morocco
2. Sub-Sahara
3. South Africa
4. Central Africa
5. West Africa

First Wave Out of Africa

1. The first wave starting from 180,000 years ago
2. Early Northern Africa migration went far but did not leave long-lasting genetic evidence outside of Africa
3. First wavers may have met Neanderthals and came back to Africa

Second Wave Out of Africa from 75,000 years ago up to LGM

1. Coastal migration toward Australia
2. Dispersal through Eurasia
3. Northwest-bound to Europe
4. East and North Asia

After LGM: 20,000 years ago, through Holocene

1. Eurasia
2. Americas

Holocene Migrations from 12,000 years ago and onward

1. Eurasia
2. Sub-Saharan Africa
3. Pacific
4. Caribbean
5. Arctic

INTRA AFRICA

MOROCCO, NORTH AFRICA

Modern humans emerged about 200,000 years ago, an established general consensus for now. Recall that this number has intrinsic uncertainties bracketing the number 200,000 due to inherent uncertainties in mtDNA mutation rates. Here is one case that I believe indicates that modern-day molecular anthropology is not entirely immune to controversy and arguments.

The 2017 discoveries of human artifacts and five specimens from Jebel Irhoud, Morocco, have been attributed to modern human, dated 300,000 years ago. This discovery in Morocco throws a monkey wrench in the story of modern humans. Can the age of 200,000 years for mtDNA Eve be wrong by 100,000 years? A more careful study of the cranial shape of the remains from the same fossils leads to a different conclusion. Although the skulls' faces are delicate and modern, the cranial structures indicate more elongated skulls, akin to earlier hominins. They might not be Homo *sapiens sapiens*, after all. The 200,000-year-old age for mtDNA Eve is still the current understanding, at least, for the time being.

The Moroccan discovery implies that hominins in Africa are wider-spread than expected, and we have more relatives in Africa than we thought. Previous beliefs that East Africa is the "Garden of Eden" need to expand to include the whole of Africa.

There are more similar discoveries in other parts of Africa from recent years that have been in the range of 200,000 years, further supporting original mtDNA findings. The Omo remains, excavated between 1967 and 1974 in Ethiopia and dated 200,000 years old, were initially thought to be the oldest known fossils of anatomically modern humans in Africa. It looks like they still are.

SUB-SAHARA

Early modern humans quickly expanded to Central, Western, and Southern Africa from the time of their emergence. They also expanded to a part of Eurasia but appeared not to have persisted. However, expansions into Southern and Central Africa resulted in the most ancient divergence of living human populations, as one would reasonably assume. Early modern human migration in sub-Saharan Africa might have contributed to the demise of late Acheulean industries about 130,000 years ago. Acheulean, from the French *acheuléen* after the type-site of Saint-Acheul, is an archaeological industry of stone tool manufacture, characterized by distinctive oval and pear-shaped "hand-axes" associated with Homo *erectus* and derived species, such as Homo *heidelbergensis*. Early modern humans either absorbed Homo *heidelbergensis* or caused their demise.

SOUTH AFRICA

The ancestors of the modern Khoisan expanded into South Africa before 150,000 years ago. This group carries the L0 haplogroup and is known to be the earliest split from Homo *sapiens* carrying the L haplogroup. This haplogroup branching is indicated on the mtDNA haplogroup migration map as well as its phylogenetic tree. By 130,000 years ago there were two ancestral populations in Africa, people with mtDNA haplogroup L0 in South Africa, ancestral to the Khoisan, and people with haplogroup L1-6 in central/eastern Africa, ancestral to everyone else, including the majority of our current population.

There was also a significant back-migration of people with Lo toward eastern Africa between 75,000 and 120,000 years ago.

The Khoisan people speak a unique language that starts with a clicking sound before uttering vowels. Their clicking language might have been the original language spoken by all modern humans. Homo *sapiens sapiens* migrated out of Africa and lost this clicking language, whereas the Khoisan retained it. The mtDNA haplogroup graph can give you a visual idea of how carriers of haplogroups Lo through L6 moved around in Africa.

CENTRAL AFRICA

Expansion into Central Africa by the ancestors of African Pygmy populations, the hunter-gatherers of the Congo basin, most likely took place before 130,000 years ago, and certainly before 60,000 years ago. African Pygmies are genetically diverse and divergent from all other human populations, suggesting they have an ancient indigenous lineage, much like the Khoisan. They are the second-most ancient modern human divergence group right after the Khoisan people.

WEST AFRICA

Modern humans may have reached the west end of the Sahara Desert near the Atlantic Ocean. There is evidence that tropical West African sites are associated with Homo *sapiens sapiens* after 130,000 years ago. Unlike elsewhere in Africa, archaic middle stone age (MSA) sites appear to persist until very late, up to 12,000 years ago, pointing to the possibility of the late survival of archaic Homo *sapiens* and crossbreeding with Homo *sapiens sapiens* in West Africa. The MSA sites, mainly attributed to archaic Homo *sapiens*, evolved locally in Africa (as opposed to the Neanderthals and Denisovans who likely evolved outside of Africa), like Homo helmeis. They lived in South Africa 260,000 years ago but did not get much of our attention because the hybridization did not have a long-lasting impact on our genes in the majority of the population.

FIRST WAVE OUT OF AFRICA THROUGH TWO CAUSEWAYS

The first wave may have started 180,000 years ago and lasted through 80,000 years ago by two routes, one northbound through the Niles Valley and the other moving east- and northeast-bound in the general direction of Eurasia.

THE MIDDLE EAST ROUTE

A part of the first migration wave was through the Nile Valley heading to the Middle East, at least into modern Israel around 120,000 to 100,000 years ago. Populations of modern humans migrated to the Levant and Europe between 130,000 and 115,000 years ago and possibly in waves as early as 185,000 years ago. These early migrations did not appear to have led to lasting colonization, and they receded by about 80,000 years ago.

A jawbone fragment with eight teeth found in Misliya Cave, Israel, has been dated between 170,000 to 194,000 years ago. Layers dating from between 250,000 and 140,000 years ago in the same cave contained tools characteristic of knapping techniques, putting the first migration date even earlier if these tools can be associated with the modern human jawbone finds. However, this type of technology could be from early modern humans. If the tools are, indeed, from early modern humans, they could be the earliest indication that modern human and archaic modern men co-located outside of Africa for a while.

In July 2019, anthropologists reported the discovery of 210,000-year-old remains of a modern human in southern Greece, more than 150,000 years older than previous Homo *sapiens* finds in Europe. The same location also featured some 170,000-year-old Neanderthal remains. Again, there is no evidence that modern humans persisted, but they may have blended into archaic Homo *sapiens*.

· · ·

THE RED SEA ROUTE AND COASTAL MIGRATION
The second route is through the present-day Bab-el-Mandeb Strait. This narrow isthmus might have been dry land with a much lower sea level on the Red Sea and the Gulf of Aden in those days. From there, they crossed to the Arabian Peninsula and settled in places like the present-day United Arab Emirates around 125,000 years ago, Oman around 106,000 years ago, and possibly reaching the middle of the Indian subcontinent around 75,000 years ago. Although no human remains have been found in these three locations, the apparent similarities between the stone tools found at Jebel Faya, UAE, those from Jwalapuram, and some from Africa suggest that the creators were modern humans.

The China Connection
There is the possibility that this first wave of expansion through the Red Sea route reached China as early as 125,000 years ago. The coastal migration route findings beginning at the Red Sea route might lend support to the claim that modern humans from Africa arrived in southern China at the border of South China and Vietnam about 100,000 years ago. A 2007 discovery of fragmentary human remains at Zhirendong, Guangxi, South China, provides insight into the dispersal of modern humans in eastern Eurasia. These human remains are dated to 100,000 years ago. They are the oldest modern human fossils in East Asia and predate the oldest previously known modern human remains in the region by more than 60,000 years. Dating results of the Lunadong teeth from similar areas, including a right upper second molar and a left lower second molar, indicate the molars may be as old as 125,000 years.

These early exits from Africa did not leave traces for genetic analyses based on the Y-chromosome or mtDNA. It seems as if these modern humans did not survive in large numbers and were assimilated by earlier emigrants, like Homo *erectus* or archaic Homo *sapiens*, like the Denisovans.

SECOND WAVE OUT OF AFRICA

COASTAL MIGRATION TOWARD AUSTRALIA

<u>Two Routes Out Of Africa</u>

The second wave of modern human migration took place about 75,000 years ago. It is this wave of migration that led to the lasting presence of modern humans throughout the world. Two migration routes are equally possible.

The first route is through Yemen. A small population in East Africa bearing the mitochondrial haplogroup L3 and numbering possibly fewer than 1,000 individuals crossed the Red Sea Strait at Bab el Mandib into what is now Yemen around 75,000 years ago, according to a couple of studies in 2003 and 2008.

A recent review has also shown support for the second and northern route through Sinai/Israel/Syria (Levant). Their descendants spread along the coastal path around Arabia and Persia to the Indian subcontinent before 55,000 years ago. The coastal migration between roughly 70,000 and 50,000 years ago is associated with mitochondrial haplogroups M (remember *Girl with the Dragon Tattoo* book?) and N, both derivatives of L3.

Either or both routes gave modern humans opportunities to blend in with Neanderthals and/or Denisovans.

Reaching Oceania And Beyond

Migrations continued along the Asian coast to Southeast Asia and Oceania, reaching Australia before 60,000 years ago. By getting to Australia, Homo *sapiens*, expanded their habitat beyond that of H. *erectus* for the first time. Denisovan ancestry is shared by Melanesians, Australian Aborigines, and smaller, scattered groups of people in Southeast Asia, such as the Mananwa, a Nigrito people in the Philippines, suggesting that interbreeding with Denisovans took place in eastern Asia. Denisovans may have crossed the Wallace Line, with Wallacea serving as their last refugium (refuge in the previous ice age). The Wallace Line is the limit of where Homo *erectus* crossed the Lombok gap reaching as far as Flores, giving rise to Homo floresiensis, but they never made it to Australia. The following map,

Figure 34, shows the probable extent of land and water at the time of the last glacial maximum (LGM), 20,000 years ago, when the sea level was probably more than 145 meters lower than today.

During this time, most of Maritime Southeast Asia formed one landmass, known as Sunda. Migration continued southeast on the coastal route to the straits between Sunda and Sahul, the

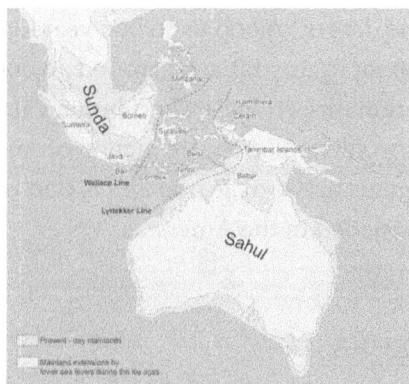

Figure 34. This figure shows the probable extent of land and water at the time of the last glacial maximum (LGM) in the Sunda and Sahul area, 20,000 years ago, and when the sea level was probably more than 145 meters lower than today. Image from Wikipedia by Maximilian Dörrbecker, CC BY 3.0, Simplification by ChrisKelly, https://creativecommons.org/licenses/by-sa/3.0/legalcode

continental landmass of present-day Australia and New Guinea. The gaps on the Weber Line are believed to be up to 90 km wide, so the migration to Australia and New Guinea would have required seafaring skills.

Those who did not go to Oceania continued their migration along the coast route, eventually turning northeast to China and finally reaching Japan before turning inland. This mtDNA haplogroup pattern provides evidence that they descended from haplogroup M and Y-chromosome haplogroup C.

Who Are the Australians, Exactly?

The sequencing of one Aboriginal genome from an old hair sample in Western Australia revealed that the individual was a descendant of those who migrated into East Asia between 62,000 and

75,000 years ago. This evidence supports the theory of a single migration into Australia and New Guinea before the arrival of modern Asians (between 25,000 and 38,000 years ago) and their later migration into North America. This migration to Australia is believed to have happened earlier than 50,000 years ago, before Australia and New Guinea were separated by rising sea levels, approximately 8,000 years ago. The early arrival in Australia and eventual isolation is supported by (1) the date of 50,000 to 60,000 years ago for the oldest evidence of settlement in Australia; (2) around 40,000 years ago for the oldest human remains; (3) the earliest human artifacts, which are at least 65,000 years old; and (4) the extinction of Australian megafauna by humans between 46,000 and 15,000 years ago, which is similar to what happened in the Americas.

DISPERSAL IN EURASIA

The population brought to South Asia by coastal migration appears to have remained there for some time, roughly 60,000 to 50,000 years ago, before spreading further throughout Eurasia. This dispersal of early humans, at the beginning of the late Stone Age 50,000 to 10,000 years ago, gave rise to major population groups in the Old World and the Americas.

In the northwest dispersal, populations associated with mitochondrial haplogroup R and its derivatives spread throughout Asia and Europe, with a back-migration of M1 to North Africa and the Horn of Africa several thousand years ago.

Europe And Neanderthal Interactions

It is certain that modern humans arrived in Europe around 40,000 years ago, possibly as early as 43,000 years ago, rapidly replacing the Neanderthal population. Contemporary Europeans have Neanderthal ancestry, borne from interbreeding in Europe. However, another theory supports that substantial interbreeding with Neanderthals ceased before 47,000 years ago (i.e., the interbreeding took place before modern humans entered Europe).

The recent expansion of the latest modern humans reached

Europe from Central Asia and the Middle east around 40,000 years ago and is a result of the cultural adaptation to the big game hunting of the subglacial steppe fauna. Neanderthals were already present both in the Middle East and in Europe at the time. The arriving populations of Homo *sapiens sapiens*—early European modern humans—interbred with Neanderthals to a limited degree. Populations of modern humans and Neanderthals overlapped in various regions such as the Iberian Peninsula and the Middle East. Interbreeding may have contributed Neanderthal genes to paleolithic, and ultimately, modern Eurasians and Oceanians.

A significant difference between Europe and other parts of the inhabited world is its high latitude. Archaeological evidence suggests humans—whether Neanderthal or Cro-Magnon—reached sites in Arctic Russia by 40,000 years ago.

Cro-Magnons are considered the first anatomically modern humans in Europe. They entered Eurasia by present-day Iran and eastern Turkey around 50,000 years ago, with one group rapidly settling in coastal areas around the Indian Ocean and another migrating north to the steppes of Central Asia. Modern human remains dating to 43,000 to 45,000 years ago have been discovered in Italy and Britain and in the European Russian Arctic from 40,000 years ago.

Modern humans colonized the territory west of the Urals, hunting reindeer especially, but they were faced with adaptive challenges: winter temperatures averaged from -20 to -30 degrees C, and shelter and fuel were scarce. They traveled on foot and relied on hunting highly mobile herds for food. They overcame these challenges through technological innovations: tailored clothing from the pelts of fur-bearing animals; constructing shelters with hearths using bones as fuel; and digging ice cellars into the permafrost to store meat and bones.

An mtDNA sequence of two Cro-Magnons from the Paglicci Cave in Italy, dated to 24,000 and 23,000 years old, identified the mtDNA as haplogroup N, typical of the older group. The presence of the N haplogroup in Italy that recent, and its presence in Iran and

Saudi Arabia much earlier, confirms their migration via the Red Sea route.

The expansion of modern human populations in Europe is thought to have begun 45,000 years ago. It may have taken them 15,000 to 20,000 years to fully colonize Europe. With the advent and flourish of ancient DNA study, David Reich has written a book published in 2018 that details the modern humans' migration and intermingling amongst themselves.

The Neanderthal Fizzle

During this time of European colonization, the Neanderthals were slowly displaced. Because it took so long for Europe to be occupied, it appears that humans and Neanderthals may have competed for resources and territories. The Neanderthals had larger brains and were physically larger overall, with a more robust or heavily built frame, suggesting they were physically stronger than modern humans. Having lived in Europe for 400,000 years, they must have been better adapted to the cold weather. The anatomically modern humans, known as Cro-Magnons, with their widespread trade networks, superior technology, and bodies, were likely better suited to running and eventually completely displaced the Neanderthals, whose last refuge was the Iberian Peninsula. After about 40,000 years ago, the Neanderthal fossil record ended, indicating its extinction. The last known population lived around a cave system on the remote south-facing coast of Gibraltar about 40,000 years ago.

From the extent of some seemingly random allele variants belonging to Neanderthals that clump together, it has been estimated that the last Neanderthal gene flow into early European ancestors occurred 47,000 to 65,000 years ago. In conjunction with archaeological and fossil evidence, interbreeding is thought to have occurred somewhere in western Eurasia, possibly the Middle East.

Some North African groups share a similar excess of derived alleles with Neanderthals as non-African populations. This evidence indicates that a backflow to Africa happened 50,000 to 60,000 years ago. Sub-Saharan African groups are the only modern human populations with no substantial Neanderthal admixture.

. . .

EAST AND NORTH ASIA

Tianyuan Man, an individual who lived near modern-day Beijing, China, around 40,000 years ago, showed substantial Neanderthal admixture. A 2017 study of his ancient DNA showed that the individual was related to modern Asian and Native American populations. The study found Neanderthal introgression of 18 genes within the chromosome 3p21.31 region (HYAL region) of East Asians. The introgressive haplotypes were positively selected in East Asian populations, rising steadily from 45,000 years ago until a sudden increase in growth rate around 5,000 to 3,500 years ago. They occur at very high frequencies among East Asian populations in contrast to other Eurasian populations (e.g., European and South Asian people). The findings also suggest that this Neanderthal introgression occurred within the ancestral population shared by East Asians and Native Americans.

A 2016 study presented an analysis of the population genetics of the Ainu people of northern Japan as the key to the reconstruction of the early peopling of East Asia. The Ainu were found to represent a more native branch than the modern farming populations of East Asia, suggesting an ancient connection with northeast Siberians. A 2013 study associated several Ainu phenotypic traits linked to Mongolians with a single mutation of the EDAR gene, dated to 35,000 years ago. Specific characteristics affected by the mutation are sweat glands, teeth, hair thickness, and breast tissue. See chapter 12.

Mitochondrial haplogroups A, B, and G originated about 50,000 years ago, and the carriers subsequently colonized Siberia, Korea, and Japan by about 35,000 years ago. Parts of these populations migrated to North America during the last glacial maximum (LGM).

POST-LAST GLACIAL MAXIMUM

EURASIA

Starting around 20,000 years ago, approximately 20,000 years after the Neanderthal extinction, the last glacial maximum forced inhabitants of the northern hemisphere to migrate to shelters (refugia, the area in which a population of organisms survives through a period of unfavorable conditions) until the end of this period.

The resulting populations are presumed to have resided in such refuges during the LGM to ultimately repopulate Europe, and the historical populations are considered their descendants. The composition of European populations was later changed by further migrations, notably the Neolithic expansion from the Middle East and the copper-using population movements associated with Indo-European expansion.

A Paleolithic site on the Yana River, Siberia, as north as 71°N, also showed evidence of modern human occupancy. The site lies well above the Arctic Circle and dates to 27,000 years ago, during glacial times. This site's human presence indicates that modern humans adapted to the harsh, cold, high-latitude, late Pleistocene environment much earlier than previously thought.

AMERICAS

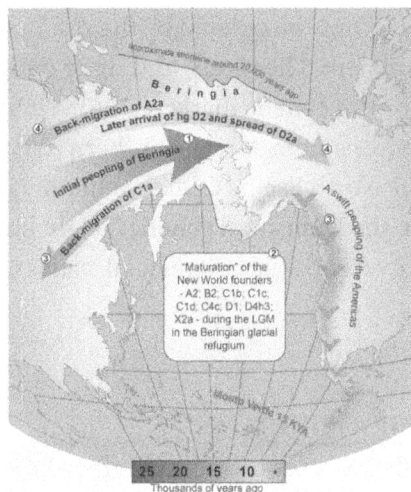

Figure 35. The gene flows in and out of Beringia. Image from
Wikipedia Erika Tamm et al. with modified background color, CC
BY 3.0, Background color by ChrisKelly,
https://creativecommons.org/licenses/by-sa/3.0/legalcode

Native ancient Americans migrated from Central Asia, crossing
the Beringia Land Bridge between eastern Siberia and present-day
Alaska. The general knowledge of how the Americas is peopled and
their mtDNA haplogroups are included in Figure 35. Modern
humans lived throughout the Americas by the end of the last glacial
period, or more specifically, the LGM, no earlier than 23,000 years
ago. Details of their migration to and throughout the American continent, including the dates and the routes traveled, are subject to
ongoing research and discussion.

Routes of migration to the Americas are also still debated. The
traditional theory is that these early migrants moved when sea levels
were significantly lower due to intermittent glaciation periods,
following herds of now-extinct Pleistocene megafauna along ice-free
corridors that stretched between the Laurentide and Cordilleran ice
sheets.

Another route proposed is that, either on foot or using primitive
boats, they migrated down the Pacific Coast to South America as far
as Chile. Any archaeological evidence of coastal occupation during

the last ice age would now be covered by the rise in sea level since then, by up to 100 meters. The recent finding of Indigenous Australasian/Denisovan genetic markers in Amazonia supports the coastal route hypothesis from Africa, Southern Asia, East Asia, south of Beringia, and the North Pacific Coast, eventually reaching South America. However, the Denisovan genetics might have reached North America a lot more recently via commercial trades in the last 300 years.

HOLOCENE MIGRATIONS

The Holocene began 12,000 years ago, after the end of the LGM. During the Holocene climatic optimum, beginning about 9,000 years ago, human populations geographically confined to refugia began re-emerging and migrating. By that time, most parts of the globe had been settled by Homo *sapiens sapiens*; however, large areas covered by glaciers were now starting to repopulate.

This period sees the transition from the Mesolithic to the Neolithic stage throughout the temperate zone. The Neolithic age subsequently gave way to the Bronze Age in Old World cultures and the gradual emergence of the historical record in the Near East and China, beginning around 4,000 years ago.

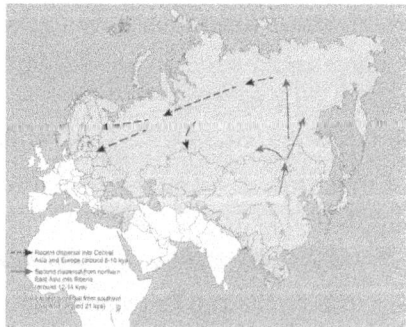

Figure 36. 1. Prehistoric migration routes for Y-chromosome Haplogroup N lineage following the retreat of ice sheets after the Last Glacial Maximum (22–18 kya). Image from Wikipedia by Hong Shi, et al., CC BY 2.5, Background color by ChrisKelly, https://creativecommons.org/licenses/by/2.5/legalcode

Large-scale migrations in the Mesolithic to Neolithic eras are thought to have given rise to the pre-modern distribution of the world's primary language families, such as the Niger-Congo, Nilo-Saharan, Afro-Asiatic, Uralic, Sino-Tibetan, or Indo-European phyla. The speculative Nostratic Theory postulates the derivation of Eurasia's main language families (excluding Sino-Tibetan) from a single proto language spoken at the beginning of the Holocene period.

Figure 36 shows prehistoric migration routes for the Y-chromosome Haplogroup N lineage following the retreat of ice sheets after the LGM (26,000 to 18,000 years ago).

Eurasia

Evidence published in 2014 detailing the analysis of a genome from ancient human remains suggests that modern native populations in Europe descended primarily from three distinct lineages: (1) Western Hunter-Gatherers derivative from Cro-Magnon populations in Europe; (2) Early European Farmers introduced to Europe from the Near East during the Neolithic Revolution; and (3) Ancient North Eurasians who expanded to Europe in the context of the Indo-European expansion. The people from the last lineage are those that European history considers barbarians. These are the people we might have identified as the Huns, the nomads, or the Turks.

Sub-Sahara Africa

The Nilotic peoples are thought to have derived from an earlier, undifferentiated eastern Sudanic group 5,000 years ago. Nilotic people are indigenous to the Nile Valley and speak Nilotic languages, which constitutes a large sub-group of Nilo-Saharan languages spoken in South Sudan, Uganda, Kenya, and northern Tanzania. The development of the Proto-Nilotes as a group may have been connected with their domestication of livestock. The 5,000-year-old Proto-Nilotes were sheep or cattle farmers, whereas their neighbors, the Proto-Central Sudanic people, were mostly agriculturalists. The eastern Sudanic group must have been considerably earlier still, perhaps around 7,000 years old. The original locus of early Nilotic speakers was presumably east of the Nile in what is now South

Sudan. The earlier Nilo-Saharan people dated to the Upper Paleolithic, about 15,000 years ago

The Niger-Congo group is thought to have emerged around 6,000
years ago in West or Central Africa. Its expansion may have been
associated with the expansion of Sahel agriculture in the African
Neolithic period, following the desiccation of the Sahara about 5,900
years ago. The Bantu expansion spread the Bantu language to
Central, East, and South Africa, partly replacing the regions' Indigenous populations. It began about 3,000 years ago and reached South
Africa about 1,700 years ago.

Indo-Pacific

The Indo-Pacific—not a common term—sometimes known as the
Indo-West Pacific or Indo-Pacific Asia, is a sea region comprising the
Indian Ocean's tropical waters, the western and central Pacific Ocean,
and the seas connecting the two in the general area of Indonesia.
Figure 37 here shows the migration paths for modern human to
finally populated the whole Indo-Pacific Area.

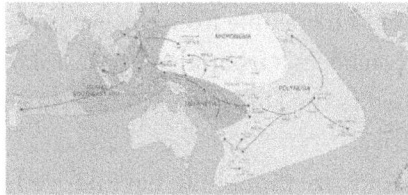

*Figure 37. This figure shows the migration paths for modern human
to finally populated the Indo-Pacific Area. Image from Wikipedia by
Obsidian Soul, with modified color scheme, CC BY 4.0, Background
color by ChrisKelly,
https://creativecommons.org/licenses/by/4.0/legalcode*

The islands of the Pacific were populated between 3,600 years ago
to 1,000 years ago. The Austronesian-speaking people, Lapita people,
settled in Near Oceania (notably the Bismarck Archipelago in Papua
New Guinea and the Solomon Islands) around 3,500 years ago. Lapita
people got their name from the archaeological site in Lapita, New
Caledonia, where their characteristic pottery was first discovered,
and they intermingled with the existing Papuan population.

Acquiring long-distance voyaging skills, they ventured into Remote Oceania, probably settling in Vanuatu and New Caledonia around 3,200 years ago, then to Fiji, Samoa, and Tonga. By about 3,000 years ago and onward, the western part of Polynesia was a loose web of thriving populations settling on the islands' coasts and living off the sea. By 2,000 years ago, Micronesia was completely colonized, and tropical eastern Polynesia, including Tahiti, was probably settled by 1,300 years ago. The last region of Polynesia to be reached was New Zealand, perhaps 700 years ago.

Caribbean

The Caribbean was one of the last places in the Americas to be settled by humans. The oldest remains are known to be from the Greater Antilles (Cuba and Hispaniola), dating between 6,000 and 5,500 years ago, and comparisons between tool-technologies suggest that these people moved across the Yucatán Channel from Central America. All evidence suggests that later migrants—from 4,000 years ago and onward—originated from South America via the Orinoco region. The descendants of these migrants include ancestors of the Taíno and Kalinago (Island Carib) people.

Prehistoric evidence from submerged caves and sinkholes (cenotes) on the Yucatan Peninsula provides strong evidence for the existence of an early pre-ceramic human settlement in southern Mexico. We have already documented three well-preserved human skeletons as old as 13,000 and 9,000 years from sites in Quintana Roo during our ongoing paleoanthropological research. The findings were associated with hearths and a diverse assemblage of late-Pleistocene megafauna.

Arctic

The last region permanently settled by human migration is the Arctic. The earliest inhabitants of North America's central and eastern Arctic are referred to as the Arctic Small Tool Tradition (AST) and existed about 4,500 years ago. AST consisted of several Paleo-Eskimo cultures, including the Independence and Pre-Dorset cultures.

The Inuit are the descendants of the Thule culture, which

emerged from western Alaska around 1,000 years ago and gradually displaced the Dorset culture.

SETTLEMENT OF THE AMERICAS

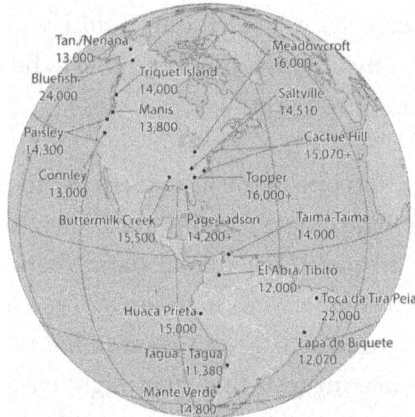

Figure 38. Humans and artifacts discover sites in America with radiocarbon dates. Image from Wikipedia by Pratyeka with more details. Add color and details by ChrisKelly, CC BY 4.0, https://creativecommons.org/licenses/by-sa/4.0/legalcode

Most research on human migration has centered around global migration patterns. The migration to and inside the Americas has not been treated with proper emphasis. For me, it is worth a special section to go over the settlement of the Americas—in other words, the peopling of the Americas.

There have been a few controversies concerning the settlement of the Americas, particularly since there is no physical evidence of human fossils, dwellings, or artifacts earlier than 15,000 years ago. Figure 38 shows the locations and ages of discovered fossils and artifacts on the America continents. Along with the LGM, it is a reasonable assumption that humans did not come to the Americas before 20,000 years ago. Thus, we have a general concept of the peopling of the Americas based on existing evidence.

America's first settlement began when Paleolithic hunter-gatherers entered North America from the North Asian Mammoth Steppe via the Beringia Land Bridge formed between northeastern Siberia and western Alaska due to the lowering sea level during the LGM. These populations expanded south of the Laurentide ice sheet and rapidly throughout both North and South America by 14,000 years ago. The earliest people in the Americas, before roughly 10,000 years ago, are known as Paleo-Indians.

The peopling of the Americas is a long-standing open question. While advances in archaeology, Pleistocene geology, physical anthropology, and DNA analyses have shed progressively more light on the subject, significant questions remain unresolved. There is a general agreement that the Americas were first settled from Asia. The pattern of migration, the timing, and the place(s) of origin in Eurasia of the peoples migrating to the Americas remain unclear. In 2019, a study by the University of Cambridge and the University of Copenhagen concluded that Native Americans are the closest relatives to the 10,000-year-old inhabitants of the Kolyma River in northeastern Siberia.

The prevalent migration models outline different timeframes for the Asian migration from the Bering Straits and subsequent dispersal of the founding population throughout the continent. Indigenous peoples in the Americas have been linked to Siberian people by linguistic factors, the distribution of blood types, and genetic composition as reflected in molecular data, such as DNA.

The Clovis First Theory refers to the 1950s hypothesis that the Clovis culture represents the earliest human presence in the Americas, beginning about 13,000 years ago. Evidence of pre-Clovis cultures has accumulated since 2000, pushing back the possible date of the first peopling of the Americas to about 13,200 to 15,500 years ago.

Scientists in Chile say they have found one footprint dating to at least 15,600 years ago, making it the earliest sign of man's presence in the Americas. The footprint was found at the Pilauco excavation in Osorno (820 kilometers—500 miles—south of Santiago), where scientists have been digging since 2007. There are other human footprints in the Americas, but none have been dated as far back.

An important observation on the settlement of America is in the genetic groups or haplogroups. It is expected that the mtDNA and Y-DNA haplogroups for a single individual or single group should be consistent, but by examining these haplogroup maps, the most striking part is in its simplicity. For example, mtDNA haplogroups are as simple as A and X, whereas the Y-DNA haplogroup is majorly Q. The implication: the founding group has been relatively small with simple and narrow gene diversities. It also attests to the young ages of the original America settlers.

SUMMARY FOR MODERN HUMAN MIGRATION

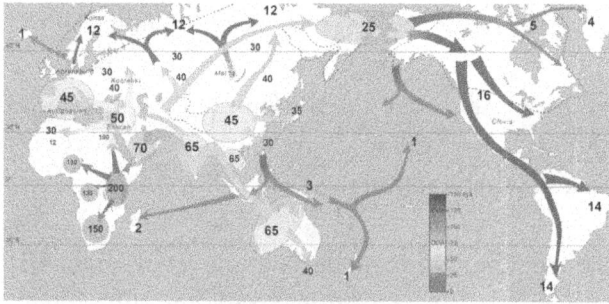

Figure 39. Overview map of the peopling of the world by early humans during the Upper Paleolithic, following to the Southern Dispersal paradigm. Image from Wikipedia by Dbachmann with modified color scheme, CC BY 4.0, Background color by ChrisKelly, https://creativecommons.org/licenses/by-sa/4.0/legalcode

We had the two charts for modern human migration according to the mtDNA and Y-chromosome haplogroups. Using these charts and the information from, say 23andme, people can trace their ancestors on both their mother and father's sides. Included in these two charts are the times for most branching points, using molecular clock techniques. That pretty much answers the big question of where we individually came from.

In the big picture, you can plot out general paths of human migration if you combine these two charts, ending with the composite migration map as shown in Figure 39. It seems as if we have fully answered the question of where we came from, except, of course, we have to qualify the answers to limit the "we" to modern humans who are 200,000 years old.

Haplogroups are in fact a fairly coarse modern human categorization that has helped us trace our ancestry and migration thus far. We utilize the mutations and the sources of the mtDNA and Y-DNA samples to correlate with each other resulting in this big modern human migration history described in this chapter. With our abilities to sequence and identify specific genes in ancient DNA and tracking their mutations, we are now able to chart out our migration history with a lot finer grid. In fact, with ancient DNAs from about 4,000 humans in our recent past, mostly from west and northern Eurasia, we are getting a better picture of our migration history since the start of the LGM. The study of similar granularities on the Easter Eurasia and the other part of the world is lagging but catching up.

FUTURE MIGRATION?

There have been 107 billion hominin individuals that have ever lived on this planet, including the current 7.8 billion, sustained by the vast expanse of space and the endless supply of resources in the form of other living organisms, animals, or plants. I cannot help but be in awe at the enormity of our species and humbled by what we have done to ourselves and our landscape.

The migration of human beings had a lot to do with following the game until we settled down for agriculture. For the 107 billion people that have lived on this planet before and after the population explosion driven by the rise of the agricultural age, we have upset nature's balance and driven many animals into extinction and prosperity. Prosperity is not necessarily a good thing. For example, the number of chickens for our consumption is in the billions. This number-based prosperity is not for the benefit of the species.

We have also altered our biological kingdom of plants for our existence. For example, we have domesticated and changed the reproduction of grains and vegetables. As our residence, the planet is now an environment of our own making. With our modern method of mobility taking no time to homogenize our species and our habitat, we are whittling down our fauna, our flora, and our diversity. We need to think hard about how we can live harmoniously with our surroundings lest we set off some positive feedback that accelerates our shrinking diversity with the ever-increasing population, setting off a runaway situation poised to total collapse.

Michio Kaku's take on humanity's future outlines the migration possibility, colonizing other planets and their moons for resources. He painted an optimistic picture of our eventual migration to exoplanets; however, the effort and cost are prohibitive in the foreseeable future, and the outcome is not apparent to warrant the tremendous resources that might find better use on earth. We still have a lot to understand about our evolution in the habitat we have helped to change. It is incumbent upon us to do what we can to optimize our living environment to evolve into a better species.

BIBLIOGRAPHY

1. "Identifying and Interpreting Apparent Neanderthal Ancestry in African Individuals," Lu Chen, Aaron B. Wolf, Wenqing Fu, Liming Li, and Joshua M. Akey, *Cell,* **180,** 677 (2020).
2. "Updated Comprehensive Phylogenetic Tree of Global Human Mitochondrial DNA Variation," Mannis van Oven and Manfred Kayser, *Human Mutation, Mutation in Brief,* **1039,** 30 (20089).
3. "Genetic clues to dispersal in human populations: retracing the past from the present," R. L. Cann, *Science,* **291,** 1742 (2001).
4. "Mitochondrial DNA and Y Chromosome Variation Provides Evidence for a Recent Common Ancestry between Native Americans and Indigenous Altaians," Matthew C. Dulik, Sergey I. Zhadanov, Ludmila P.

Osipova, Ayken Askapuli, Lydia Gau, Omer Gokcumen, Samara Rubinstein, and Theodore G. Schurr, *The American Journal of Human Genetics*, **90**, 229–246 (2012).

5. "Major genomic mitochondrial lineages delineate early human expansions," Nicole Maca-Meyer, Ana M González, José M Larruga, Carlos Flores, and Vicente M Cabrera, *BMC Genetics*, **2**, 13 (2001).

6. "Modern Humans Did Not Admix with Neanderthals during Their Range Expansion into Europe," Mathias Currat and Laurent Excoffier, *PLoS Biology*, **2**, 12 (2004).

7. "Human Dispersal Out of Africa: A Lasting Debate", Saioa López, Lucy van Dorp, and Garrett Hellenthal, *Evol Bioinform Online*, **11**, 57–68 (2015).

8. "Pre-Clovis occupation of the Americas identified by human fecal biomarkers in coprolites from Paisley Caves, Oregon," Lisa-Marie Shillito, Helen L. Whelton, John C. Blong, Dennis L. Jenkins, Thomas J. Connolly, and Ian D. Bull, *Science Advances*, **6**, 29 (2020).

9. *"The Future of Humanity: Terraforming Mars, Interstellar Travel, Immortality, and Our Destiny Beyond Earth,"* Michio Kaku, Anchor Publisher, 2018.

10. *"Who We Are and How We Got Here: Ancient DNA and the New Science of the Human Past"*, David Reich, Vintage Publisher, 2018.

14

RECENT ANTHROPOLOGICAL DISCOVERIES

Ｎew anthropological discoveries have not stopped happening. Hardly a day passes without a popular science report, news clip, Internet blip, or academic alert about findings claiming significant implications for our evolution.

Not all anthropological discoveries are for human evolution, although a few categories are of particular interest. They could be discoveries of new fossils with verified dating and corroborating DNA studies. It might be a re-examination of older fossils with modern dating and a new DNA study, or new a DNA study of unknown remnants that are eventually identified as hominins. There are also studies of population dispersals with broad demographic participation and the analysis of full hominin genomes.

Besides the relevant research categories, I exercise my judgment based on two criteria for continued review. The first is about how significant the impact will be for human evolution. The second is about how solid the data and analyses, and how logical and reasonable the conclusions are. Finally, I will dig deep into the research, but only from investigators with proven track records, published in reputable professional journals.

In the end, the studies included in this chapter usually have an implication for hominin identification, ages, ancestral lineage, migration, dispersal, and finally, the relevance for human evolution and how it helps answer the question of where we came from.

The basic principle behind evolution is clear and straightforward, just a few items connected in a close feedback loop as described in chapter 3, but each item and/or box entails variables that have interacted with each other for millions of years. The variability of the evolutionary outcome is astronomical, considering hundreds of thousands of generations of genetic mixing and millions of mutations creating unexpected features. Unless we have enough calculating power with artificial intelligence to manage it, the principle of evolution's simplicity will always be obscured by complex outcomes.

We have been unraveling this evolutionary complexity for the past 150 years and by thousands of dedicated scientists. The basic human evolutionary story is quite reasonable and logical at this point. More importantly, the current theories on human evolution are evidence-based accumulated and credible discoveries. As such, any claims or changes to the status quo must live up to the same level of critical scrutiny and peer reviews and most of them have. Irrespectively, as credible or earth-shattering discoveries may claim to be, they will, at best, modify existing theories with minor details that do not shake the foundation of our current understanding.

In modern-day, super-fast, Internet-based communications, new anthropological studies and discoveries reach fellow researchers and the general public in no time. If they have the opportunity to be revolutionary, they will seep into every fabric of our culture quickly. Textbooks will make changes, public opinions and debates will ensue, and fiction writers will have new stories to make more money. Further debates to settle the argument will either ratify or reject the new theories, but most importantly, for academia as well as the general public, if discoveries lead to the inevitable modification of prevailing views, it is important to face whatever science will reveal without prejudging. We should be mature enough to handle any findings, including implications beyond science, with social, political, ethical, or religious implications.

This chapter lists some of the more notable discoveries over the past few years. It is not the intent to simply list the findings, however. Rather, they are included in this chapter because they have significant implications that we will elucidate as we go along. Some of them were mentioned earlier in this book, and we will not elaborate further except when more details are needed.

2017

HOMO NALEDI'S MOSAIC PAST, MAY 2017

We mentioned Homo naledi in chapter 11 as being contemporary with Homo *erectus* and Homo *heidelbergensis*. However, their morphology has pegged them as being a lot older, likely 2,000,000-years-old. They are a group that does not easily fit into our direct ancestral line.

Excavations started as early as 2013 in the Rising Star cave system (also known as Westminster or Empire Cave) located in the Malmani dolomites in the Bloubank River Valley, approximately 30 miles north of Johannesburg, South Africa. In 2015, a discovery from deep inside a cave in South Africa was announced. Dr. Lee Berger from the University of Witwatersrand in South Africa and his team recovered one of the largest assemblages of fossil hominins in the Dinaledi Chamber of the cave system, and it was designated as being a Homo naledi.

In addition to the wealth of fossils, including many individuals, what makes these fossils particularly striking is their hodgepodge of physical characteristics. For instance, Homo naledi has a modern, human-like collarbone (clavicle), leg, ankle, and foot, while sharing hand and pelvis features with earlier species like Australopithecus *afarensis*. This unique combination of modern and ancestral traits is found across Homo naledi fossils, and it led researchers to initially speculate that they could be up to 2,000,000-years-old. This was before the team had secured reliable dating.

The research team reported two new follow-up findings in May 2017. The first is that even after Berger's team recovered at least 15

337 from where we came

individuals from the Dinaledi chamber, they continued excavating in a second chamber in 2013 and found 130 more fossils from four more individuals, including two adults and one child. One of the new specimens, a male nicknamed "Neo" after the Sesotho word for "gift," is one of the most complete hominin fossils ever discovered.

The second finding was by combining six different dating techniques, yielding a surprising result: the Homo *naledis* dated to between 236,000 and 335,000 years young. They would have shared the planet with Homo *erectus* and Homo *heidelbergensis*, and even our archaic Homo species, Homo *sapiens*. Located in South Africa, it is not likely that they met Neanderthals or Denisovans, but their antiquated attributes solidify them as being a genus of Homo but not Homo *sapiens*.

Their brain size puts them in the category between Australopithecus and Homo genera. The persistence of small-brained humans for so long in the middle of bigger-brained contemporaries confirms that the last step of human evolution toward cognition and intelligence is the brain.

ANCIENT HUMAN DNA DISCOVERED IN THE DIRT, MAY 2017

A team from the Max Planck Institute for Evolutionary Anthropology in Leipzig, Germany, published their discovery of ancient DNA from mammals in sediments from caves in Europe and Asia in the journal *Science* in May 2017. This discovery was remarkable because it did not involve finding fossils or artifacts or anything we usually associate with the past. Instead, researchers found ancient human DNA in the dirt.

While this sounds like something out of a science fiction novel, it really happened. The Max Planck team collaborated with several other groups excavating caves in Belgium, Croatia, France, Russia, and Spain with known early human occupation. Together, they collected 85 sediment samples from seven archaeological sites varying in age between about 14,000 and 550,000-years-ago. They found fragments of mitochondrial DNA from 12 different families of mammals in the sediment, including DNA from extinct animals like woolly mammoths, woolly rhinos, cave hyenas, and cave bears.

The most exciting discoveries of ancient human DNA is in nine of those 85 samples from four of the sites. Eight had Neanderthal DNA, and one had Denisovan DNA. In some cases, the researchers could even tell that they had come from more than one individual from the specific DNA sequences. This discovery is crucial for the research into human evolution as it allows for the identification of the presence of hominins at prehistoric sites and in layers where their fossils have yet to be discovered. This pushed back the known hominin occupation of Denisova Cave in Siberia by tens of thousands of years. It also demonstrates that it is possible to extract DNA from samples stored at room temperature for thousands of years, like those previously collected for dating purposes, understanding site formation processes, or reconstructing ancient environments.

HOMO SAPIENS FROM MOROCCO OVER 300,000 YEARS OLD, JUNE 2017

We mentioned these Homo *sapiens* in the history of our human migration and categorized them as Homo *sapiens*, though they are of the archaic type. In 1961, miners stumbled upon a nearly complete fossil human skull in Jebel Irhoud, Morocco, sparking a decades-long journey to understand who these individuals were and their place in our evolutionary story. Paleoanthropologist Jean-Jacques Hublin at the Max Planck Institute of Evolutionary Anthropology in Leipzig, Germany, started new excavations of the cave in 2004, hoping to date remaining sediment still in place and tie it to layers in which fossils were found in original excavations. In 2007, researchers from Hublin's team published a date of 160,000 years for a juvenile mandible from this site, called Jebel Irhoud 3, based on radiometric dating (uranium series/electron spin resonance) of one of its teeth.

As the excavation continued, Hublin's team uncovered not only sediment they could date but many new human fossils, including teeth, jaws, partial skulls, and arm and leg bones from at least five individuals, including an adolescent and a child, bringing the total number of individuals at the site to 22. The new human fossils were mainly in the same layer that contained butchered animal bones. They also burned flint stone tools, which indicated they had control of fire, which allowed the research team to estimate the age of the tools using thermoluminescence dating.

On June 8, 2017, the team announced that the new fossils were between about 280,000 and 350,000-years-old. This dating matches the team's new dating for the Jebel Irhoud 3 mandible (using improved radiometric dating) to 254,000 to 318,000-years-old.

Like Neanderthals, the face, teeth, and lower jaw of the Moroccan fossils look more modern or specialized, while their braincases have more ancestral features like an elongated shape. The team suggests that this group of early Homo *sapiens* were not necessarily our ancestors but a part of a large, pan-African population that eventually evolved into modern humans.

MODERN HUMANS ARRIVED IN AUSTRALIA 65,000 YEARS AGO, JULY 2017

The earliest peopling of Australia has long been a fascinating and sometimes contentious subject. Estimates from previous research were that *Homo sapiens* arrived in Australia by about 47,000 years ago, and possibly as long ago as 60,000 years ago. On July 19, 2017, Dr. Chris Clarkson and his team from the University of Queensland announced results from a new excavation at an aboriginal rock shelter called Madjedbebe in the journal *Nature*, which pushed back the human occupation of Australia to 65,000 years ago.

While this site was excavated in the 1970s, new digs—in 2012 and 2015—recovered over 10,000 new artifacts from the site, including the earliest known edge-ground axes (stone axes that would have had handles). The site had been previously radiocarbon dated, but radiocarbon cannot accurately date sediments much older than 50,000 years. Clarkson's team used optically stimulated luminescence (OSL, see chapter 6) dating on 52 samples of sediment surrounding lithic artifacts in the deepest layers to get the new, ancient dates. Using multiple dating techniques, they showed that the range of artifact deposits at the site ranged from 10,000 years ago back to 65,000 years ago.

They also conducted extensive studies of the stone tools to understand early technological advancements of Native Australian settlers. They examined ancient plant remains preserved at the site to understand what plants people may have eaten, and they analyzed the size distribution of sediment grains to investigate the ancient soil. All of these methods came together to tell the story of a people who ground a variety of foods, including seeds, fruits, other plants, and animals, eating nuts and yams, making ochre "crayons," and using reflective pigment 65,000 years ago in northern Australia.

Interestingly, this finding overturns the hypothesis that Homo *sapiens* drove Australia's megafauna to extinction soon after arriving on the continent. The climate and fossil data show a decline in Australian megafauna at 45,000 to 43,100 years ago, well after the new evidence for human arrival as early as 65,000 years ago. Researchers excavating the site worked closely with the local aboriginal community to acknowledge the importance of this site and ensure the site's ownership and stewardship stayed with its ancestral people.

2018

THE EARLIEST MODERN HUMAN OUT OF AFRICA? JANUARY 2018

We covered this discovery as a part of the human migration story in chapter 13 while exploring the occupants in a cave in Israel where the presence of modern humans predated Neanderthals. In the end, it seems that these modern human emigrants from Africa that early either faded away or were assimilated by Neanderthals.

Every person alive on the planet today is a Homo *sapiens*, and our species evolved around 200,000 years ago in Africa. In January of last year, a team of archaeologists led by Israel Hershkovitz from Tel Aviv University discovered a modern human upper jaw in

Misliya Cave on the western slope of Mount Carmel in Israel. The site had previously yielded flint artifacts dated to between 140,000 and 250,000 years ago, and the assumption was that these tools had been made by Neanderthals, who also occupied Israel at the time, but tucked in the same layer of sediment as the stone tools was a Homo *sapiens* upper jaw. Dated to between 177,000 and 194,000 years ago by three different dating techniques, this find pushes back evidence for modern human expansion out of Africa by roughly 40,000 years. It also supports the idea that there were multiple waves of modern humans migrating out of Africa at that time.

INNOVATING AND INTELLIGENT MODERN HUMANS, MARCH 2018

At the prehistoric site of Olorgesailie in southern Kenya, years of careful climate research and meticulous excavation explored both archaeological and paleoenvironmental records to document behavioral changes in modern humans in response to climatic variation. The research team that led this discovery was headed by Rick Potts of the Smithsonian's National Museum of Natural History and Alison Brooks of George Washington University.

The artifacts show a shift from the larger, clunkier tools of the Acheulean, characterized by teardrop-shaped hand axes, to the more sophisticated and specialized tools of the Middle Stone Age (MSA). These MSA tools were dated to 320,000 years ago, the earliest evidence of this type of technology in Africa. They also found evidence that one of the rocks used to make MSA tools—obsidian, a non-crystalline black glass loaded with soot—was obtained from at least 55 miles (95 kilometers) away. Such long distances led the research teams to conclude that obsidian was traded in social networks. The distance is much farther than foraging modern human groups typically travel in a day.

On top of this, the team found red and black rocks (pigments) used for coloring material on the MSA sites, indicating symbolic communication, possibly used to maintain social networks with distant groups.

Finally, all of these innovations occurred during a time of great climate and landscape instability and unpredictability, with a significant change in mammal species. In the face of this uncertainty, early human members of our species seem to have responded by developing technological innovations, greater social connections, and symbolic communication.

This discovery casts our ancient ancestors as involved in long-distance trade, using color, and making the oldest MSA tools in Africa as early as 300,000 years ago. Most likely, they were not the modern humans we expected to engage in such activities.

ART-MAKING NEANDERTHALS, FEBRUARY 2018

Nearly 350 art containing prehistoric caves have been discovered in France and Spain. These cave paintings are believed to be artistic representations created by modern humans. They range from a depiction of several human figures hunting pigs in the caves in the Maros-Pangkep karst of South Sulawesi, Indonesia, dated to over 43,900-years-old to figurative cave paintings of a bull dated to 40,000 years ago in Lubang Jeriji Saléh cave, East Kalimantan, Borneo, and the depiction of a pig with a minimum age of 35,400 years at Timpuseng Cave in Sulawesi, Indonesia; and who has not have heard of the European figurative cave paintings of Chauvet Cave in France, dated 35,000 to 30,000 years ago. Australia has also yielded cave paintings but at a younger age.

It seems as though these cave paintings are sophisticated and date younger than 50,000-years-old, but discoveries—including one made in 2017—invariably changed the notion of cognitive and intelligence divide between modern humans and Neanderthals. A team led by Alistair Pike from the University of Southampton found red ocher paintings—dots, boxes, abstract animal figures, and handprints—deep inside three Spanish caves. The most amazing part? These paintings date to at least 65,000 years ago, a full 20,000-25,000 years before Homo *sapiens* arrived in Europe.

The paintings' ages were determined using uranium-thorium dating of white crust, made of calcium carbonate (calcite) forming on top of the paintings after water percolated through the rocks. Since the calcite precipitated on top of the paintings, the paintings must have been there first, making them older than the calcite. The age of the paintings suggests that Neanderthals made them. It has changed the common belief that symbolic thought, representing reality through abstract concepts, was a uniquely modern human ability.

THE OLDEST MODERN HUMAN FOOTPRINTS IN NORTH AMERICA, MARCH 2018

We recall that Mary Leakey and her team discovered the Laetoli footprints, which were dated as old as 3,600,000 to 3,800,000 years, most likely left behind by Australopithecus *afarensis*. We can infer their morphology and movement and put them in the right place on our family tree. Fast forward to 2018—a discovery revealed the oldest footprints in North America from vintage modern humans. Before getting into the details of the discovery, it should be duly noted that Duncan McLaren led the research team from the University of Victoria with representatives from the Heiltsuk and Wuikinuxv First Nations, both Canadian Native American, so they come by their keen interest in heritage and involvement in Native cultural studies naturally.

The 29 footprints discovered had been made by at least three individuals on the tiny Canadian island of Calvert. The team used Carbon-14 dating of fossilized wood, found in proximity with the footprints, to 13,000-years-old. This site may have been a stopover on a late coastal human route while migrating from Asia to the Americas. Because of their small size, it is thought that some of the footprints might have been made by a child who would have worn about a size seven kids' shoe today, had they worn shoes.

As humans, our social and caregiving nature is essential to our survival. One of the research team members, Jennifer Walkus, mentions why finding children's footprints are particularly noteworthy: "Because so often kids are absent from the archeological record. This discovery makes archaeology more personal." Any site with preserved human footprints is pretty unique, as there are currently only a few dozen in the world. We later see in another recent discovery that a single modern human footprint in South America has been dated to even earlier than his discovery.

Calvert Island was still an island during the last ice age, indicating that prehistoric people used boats to reach it, McLaren said. The footprints were likely left "by a group of people disembarking from watercraft and moving toward a drier central activity area to the north or northwest," the researchers wrote, speculating on the possibilities.

THE FIRST HUMAN GENERATION WITH MIXED ANCESTRY, JANUARY 2018

As is already mentioned, species boundaries are, at best, guidelines for taxonomic purposes. The subspecies of Homo *sapiens* do not have insurmountable genetic dividing lines between them. A discovery from Denisova Cave in Siberia added to the complicated history of Neanderthals and other ancient human species, as we saw in chapter 10.

While Neanderthal fossils have been known for 150 years, Denisovans are a population of hominins that were only discovered in 2008 based on the sequencing of the genome from a 41,000-year-old finger bone fragment from Denisova Cave, which was also inhabited by Neanderthals and modern humans (and with whom they also mated). While all known Denisovan fossils could fit into one of your hands, the amount of information we can gain from their DNA is enormous.

In early 2018, a discovery was made from a fragment of a 2 cm long bone fragment identified as coming from a 13-year-old girl, nicknamed "Denny," who lived about 90,000 years ago. As it turns out, she was the daughter of a Neanderthal mother and Denisovan father. A team led by Svante Pääbo from the Max Planck Institute for Evolutionary Anthropology in Leipzig, Germany, was first to look at her mitochondrial DNA to find that it was Neanderthal—or rather, her mother was a Neanderthal. They also sequenced her nuclear genome and compared it to the genomes of other Neanderthals and Denisovans from the same cave and to a modern human with no Neanderthal ancestry. They found that about 40% of Denny's DNA fragments matched Neanderthal genomes, and another 40% matched Denisovan genomes. The team realized this meant that she had acquired one set of chromosomes from each of her parents, who must have been two different types of early humans.

Since her mitochondrial DNA was Neanderthal, the team could say with certainty that her mother was a Neanderthal and her father, Denisovan. However, the research team deliberately avoided using the word "hybrid" since the nuptial was more like mixed marriage in modern days. Denny is a "first-generation person of mixed ancestry" and might be the most fascinating person who has had her genome sequenced.

2019

NEANDERTHALS AND DENISOVANS COULD HAVE LIVED SIDE BY SIDE FOR TENS OF THOUSANDS OF YEARS, JANUARY 2019

It is reasonable to assume that Neanderthals and Denisovans occupied the same time and space for a while in the past, which is confirmed through genetic studies. Two papers in early 2019 from the Max Planck group confirmed they lived side by side for tens of thousands of years, and they summarized the relationship in a lively account.

They analyzed bones, artifacts, and sediment from Denisova Cave in southern Siberia, which is dotted with ancient-human remains, to provide the first detailed history of the site's 300,000-year occupation by different ancient humans' groups. "We can now tell the whole story of the entire cave, not just bits and pieces," says Zenobia Jacobs, a geochronologist at the University of Wollongong, Australia, who co-led one of the studies.

Hominin Hotspot: Denisova Cave

A few Soviet archaeologists began unraveling the story of Denisova Cave at the foot of the Altai Mountains in the early 1980s. Since then, scientists have found fragmentary remains of nearly a dozen ancient humans at the site. The cave became world-famous in 2010 after an analysis of the DNA from a tiny hominin finger bone found that the creature was Denisovan, distinct from both modern humans and Neanderthals.

Additional sequencing of mitochondrial DNA and nuclear DNA in bone remains from the cave found that Denisovans were a sister group to Neanderthals and might once have lived across Asia, where they interbred with the ancestors of some humans still residing there. The genetic analysis and their relationships with Neanderthals and modern humans are the main subject of chapter 10.

Dating Difficulties

Most of the cave's remains are older than the 50,000-year limit of radiocarbon dating techniques for organic materials. Efforts to use other methods to date the sediments have been hampered by the lack of a good map of the cave's geological layers. Many scientists worry that disturbances in the cave, such as animal burrows, have scrambled its contents such that the remains and artifacts no longer sit in sediment of similar age. To overcome these challenges, researchers led by Jacobs and Wollongong geochronologist Richard Roberts used optically stimulated luminescence (OSL) techniques to determine when an individual grain of soil was last exposed to light (See chapter 6), thus the age of the sediment. This technique allowed them to identify cave regions in which the soil had been disturbed, and adjacent grains returned wildly different dates. They could then omit those areas when dating sediment from the same geological layer as hominin remains and tools.

The first signs that any ancient-human species had occupied the cave are stone tools—excavations began in the 1980s—dating to around 300,000 years old, but the researchers could not work out whether they had been made by Denisovans or Neanderthals. The cave's Denisovan remains (including some DNA that had leached into the soil) date to between 200,000 and 55,000 years ago, whereas the oldest Neanderthal remains are around 190,000-years-old, and the youngest date to some 100,000 years ago.

The researchers cannot precisely determine when the groups lived together or whether they ever shared the cave, but the existence of Denny, the mixed ancestral individual who lived around 90,000 years ago, means that the groups must have lived close enough to meet. Furthermore, Denny's father harbored a sliver of older Neanderthal ancestry, suggesting that his ancestors had previously interbred with Neanderthals. This detail is used to reconstruct the Homo *sapiens* family tree, including Neanderthals, Denisovans, and modern humans, in chapter 10.

There is the possibility that modern humans might also have lived in the cave. Bone pendants and tools similar to those made by early modern humans in Europe found in the cave's younger layers date to between 49,000 and 43,000-years-old, reports a team led by archaeologists Katerina Douka from the Max Planck Institute for the Science of Human History in Jena, Germany, and Tom Higham from the University of Oxford, UK, in the second *Nature* paper. The researchers dated one hominin bone to around 46,000-50,000 years ago but could not retrieve any DNA to investigate to which species it belonged.

No other modern human remains from this period have been found in Denisova Cave or the wider Altai region. For this reason, the Russian archaeologists who spearheaded the site's excavation have argued that Denisovans made the artifacts, which are more sophisticated than the site's older stone tools, but Higham would like to see more proof before linking the artifacts to any group. It is possible that Denisovans could have made the artifacts, and the Russian researchers are right. At the moment, with the evidence we have, we can't be sure.

Hybrids similar to Denny are other suggestions as to who had made the pendant, says Robin Dennell, an archaeologist at the University of Exeter, UK, and author of an accompanying essay on the study. It is also possible that whoever made the artifacts was influenced by contact with modern humans, he says. "I would be very surprised if the sophisticated artifacts at Denisovan were made by Denisovans or Neanderthals with no input from our species." By "our species," Dennell means modern humans.

Could the lives of Neanderthals, Denisovans, and modern humans have overlapped in time and space around 43,000 years ago? It is still an open question.

EARLY MIGRATION OUT OF AFRICA, JULY 2019

In July 2019, anthropologists reported the discovery of the 210,000-year-old remains of an Homo sapiens *sapiens*, modern human and the 170,000-year-old remains of a Neanderthal in Apidima Cave in southern Greece, more than 150,000 years older than previous modern human finds in Europe. As we speculate what happened during the discussion on modern human migration, it is likely that this early wave of modern humans migrated out of Africa but could not sustain their long-term presence. They might have been assimilated by Neanderthals.

HOMO LUZONENSIS IN THE PHILIPPINES, APRIL 2019

It has been made clear that the early human family tree is interwoven like a massive shrubbery. The simplified phylogenetic tree in chapter 5 is not meant to be complete and has bypassed most of the side spurs that do not factor into the direct ancestors of modern humans. On the one hand, a few Australopithecine species—like A. *africanus*, A. *afarensis*, and A. *sediba*—all exclusively evolved in Africa. On the other hand, quite a few more branches sprung up after Homo *erectus* migrated out of Africa. They most likely evolved from the H. *erectus* ancestors at their migration destinations. We have seen Yuanmou Man, Homo *antecessors* (mainly in Europe), Peking Man, and Java Man, to name a few. Now, we can add another to the list: Homo *luzonensis*.

In April 2019, researchers in the Philippines announced that they discovered a species of small-bodied ancient humans previously unknown on Luzon Island, dated to at least 50,000 to 70,000 years ago.

This hominin is similar to Homo naledi in that it has a mishmash of physical features like a patchwork of ancient and more advanced features, although smaller in size. This hominin was identified from a total of seven teeth and six small bones. The small fossil's curves and grooves reveal an unexpected mix of both ancient and more advanced traits. The small size of the teeth and relatively simple shape points to a more "modern" individual. Still, one upper premolar has three roots, a trait found in fewer than three percent of modern humans, which may be an indication of mutation EDAR gene (see chapter 12). One of the foot bones resembles those of ancient Australopithecines, a group that includes our famous human relative, Lucy, who trekked across Africa roughly 3,000,000 years ago.

New York University anthropologist Shara Bailey, an expert on ancient teeth, notes that South Africa's Homo *naledi*—discovered by a team including National Geographic grantee Lee Berger—also has features that look both ancient and modern. She takes the two discoveries as a sign that "mosaic" evolution was more common among hominins than once thought.

Paleoanthropologists knew that archaic hominins such as Homo *erectus* ventured over land bridges into parts of what is now Indonesia nearly a million years ago, but farther east, beyond the Wallace Line, it was thought that these hominins ran into ocean currents considered impassable without boats. Luzon seemed especially tricky for ancient hominins to reach, as it was never connected to the mainland by land bridges, even during LGM time. Our ancient ancestors' seafaring ability may not have been such a rarity after all.

While many scientists lauded the research for its thoroughness, defining a species from just 13 small bones and teeth is particularly tricky without corroborating DNA evidence. Though the scientists attempted to extract DNA, they were unsuccessful, as is common for samples that have stewed for millennia in the heat and humidity of tropical locales. However, we have seen that teeth can bear genetic evidence as to what the owners might have been, so it will be interesting to find out if these samples can clarify genetic attributes.

One thing remains clear: Southeast Asia was probably home to more diverse hominin species than current fossils let on.

ONE 15,600-YEAR-OLD HUMAN FOOTPRINT IN SOUTH AMERICA, APRIL 2019

Scientists in Chile have found a single footprint, dating to at least 15,600 years ago, making it the earliest sign of man's presence in the Americas. The footprint was found at the Pilauco excavation in the city of Osorno (820 kilometers south of Santiago), where scientists have been digging since 2007. Archeologists from the Austral University of Chile said the footprint was first spotted in 2011 next to a house. It took years for paleontologist Karen Moreno and geologist Mario Pino to confirm that the print was, indeed, human. As we have seen, there are other human footprints in the Americas, but none have dated as far back.

It was speculated that the footprint appears to be that of a barefoot male modern human, weighing about 70 kilograms (155 pounds). Another footprint found at a site south of Osorno was determined to be about 1,000 years more recent.

This area in Chile has proven rich in fossils, including evidence of an ancestor of today's elephants and American horses, and a more recent human presence. It might be fruitful to continue looking for signs that modern humans might have been at these locations. However, some of this evidence might be under the sea, where water levels were lower on the coasts during the glacial period.

I hesitated for a while to include it in this list because the evidence of the discovery of a single footprint is thin and speculative. In the end, implications for early modern human presence in South America is more thought-provoking than concrete proof.

. . .

HUMAN HANDEDNESS, NOVEMBER 2019

In November 2019, a new study was made public on *bioRxiv*—a preprint server for biology—providing insight into genetic determinants of left-handedness and ambidexterity. By combining data from more than 30 different studies, the authors managed to gather an impressive dataset of more than 1,700,000 individuals. Overall, there were 1,534,836 right-handers, 194,198 (11%) left-handers and 37,637 (2.1%) ambidextrous individuals in the dataset. Using this dataset, the authors conducted the world's largest genome-wide association study (GWAS) of handedness.

GWAS is a commonly used genetic research technique to link genetic variation in the brain, behavior, and even physical features. Participants give DNA samples (e.g., saliva, oral mucosa, or blood sample), and DNA is extracted from the samples. Scientists then analyze the entire genome of the samples by looking at millions of single nucleotide polymorphisms (SNPs). By testing a lot of individuals from right-handers and a lot of individuals from left-handers and comparing these SNPs systematically, scientists can identify which genes differ between the two groups.

The investigators found 41 genetic loci associated with left-handedness and seven associated with ambidexterity that reached statistical significance in the study. These are far more than any previous studies identified in smaller samples.

These significant findings suggest that handedness, like many other complex traits, is highly polygenic. Genetic variants predisposing left-handedness may underlie some association with psychiatric disorders observed in multiple observational studies.

This work, as impressive as it is, has not been peer-reviewed when made public initially. At this time, I include this study because of its implication when using GWAS and the potential for connecting genes to macroscopic human traits and behaviors.

. . .

MOVE OVER DNA—ANCIENT PROTEIN STARTs TO REVEAL
HUMANITY'S HISTORY, MAY 2019

This title is from a news clip from the magazine *Nature*, high-lighting anthropology's new research tool, but research results based on the new ancient geometric tool has contributed significantly to construct the reach of roaming Denisovan territories in our discussion on human migration in chapter 13.

Sometime in the past 160,000 years or so, a Denisovan lived and passed away in a cave high on the Tibetan Plateau in China. After millennia, the remains of a part of jawbone with some teeth were gradually coated in a mineral crust, and the DNA from this ancient ancestor was lost to time and weather, but some signals from this person's past existence persisted.

Proteins lingered deep in the hominin's teeth, degraded but still identifiable. When scientists analyzed them, they detected collagen, a structural support protein found in bone and other tissues. In its chemical signature was a single amino-acid variant that is not present in the collagen of modern humans or Neanderthals. It flagged the jawbone as belonging to a member of the mysterious hominin group called Denisovans.

The discovery of a Denisovan in China was a significant landmark. It was the first individual found outside Denisova Cave in Siberia, where all other remains of its kind had been previously identified. The site's location on the Tibetan Plateau, more than 3,000 meters above sea level, suggested that Denisovans had lived in icy cold, low-oxygen environments. In light of the presence of Denisovan genes in modern humans, particularly those in Indo-Pacific regions, the discovery of a Denisovan at this location should not be such a surprise.

The finding also marked another milestone: it was the first time an ancient hominin was identified using only proteins. It is one of the most striking discoveries yet for the fledgling field of paleoproteomics, in which scientists analyze ancient proteins to answer questions about the history and evolution of humans and other animals. Scientists had previously recovered proteins from 1,800,000-year-old animal teeth and a 3,800,000-year-old eggshell. Now, they hope that paleoproteomics could be used to provide insight into other ancient hominin fossils that have lost all traces of DNA. By looking at variations in these proteins, scientists hope to answer long-standing questions about the evolution of archaic human groups, such as which lineages were direct ancestors of Homo *sapiens*.

We have seen how full genomes have deciphered human speciation, the Homo *sapiens* family tree, modern human ancestral lineages, and migration histories. Hopefully, this new tool can help unlock more human mysteries and construct more detailed and better phylogenetic trees.

The full science and potential of paleoproteomics anthropology is, however, still very young. We might see the day when modern humans and early humans are better connected on the family tree on the molecular level, either through DNA or proteins.

2020

WE COOKED STARCHY FOOD IN SOUTH AFRICA 170,000 YEARS AGO, JANUARY 2020

According to a publication by scientists from the University of the Witwatersrand, South Africa, they have discovered that starchy food was cooked and consumed by our South African ancestors 170,000 years ago.

The inhabitants of the Border Cave in the Lebombo Mountains on the Kwazulu-Natal/eSwatini border were cooking starchy plants 170,000 years ago, according to Professor Lyn Wadley, a scientist from the Wits Evolutionary Studies Institute at the University of the Witwatersrand, South Africa (Wits ESI). This discovery is much older than earlier reports for cooking similar plants, and it provides a refreshed insight into the behavioral practices of early modern humans in South Africa. It also implies that they shared food and used wooden sticks to extract plants, mostly tubers, from the ground.

During the excavation, scientists recognized the small, charred cylinders as rhizomes, underground stems including bamboo, ginger, turmeric, lotus, and many types of ferns. Some of these rhizomes are edible and sought out as a delicacy these days. They are often nutritious and carbohydrate-rich with a high energy value, approximately equivalent to barley, wheat, or rice. While they are edible raw, the rhizomes are fibrous and have high-fracture toughness until they are cooked, when they are easier to peel and digest.

The presence of these rhizomes implies that they could have provided a reliable, familiar food source for early humans trekking within—or even outside of—Africa. Hunter-gatherers tend to be highly mobile, so the wide distribution of a potentially staple plant food would have ensured food security.

YET ANOTHER ARCHAIC GROUP IN HOMO SAPIEN FAMILY TREE, FEBRUARY 2020

The Max Planck Institute group speculated as early as 2010 that there might be a third group of archaic Homo *sapiens* when Denisovans were discovered. However, it was not determined exactly where and when that group came into the picture.

A report in February 2020 indicates there is another group of archaic Homo *sapiens* who interbred with Homo *sapiens* in West Africa approximately 43,000 years ago. The genetic data analysis reveals a substantial contribution of archaic ancestry in shaping the gene pool of present-day West African populations.

This discovery indicates there may still be more archaic Homo *sapiens* who contributed to the modern human gene pools. If you try to include all of them on our Homo *sapiens* family tree like the ones we discussed in chapter 10, there will be quite a few more subspecies to add.

EARLIER THAN LGM MIGRATION TO MEXICO? JULY 2020

We have dedicated a full section to the peopling of the Americas in chapter 13, but this new discovery provides possible evidence that modern humans might have been present in Mesoamerica before the last glacial maxima started 26,000 years ago. Recent investigations provide evidence of a human presence in the northwest region of Mexico, the Chiapas Highlands, Central Mexico, and the Caribbean coast as early as 30,000 years ago. This timeframe predates that of the Clovis culture and could open new directions for research.

Artifact evidence at the site corroborates previous findings of a culture dating to LGM in the Americas (26,500-19,000 years ago). This evidence pushes back dates for human dispersal to the region as early as 33,000-31,000 years ago.

These reportedly early dates are outliers of the prevailing concept that Native Americans came to the Americas no earlier than 25,000 years ago. We have to re-ascertain the validity of data, but we also need to recognize that this might be a special exception if true.

A June 2015 report suggests that Denisovan ancestry in Native Americans is derived either from a common ancestry line with—or gene flow from—the common ancestor of New Guineans and Australians. This suggestion may point to a more complex history involving East Eurasians and Oceanians than previously suspected. There is the possibility that an Indian tribe (Maidu) in Northern California, USA, interbred with Native Hawaiians who were brought to the sugar fields in California some time ago. This possibility is certainly a viable explanation for how Denisovan genes are present in North America.

A 2012 study indicates some Denisovan genes reach as far as South America without offering any plausible explanation. It is not clear how ancient Denisovan genes ended up in South America in Native Americans. This begs the question of how Denisovan genes got into South American Native Americans other than interbreeding between Hawaiians and Native Americans. This most recent, yet to verify evidence of human activities in Middle America as early as 33,000 years ago may speak of the possibility of Denisovans reaching America that early, but this line of reasoning is still highly speculative.

. . .

GENETIC RISK FACTOR FOR SEVERE COVID-19 INHERITED FROM NEANDERTHALS, SEPTEMBER 2020

This most recent study links a gene cluster on chromosome 3 to severe COVID-19 cases. This discovery is covered in chapter 10 and will not repeat it except to highlight how much macroscopic insight we can gain by studying human evolution at the microscopic level.

2021

NEANDERTHALS AND HUMANS HAVE THE SAME AUDITORY CAPACITY, MARCH 2021

We noted before that not only Neanderthals have the similar throat structures, they can almost utter the same sound and voices as humans by simulation. Neanderthals are also found to have similar auditory capacity as humans. Detailed 3-D analysis of Neanderthals and human ear structures points to similar audio responses as modern humans. They have similar high frequency responses up to approximately 5 KHz and can hear the 8th octave of the middle C (4th) note. I know I have trouble hearing that.

SUMMARY

You might have noticed that the latest discovery in the list was as recent as March 2021. This chapter is, in reality, a live document. A few recent discoveries have already made it into other chapters, modifying our stories to some extent. Credible findings and evidence will continue to fuel our evolutionary stories' frequent changes if proven beyond reproach. In that sense, this book is also a live document that will need periodic updates. I opted for e-publishing this book because I can keep up with anthropological advances as soon as they prove worth updating.

BIBLIOGRAPHY

1. "Denisovan Ancestry in East Eurasian and Native American Populations," Pengfei Qin and Mark Stoneking, *Molecular Biology and Evolution*, **32**, 2665–2674 (2015).
2. "U-Th dating of carbonate crusts reveals Neandertal origin of Iberian cave art," D. L. Hoffmann, C. D. Standish, M. García-Diez, P. B. Pettitt, J. A. Milton, J. Zilhão, J. J. Alcolea-González, P. Cantalejo-Duarte, H. Collado, R. de Balbín, M. Lorblanchet, J. Ramos-Muñoz, G.-Ch. Weniger, A. W. G. Pike, *Science,* **359**, 912-915 (2018).
3. "Terminal Pleistocene epoch human footprints from the Pacific coast of Canada," Duncan McLaren, Daryl Fedje, Angela Dyck, Quentin Mackie, Alisha Gauvreau, Jenny Cohen. *PLOS,* March 28, 2018, https://doi.org/10.1371/journal.pone.0193522
4. "Timing of archaic hominin occupation of Denisova Cave in southern Siberia," Zenobia Jacobs, Bo Li, Michael V. Shunkov, Maxim B. Kozlikin, Nataliya S. Bolikhovskaya, Alexander K. Agadjanian, Vladimir A. Uliyanov, Sergei K. Vasiliev, Kieran O'Gorman, Anatoly P. Derevianko & Richard G. Roberts, *Nature,* **565**, 594-599 (2019).
5. "Age estimates for hominin fossils and the onset of the Upper Palaeolithic at Denisova Cave," Katerina Douka, Viviane Slon, Zenobia Jacobs, Christopher Bronk Ramsey, Michael V. Shunkov, Anatoly P. Derevianko, Fabrizio Mafessoni, Maxim B. Kozlikin, Bo Li, Rainer Grün, Daniel Comeskey, Thibaut Devièse, Samantha Brown, Bence Viola, Leslie Kinsley, Michael Buckley, Matthias Meyer, Richard G. Roberts, Svante Pääbo, Janet Kelso & Tom Higham, *Nature,* **565**, 640-644 (2019).
6. "A new species of Homo from the Late Pleistocene of the Philippines," Florent Détroit, Armand Salvador Mijares, Julien Corny, Guillaume Daver, Clément Zanolli, Eusebio

Dizon, Emil Robles, Rainer Grün & Philip J. Piper, *Nature*, **568**, 181-186 (2019).

7. "American Indians, Neanderthals, and Denisovans: Insights from PCA Views," German Dziebel, *Anthropogenesis Blog*, March 2012.

8. "Genome-wide association study identifies 48 common genetic variants associated with handedness," Gabriel Cuellar Partida, Joyce Y Tung, and 116 more contributors, https://doi.org/10.1101/831321, Nov (2019).

9. "Recovering signals of ghost archaic introgression in African populations" Arun Durvasula and Sriram Sankararaman, *Science Advances*, **6**, Feb (2020).

10. "A late Middle Pleistocene Denisovan mandible from the Tibetan Plateau," Fahu Chen, Frido Welker, Chuan-Chou Shen, Shara E. Bailey, Inga Bergmann, Simon Davis, Huan Xia, Hui Wang, Roman Fischer, Sarah E. Freidline, Tsai-Luen Yu, Matthew M. Skinner, Stefanie Stelzer, Guangrong Dong, Qiaomei Fu, Guanghui Dong, Jian Wang, Dongju Zhang & Jean-Jacques Hublin, *Nature*, **569**, 409-412 (2019).

11. "Early modern humans cooked starchy food in South Africa, 170,000 years ago," ps://phys.org/news/2020-01-early-modern-humans-cooked-starchy.html.

12. "Evidence of human occupation in Mexico around the Last Glacial Maximum," Ciprian F. Ardelean, Lorena Becerra-Valdivia, Mikkel Winther Pedersen, Jean-Luc Schwenninger, Charles G. Oviatt, Juan I. Macías-Quintero, Joaquin Arroyo-Cabrales, Martin Sikora, Yam Zul E. Ocampo-Díaz, Igor I. Rubio-Cisneros, Jennifer G. Watling, Vanda B. de Medeiros, Paulo E. De Oliveira, Luis Barba-Pingarón, Agustín Ortiz-Butrón, Jorge Blancas-Vázquez, Irán Rivera-González, Corina Solís-Rosales, María Rodríguez-Ceja, Devlin A. Gandy, Zamara Navarro-Gutierrez, Jesús J. De La Rosa-Díaz, Vladimir Huerta-Arellano, Marco B. Marroquín-Fernández, L. Martín

Martínez-Riojas, Alejandro López-Jiménez, Thomas Higham & Eske Willerslev, *Nature* (2020). https://doi.org/10.1038/s41586-020-2509-0

13. "The major genetic risk factor for severe COVID-19 is inherited from Neanderthals", Hugo Zeberg and Svante Pääbo, *Nature,* (2020). https://doi.org/10.1038/s41586-020-2818-3

14. "Neanderthals and modern humans have similar auditory and speech capacities", Mercedes Conde-Valverde, Ignacio Martínez, Rolf M. Quam, Manuel Rosa, Alex D. Velez, Carlos Lorenzo, Pilar Jarabo, José María Bermúdez de Castro, Eudald Carbonell and Juan Luis Arsuaga, *Nature Ecology and Evolution,* (2021). DOI 10.1038/s41559-21-01391-6

15

WE CAN BE A BETTER SPECIES

This book was initially planned to memorialize what I learned about human evolution and the experience of acquiring the knowledge. As a physicist, I consider that I have truly learned something when everything looks reasonable through the lens of physics and can logically fit together. I believe there must be cause-and-effect causality in all evolutionary events, and the common logic should thread through the whole evolutionary process without fail. The first objective of this book, then, is to convey my learned knowledge with such a vision. I have taken my messy notes I took through classes, reading, theorizing, and deliberation, and organized them into an evolutionary story with a physical logical theme. I hope this book gives readers an evolutionary story from one physicist's perspective and find that there is an encompassing principle dictating the activities and outcome.

As I dive further into human evolution, I realized how close we are to each other biologically and genetically, yet wars and violence always permeates all facets of human life in oral and written history. We are definitely missing something that this closeness cannot translate into a more benign human behavior toward each other. The second objective is an attempt to awaken our innate empathetic nature that I believe is the key to to improve ourselves as a species.

ACHIEVING THE FIRST OBJECTIVE

Although it has been more than five years since I started on human evolution, I am hopelessly stuck as an amateur anthropologist but happy to be one. I am well aware that I am not an expert in any of individual disciplines needed for a wholesome human evolutionary picture. I am not a biologist and cannot understand the intricate interaction between organisms or how base pairs are arranged to form double helices. I am not a chemist and cannot understand how oxygen concentration affects the mutation of mtDNA. I am not a geneticist since I cannot effortlessly connect genes with specific human traits or use parsimony algorithms to identify the most likely phylogenetic trees, or how they are passed down through generations. A mathematician, I am not, and I cannot determine the probabilities of different speciation scenarios. I am also not a traditional anthropologist who can envision ancient human gaits based on the anatomy of fossil evidence, nor am I an evolutionary psychiatrist who can postulate, with sound assumptions, what drives the social dynamics of early human groups. I am not a populationist who can understand the dynamics of migration and growth. The modern-day artificial intelligence scientist—of which I am not one—is needed to decipher correlations between traits and genomes through massive GWAS analysis. After the last few years' immersion in every facet of human evolution, I have a pretty good idea of our roots but I am at best a generalist in anthropology.

As a physicist, I used quantum physics to improve the efficiency of excimer lasers generally used in optical projection lithography in nanometer scale semiconductor manufacturing. I correlated, through quantum physics, the behavior of super-cold hydrogen in laboratories and similar features found on our outer giant planets of Uranus and Neptune. As an engineer, I designed highly reliable and fast communication backbones so that cloud computing, storage, and Internet of Things had the infrastructure on which to ride.

By employing the same analytical skills of sorting through complex problems logically, I have articulated the evolutionary principle for the foundation of all organisms, including humans (chapter 3). Under the cause and effect umbrella, every evolutionary activity behaves according to the governance of the principle in an orderly manner amid seemingly chaotic biological activities and phenomena.

We have a crude answer to humans' earliest question of "where did we (the human species) come from?" when we first became our own species. With a reasonable level of confidence, we understand how we evolved into a new and different species 7,000,000 years ago from a common ancestor between humans and chimps. That theory of speciation is substantiated by massive data analysis based on DNA from humans, archaic humans, and our primate relatives (chapter 11). We constructed a simplified phylogenetic tree from that point on, focusing on us, modern humans, starting from when we bid adieu to the chimps (chapter 5). Whenever possible, we made connections between genetic evidence and fossil evidence to help solidify our ancestral lines. We also included as many genetically related Homo sapiens as we could in our family tree (chapter 10).

As for modern humans, we found out that we have a short family lineage traceable to Africa as our homeland and at a time of 200,000 years ago (chapter 9). We defined ourselves as modern humans, a distinct species different from any other living organism, through DNA analysis. We also found out that as a species, we shared an overwhelming majority of our genes. The differences and varieties within us are simply nature's means to assure species diversity and longevity (chapter 12).

Molecular anthropology is complicated and needs intense, indepth training to be conversant. Still, we dabbled in the basics of DNA and molecular clocks in two chapters to date the ages of traits, and thus, our ancestors (chapters 8 and 9). With the essential background of molecular anthropology on haplogroups, we combined macroscopic and microscopic evidence to plot our migration throughout our land (chapter 13).

The previous chapters have thoroughly outlined our transformational journey from ape to human based on evolutionary principles with sound logic. The answers to "Where did we come from?" can be considered pretty much in hand. The first objective of articulating my level of human evolutionary knowledge, however superficial, can be regarded as accomplished.

The current status of evolutionary theory is well established and seems relatively stable at its foundation. However, there are continuing quests to improve our understanding of evolution built on this solid foundation, utilizing ever-advancing science and technologies. The knowledge base behind who we are will continue to accumulate, improve, and expand. Readers who become well-versed in the big and logical evolutionary picture can now interpret theories with their own understanding as long as they are consistent with the cumulative knowledge.

ACHIEVING THE SECOND OBJECTIVE?

Where are we with respect to the second objective? I have planned to invoke and remind us of our innate and genetically built-in goodness toward each other. I hope we think twice about the impact on our fellow humans before any decisions are made because of this reminder. Subsequently, this little extra step of consideration could be a seed and means to stem our propensity of ill will toward each other, rendering a better human species.

This last chapter gives a final push and attempts to hit home the point of our closeness and achieves the second objective . The hope is that we appreciate this feeling, take advantage of the underlying human quality, and channel it for the betterment of our species.

WE ARE REALLY CLOSE

Let us explore this "closeness" a little further to get a better feel for the second objective. The three aspects illustrated below should provide a good perspective.

BIOLOGICAL BROTHERHOOD AND SISTERHOOD

One of the most memorable quotes describing the significance of the pioneering work by Cann et al. in 1987 (see chapter 9) is by Stephen Jay Gould, who says: "This idea (referring to the single source of our Adam and Eve) is tremendously important...There is a kind of biological brotherhood that's much more profound than we ever realized." Stephen Jay Gould was an American paleontologist, evolutionary biologist, and historian of science. Recall that he was one of the two people who invented the concept of punctuated equilibrium. A quick reminder of the conclusion of Cann's work: all human beings living today, without exception, have a few common ancestors hailing from Africa a mere 200,000 years ago, or about 8,000 generations ago. That conclusion cast in stone that we are not just close—every one of us, we are family.

Gould's statement was very appropriate at the time, some 30 years ago, and it is even more so today.

Our Genetic Closeness

Out of the 25,000 genes in our genome, only about 150 are different. These genes actively participate in the evolutionary process. The rest are building blocks used to replicate ourselves as with identical twins. In our discussion on commonalities and varieties, we realized that what makes us a unique species is the commonalities that tell us apart from other animals. This alone should give us a warm and fuzzy feeling for others already.

Our variety and diversity are the results of the cross-pollination of these few genes. This diversity is the primary source for people with different talents who generate new ideas with the expertise to accelerate our collective knowledge when it comes to science, engineering, technology, and the arts to enrich culture and our lives. These minor differences in genes are most beneficial for human beings. How could we not appreciate the variety of our close family members?

As diverse as we are from minute genetic differences, there are many more variations than simple, "hard-wired," genetic diversity to help us march through our evolution. There is another layer of complexity on top of the hard-wired genes that further enhances their ability to create varieties of human beings that adapt to environmental challenges. There is a set of instructions that tell genomes to express or suppress specific genes on the fly in response to the environment to which the genomes and organisms are exposed. This set of instructions also resides in various parts of the genome. The study of these soft-wired instructions entails the primary subjects of epigenetics. Even though identical twins have identical genomes at the beginning of their lives, they can be very different at birth or later in their lives because of these on the fly instructions in action. Through the processes we call epigenetics, the rest of the genome plays an important role in controlling how the 150 different genes are presenting themselves and expressed as phenotypes. The diversity of what we observe in all of us now is nothing compared to the possibilities these nearly identical genomes can generate.

Whatever variety or versatility we see outwardly is the result of these minute differences in the permutation and combination of the genes involved.

Our Physical Closeness

All 7.8 billion of us look very much alike anatomically with some apparent variety, as we enumerated in chapter 12, but there is no danger that any of us may be mistaken as non-human with just a glance at each other. A few simple facts go beyond just our appearance to illustrate our closeness.

Our body parts are interchangeable! Of course, this is not as simple as it sounds. My nephew had an eye infection with keratitis bacteria due to infrequent contact lens cleaning ten years ago. This cyst-forming microorganism usually causes the cornea to become inflamed. For one in every four people infected, the disease results in the loss of most of their vision, and even blindness in some cases. My nephew's left eye went blind and needed a cornea transplant. The transplant was a success since a cornea transplant is considered the least intrusive to the Major Histocompatibility Complex. Yet, he was on immunosuppression treatment for at least two years due to the MHC.

Histocompatibility is our immune system's ability to attack tissues that are not genetically compatible with our genes on the cellular level. Human organ transplantation requires donors that are a genetic match as well as willing to participate in such deeds. Our genetic closeness is the first step toward the success of organ transplants. Histocompatibility is the built-in protective mechanism that allows our species to retain its integrity to maintain survival viability. We are not just close to each other by birth; we are close to each other by necessity. As xenotransplantation is not yet practical, human body parts are still the most viable organ transplant sources, along with the help of immunosuppression treatment.

Our body parts are not 100% interchangeable, per se, but they are our best matches.

HOW HUMAN BEINGS FARED AS A SPECIES

Since we are so close to each other in many aspects, it is interesting to see how this translates to our existence as a species. More specifically, we should zoom out and review how human beings have fared in the grand scheme of our evolution as a species.

I should emphasize that when we judge how our species fares in the evolutionary process, we refer to ourselves as a single entity and not specific individuals. If we succeed, it is as a whole species, and the same goes if it fails. Our success or failure is a result of the collective effort of all individuals, although each might contribute to different aspects of the feat.

WE HAVE NOT FARED WELL

Wars, Colonialism, Imperialism

We depend on various resources to survive as individuals and social groups. To make resources available to all, we help each other acquire and share them in good and lean times. However, somewhere along the way, we made a wrong turn, even when we did not lack the necessary resources. In particular, as the social groups grew larger, we instigated ideologies to keep groups united and fend off strangers in the name of the greater good even when the danger is minimum. When resources are truly scarce, or ideologies clash with other social groups, the interaction between groups escalates to war whenever there are slight perceived existential threats. We have tried our hardest to annihilate other groups of human beings to survive in the name of the greater good.

As such, we have almost always engaged in conflict, war, or we are on the brink of war through history immemorial, but the enormity of the evil of which we are capable of inflicting on our fellow human beings through war—again, in the name of the greater good—never fails to render all of us speechless. Animals, who only kill for food or protect their young, are more humane than our species has proven to be. We sometimes kill for no reason at all. It seems there is an abundance of hatred because of our biological prosperity and not because of a lack of resources. It is fair to say that we are even worse than animals in some respects.

The war of resources and ideologies went global and devolved into massive colonialism and imperialism in the 15th through 20th centuries. The motivation behind this is nothing short of greed, ideology, heroism, and the egotism of the states, resulting in unspeakable atrocities. Wars, colonialism, and imperialism have killed a significant portion of our species.

In fact, colonialism and imperialism have been rampant for thousands of years in our history, not just in the past 500 years, although these -isms were invented of late. For example, Genghis Khan was definitely a hero in most aspects, but during his rampage through Asia and Europe he was a ruthless murderer in the names of making the world Mongol Empire's pastures. In the 13th century, he and his empire slaughtered fifty million innocent people in a mere 100 years. Considering the old world had a population of 250 million at the time, Genghis Khan's actions toward our own species is utterly unforgivable.

Inequality and Slavery

As the social groups became bigger, resources needed to be allocated within and traded between groups. Rules and structures were created to ensure we did not trample on others' toes for the group's greater good, but again, we took a wrong turn. We mistook structures —be they chiefdoms, monarchies, and republics—as permission to construct caste systems dividing us into classes to function as different parts in the machine of social groups. We assign classes to people to serve different purposes within social groups for various functions. Slavery was a natural outgrowth of caste inequality, which was encouraged, you guessed it, for the greater good of the group. We certainly do not treat our fellow humans the same as we would like to be treated.

Racism

War, colonialism, imperialism, ideology, and inequality have perpetuated racism collectively, because of our intrinsic varieties. Most of the time, this is cited in the name of the greater good of some groups. We executed genocide simply because we were different in the smallest details. There seems to be no end to the evil we will do to each other.

If we are not convinced about our genetic closeness and that race is meaningless (chapter 9), we are not intelligent enough to be considered human beings and do not deserve to be counted as a part of our species. Instead, the apparent superficial varieties and differences that so enrich our species should be cherished. Still, global racism rages on.

Warring With Our Environment

We wage another war against the environment in which we live, and that may have substantially altered the path of our evolution and possibly change our futures. We owe our existence to this environment, together with all the other ingredients that feed into this huge evolutionary crucible.

We need a feedstock to keep the evolutionary process moving nonstop. We also need the environment to mediate the process of natural selection. We were not capable of appraising the impact of our evolution on the environment in the early days, but we continue to be oblivious to the changes to our environment that are partly our own doing these days, even if we are intelligent enough to know better.

We gobble up resources without considering the consequences. We have driven many animals to extinction in the last few hundred thousand years. For example, according to statistical analysis, the rate of the extinction of species per year is 1,000 times faster than before modern humans came onto the scene. A more recent study published in 2020 shows that brain expansion to the rate of carnivore extinction in East Africa happened in close synchronicity. It looks like the more intelligent we become, the more devastation we cause the global fauna on which we feed.

Fast forward to the 21st century; we continue to relentlessly and greedily use up natural resources, including fertile ground, metals, fossil fuels, rare earth metals, plants, land, and of course, water. We keep splurging with the false hope (are we not supposed to be intelligent enough to know better?) that we can always find replacement resources and land somewhere else on the planet. The hope is that even if we run out of space and resources, we can move to other planets since we have the will and technology to do it—just ask Elon Musk. However, despite how smart and technologically advanced we are, there is only one earth on which we are trapped for the foreseeable thousand or so years. This begs the question, are we really so intelligent if we do not know what might be coming?

Michel Mayor, who should be very believable from his vantage point of being the first to search and find exoplanets, exclaimed that migrating to exoplanets is just impossible. Mayor, a Swiss physicist who won the 2019 Nobel Prize in physics, said he felt the need to "kill all the statements that say, 'OK, we will go to a livable planet if one day life is not possible on Earth.'" If we are talking about exoplanets, this could not be clearer: we will not migrate there. The reason might sound too naive and simple to most people, had he not won a Nobel Prize: it will take too long to get there. As far as I know, the nearest inhabitable exoplanet is four light-years away or 40 trillion kilometers from earth.

Bottom line? We have to survive in our sandbox, the place on which we evolved: Earth. Modern-day species survival is very different from our evolutionary past. In the olden days, we were able to keep expanding into new territories whenever we ran out of resources when we started our first migration from Africa. We have since run out of new and unexplored spaces and environments. We are now at the point at which we have to think about our evolutionary goals and behave accordingly with respect to our living quarters.

WE ARE DOING PRETTY WELL, TOO

It seems that something must have gone right in our evolution to make us so successful at growing our population to such vast numbers, all 7.8 billion human beings. If so, why do we so often resort to violence and mutual destruction with the possibility of annihilating ourselves as a species? We cannot help but ask if there are any redeeming qualities left in us other than our numbers? The answer is a resounding yes.

Humanity

Just like any other social animal, we do not survive as individuals. We have naturally adopted humanity and a group survival instinct, taking care of each other as any social animal would. We stay together to ensure we have as much security as possible in the most basic social unit of a family. Strong family values enable us to expand our humanity to fellow human beings. We support each other with materialistic and emotional needs. Though minor squabbles happen once in a while, we can generally look past it and eventually appease each other.

Language, Intelligence, Communication, And Culture

Human evolution also brings about our ability to vocalize through our anatomy and intelligence. We can vocalize information and thoughts in a language that is said to advance hand in hand with our intelligence. The exchange between two or more individuals using language constitutes the backbone of communication. Not only does it raise our knowledge base, but it also gives intelligence the depth to understand abstract concepts and thoughts and articulate beyond the physical part of our evolution. We have created culture in every aspect of our lives due to verbalized and written communications. There is no single cultural achievement in science, technology, music, art, and knowledge that is not borne out of intelligence and the ability to communicate with other humans.

Fostering Kinships

We found and built shelters to keep us from harsh climates and imminent and perceived danger, not just for our immediate family but also for other families and fellow citizens. We hunted for food in coordinated efforts, either big game by males under patriarchy or small animals by females for our livelihood. We cooked and shared the food with everyone circling the fire in our shelter and shared stories of our outings or families in hunter-gatherer times. We built camaraderie by getting to know each other through these intimate interactions. A fringe benefit of these fireside chats was further exercising our brains while devouring rich and nutritious cooked meat beneficial for brain growth. We became farmers and raised crops to continue the expansion of our species. Resources became a lot more abundant to sustain larger, related groups. We succeeded in expanding populations far beyond families and tribes.

Managing Population With Intelligence

While we were becoming more numerous, the close interaction with each other and between social groups created friction because we continuously strived for better food and mating resources. We had to set rules, guidelines, and boundaries within ever-growing groups so everyone in the group had a fair share of resources while making sure we did not trample on the well-being of our group-mates. These rules, which eventually led to regulations and laws, seem artificial but had their origins in goodwill with the intent of taking care of one another.

It is very fortunate that, besides growing in numbers, human beings also evolved the skills and intelligence to recognize the importance of setting boundaries and putting organizations together to manage increases in population size. We invented and enforced rules to ensure we did not obstruct the paths to other people's welfare. We have managed all 7.8 billion of us in a mostly ordered manner through rules, regulations, organizations, and governments.

Enlightenment

In the face of various artificial and self-inflicted tragedies, we eventually managed to steer our civilization through the "ENLIGHT-ENMENT" age, which puts humanism, reason, liberty, and freedom ahead of our shortcomings. This enlightenment led to the creation of republics and democracy, which also brought us prosperity and a more equitable world.

Even though Enlightenment alone was not enough to stem WWI and WWII, we became more conscious about our behaviors and set standards for right and wrong from the point of view of humanism. Luckily, we have not had a major war or conflict since WWII, 80 years ago. According to Steven Pinker, we have improved our lives tremendously while reducing disputes and conflicts to a large extent because Enlightenment works pretty well. Overall, we are not doing too badly, indeed.

EMPATHY AND HUMAN DUALITY

WE ARE A SPECIES WITH FLAWS

An unavoidable assessment of the human species is that we are simultaneously benevolent and malevolent. Nature has given us all the needed materials lets evolution happen without interference. It also gave us a set of ground rules and the randomness with which evolutionary events are triggered, but nature did not make a judgment as to how evolution or its outcome—us, in particular—would be successful or not. If we consider ourselves the most intelligent creation on earth, it is then our responsibility to judge how we fare as a species because we are no longer passive participants in our evolution. By just reviewing how we have done, the good deeds we performed, and the atrocities we committed, I can categorically say that we have serious flaws.

As we are now a part of evolution, we owe it to ourselves to find the root cause of the bifurcation between being malevolent and benevolent at the same time. The least we should do is to figure out how we can maximize benevolence and minimize malevolence. We might use the seemingly lofty and noble yet reasonable goal of "with malice toward none, with charity for all" as a guideline.

THE ROOT CAUSE OF HUMAN DUALITY: EMPATHY

It seems that we are stuck with this good and evil duality, like it or not. Meanwhile, good and evil are not mutually exclusive; they are present hand in hand, and we cannot be all good or all bad all the time. I have concluded that the root cause of this duality is our innate empathic nature. We could even say empathy is in our genes since it is inherently and deeply rooted in all of us since before we became humans.

Empathy Manifested

Empathy is the ability to understand and share the feelings of others around you. As we have already found out, all primates have the capacity for empathy but differ in degrees among species.

It is most instructive to observe how empathy manifests itself in primates in their natural habitat, as untainted by cultures or social structures as possible. Primatologist Frans de Waal is well-versed in primate social behavior, including conflict resolution, cooperation, inequity aversion, and food-sharing. He has found that within social group sizes of ten and 20 as the upper limit of primate groups, they exhibit a few empathetic behaviors.

All primates have the capacity to resonate their feelings among individuals. They share emotions without being prompted to do so.

As such, this is the most unambiguous indication of the natural capacity for empathy. According to Waals, by measuring the expression of distress and arousal in great apes and how they cope, he confirmed that efficient, emotional regulation is an essential part of empathy. Empathy is what allows great apes and humans to absorb the distress of others without being overly distressed themselves. This capacity of feeling the pain, grief, or sorrow of other members of the group is a fundamental sign of empathy.

Primates also exhibit equitable sharing of materialistic possessions. One of the most illuminating examples is demonstrated by letting chimps play the Ultimatum Game. Chimps respond in the same way as human children, preferring equitable outcomes rather than the undesirable result of not having it. This mentality of sharing limited resources is a strong indication that the desire for the well-being of others is similar between chimps and humans. It has also been observed that chimps might reciprocate food transfer by giving food most often to those who have given food back to them most often. Food transfer might be part of a more generalized form of reciprocity in which individuals exchange various types of resources and services.

Settling conflicts and reconciliation are a part of life in the world of primates. Depending on the exact primate species and resources available, they seem to function well in sizes ranging from less than ten and up to 20 as the upper limit. The usual squabbles or competition for resources and love from one another is typical among members, but what keeps them together and maintains harmony is undoubtedly empathy, according to de Waal. When some unavoidable disagreements or scuffles arise, "reconciliation" for reunions is common not long after a conflict, while the memory is still fresh. This reconciliation is a step to soothe bad feelings that might ruin group harmony and reduce the group's ability to work together when external threats arise and is a fundamental reason why broader conflicts do not build-up to the level of war.

Empathy in Human Beings

We see that primates resonate emotions naturally in their native settings. They share resources equitably when possible. Even when conflicts arise and devolve into scuffles, they have the instinctive social skills to appease engaging parties. All of these characteristics seem to work well in social groups of relatively few individuals in non-human primates. It would not be too far of an extension to believe that we human beings share the same empathy because we are primates, after all. The major difference is that human's social groups were in the order of 30 to 150 during the stone ages. Empathy has to work a lot harder to have the same appeasing effect on all fronts. In particular, it is not clear if we have evolved enough brain-power to handle the highly dynamic social complexity brought about by much larger group sizes.

BIFURCATION TOWARD DUALITY: TRUE AND MANUFAC-TURED EMPATHY

According to R. I. M. Dunbar, our neocortex, the set of layers of the mammalian cerebral cortex involved in higher-order brain functions such as sensory perception, cognition, generation of motor commands, spatial reasoning, and language, has also evolved to handle group sizes that are comfortable to us. Our evolution may not have anticipated that we would discover and develop all sorts of resources to sustain group sizes substantially larger than 150. As a result, our cognition and intelligence invented means to allow for fast population growth, leaving the slower evolutionary process on the overused neocortex behind. The neocortex is stuck on being able to deal with smaller group sizes, the instinctual empathetic capacity cannot catch up with the growing population. As was famously exclaimed by Tony Stankus in *Our Modern Skulls House A Stone Age Brain*, we have been unable to effectively use our insufficient empathic capacity to handle complex human factors in large group sizes.

As our populations grew faster than we could handle by instinct, our intelligence (also using the same busy neocortex) invented rules, hierarchies, and organizations to make sure that "empathy" was "institutionalized" to deal with social issues our instinctive empathy could not. This institutionalized empathy is manufactured and forced empathy rather than natural and genuine.

Genuine empathy is the beginning of morality, leading to sympathy, compassion, morality, ethics, rules, and finally, laws while societies are getting larger. Institutionalized empathy has managed our orderly growth...most of the time, but it is often disguised as being "for the greater good" of social groups. It is also very likely that as soon as empathy is institutionalized, we stop feeling genuine empathy and are left with an artificial one. We start to use institutionalized empathy to cover up our greed and selfishness in the name of the greater good. It seems justified to instigate fighting, violence, war, and atrocities.

Manufactured empathy has been beneficial for humans, nonetheless. It has served humans well when used properly since it was borne out of true empathy, after all. It is the glaring complacency of misusing manufactured empathy that had been our downfall.

It is at this juncture we bifurcate into a simultaneously benevolent and malevolent species.

WE CAN BE A BETTER SPECIES

Having taken a look at how we have fared as a species, we can conclude that we do have what it takes to grow our population to phenomenal sizes by taking care of each other, either through genuine or manufactured empathy. At the same time, we have also committed a plethora of atrocities toward each other in the names of greater good through manufactured empathy. It is blatantly apparent that we should maximize the benevolence empathy brings about and minimize the malevolence when manufactured empathy is misused to bring about a healthier species.

I am not aware of any existing practical philosophies, rules, codes of conduct, or doctrines that can easily further the benevolence and rein in the malevolence through empathy. As a result, I resort to repeatedly emphasizing the feeling of closeness so empathy can be reawakened to be more spontaneous than manufactured. If we zoom out to look at the human species as a whole, our species' future depends on how well we can use our intelligence to fill in the gaps between the genuine and manufactured empathy that nature has not bridged.

On the one hand, reawakening our empathy may seem too insignificant to steer the whole humanity toward benevolence and away from malevolence. On the other, inciting empathy should be a good macroscopic starting point that will eventually permeate through the humanity. I maintain that as long as we keep empathetic thoughts in our mind whenever we make decisions that affect more than ourselves, my second objective will be a resounding success.

In 1947, Einstein worked with the Emergency Committee of Atomic Scientists, based in Princeton, New Jersey. As part of that group, he penned a letter that read in part:

We scientists believe upon ample evidence that the time of decision is upon us—that what we do, or fail to do within the next few years will determine the fate of our civilization...In the shadow of the atomic bomb, it has become apparent that all men are brothers. If we recognize this as truth and act upon this recognition, mankind may go forward to a higher plane of human development.

The urgency of this statement 70 years later remains the same.

Counting on us to realize that we are brothers in the shadow of the atomic bomb is overly pessimistic. I am taking a much more optimistic point of view. First of all, it should not take another event like the atomic bomb to enlighten us about our deficiency as a species. Now that we understand our evolution, we should be instinctively aware that we are brothers, period, per Steven Jay Gould. I am also optimistic because against the enormous odds of our being here, we are here, and we have prevailed, irrespective of the arduous and challenging evolutionary process we endured. As acrimonious as we treat each other at times, we still manage to prosper due to our innate empathy and our derived emotion and morality for each other.

Going forward, we should bear in mind that we are all close kin to every other living human being and how fortunate we are to have evolved and created culture and the world as we know it. As long as we dig deeply into our empathetic selves whenever we make decisions that affect our fellow humans, we should be fine and can be a better species.

BIBLIOGRAPHY

1. "Brain expansion in early hominins predicts carnivore extinctions in East Africa," Søren Faurby Daniele Silvestro Lars Werdelin Alexandre Antonelli, *Ecology Letters*, (2020), https://doi.org/10.1111/ele.13451.
2. "On the universality of human nature and the uniqueness of the individual: The role of genetics and adaptation," Tooby, J. & Cosmides, L, *Journal of Personality*, **58**, 17-67 (1990).
3. Chapter 1 in "The psychological foundations of culture," Tooby, J. & Cosmides, L. in "The adapted mind: Evolutionary psychology and the generation of culture" (ed. J. Barkow, L. Cosmides, & J. Tooby), 19-136. Oxford University Press Publisher (1992).
4. "The biodiversity of species and their rates of extinction, distribution, and protection," SL Pimm, CN Jenkins, R Abell, TM Brooks, JL Gittleman, LN Joppa, PH Raven, CM Roberts, and JO Sexton, *Science*, **344**, (2014).
5. "Our Modern Skulls House a Stone Age Brain: An Overview and Annotated Bibliography of Evolutionary Psychology, Part I," Tony Stankus, *Journal of Behavioral & Social Sciences Librarian*, **30**, 119-141 (2011).
6. *"The age of empathy: Nature's Lesson for a Kinder Society,"* Frans de Waal, Crown Publisher, (2009).
7. "Neocortex size as a constraint on group size in primates," Dunbar, R. I. M., *Journal of Human Evolution*, **22**, 469–493 (1992).
8. "Co-evolution of neocortex size, group size and language

in humans," R. I. M. Dunbar, *Behavioral and Brain Sciences,* **16**, 681-735 (1993).

9. *"Enlightenment Now, The Case for Reason, Science, Humanism, and Progress,"* Steven Pinker, Penguin Books Publisher, 2018.

ABOUT THE AUTHOR

Chris Young Kelly is an experimental physicist turned engineer. His primary research focus was on the quantum behavior of the materials responsible for lasers used in nanometer scale photolithography for modern semiconductor industries. He also studied the quantum characteristics of Neptune's and Uranus' atmospheres by recreating their environments under laboratory conditions.

As an engineer, his professional work directly impacted our daily lives. He helped lay the foundation for the current high-speed communications infrastructure, particularly the optical portion, enabling the massive Internet traffic for streaming, IoT, data storage, etc.

He became a corporate executive in later years and taught graduate-level engineering courses at Stanford University as a visiting professor. He is also an entrepreneur and investor in high-tech industries.

As a prolific technical journal writer with over 100 peer-reviewed publications to his credit, Chris has turned his attention to popular science writing in recent years.

Chris is an avid reader, traveler, hiker, Tai Chi practitioner, and a high handicap golf enthusiast. He makes his home in Northern California with his wife, Wendy, a tabby cat, Meowmy, and a golden retriever, Buddy.

You can reach Chris at cykelly60@gmail.com.

www.ingramcontent.com/pod-product-compliance
Lightning Source LLC
Chambersburg PA
CBHW070901030426
42336CB00014BA/2279